TWAYNE'S WORLD AUTHORS SERIES

A Survey of the World's Literature

GERMANY

Ulrich Weisstein, Indiana University

EDITOR

Christoph Martin Wieland

TWAS 528

Christoph Martin Wieland

CHRISTOPH MARTIN WIELAND

By JOHN A. McCARTHY

University of Pennsylvania

TWAYNE PUBLISHERS
A DIVISION OF G. K. HALL & CO, BOSTON

Library of Congress Cataloging in Publication Data
McCarthy, John Aloysius, 1942-
Christoph Martin Wieland.

(Twayne's world authors series; TWAS 528: Germany)
Bibliography: p. 180–88
Includes index.
1. Wieland, Christoph Martin, 1733–1813.
2. Authors, German—18th century—Biography.
PT2569.M3   838'.6'09 [B]   78-14338
ISBN 0-8057-6369-4

Contents

About the Author

John A. McCarthy, born in 1942 in St. Clair, Michigan, studied English, German and Psychology at Oakland University where he took an A. B. degree. He later continued his studies with the help of scholarships at the University of Munich and the State University of New York at Buffalo, taking both his M.A. and Ph.D. degrees in German from the latter institution. After having taught at Buffalo and Oakland University, Professor McCarthy went to the University of Pennsylvania, where he has served as Undergraduate Chairman and is currently an Assistant Professor of German, teaching German language and literature courses and courses in European literature of the eighteenth and nineteenth centuries.

Professor McCarthy has published scholarly articles and reviews both in the United States and abroad, in English and in German, on Büchner, Schiller, Wieland and on the essay form. His study, *Fantasy and Reality: An Epistemological Approach to Wieland*, was published in the series *Europäische Hochschulschriften* in 1974. In addition, Professor McCarthy serves in various editorial capacities.

Preface

In the following study I attempt to present to an American audience Christoph Martin Wieland (1733–1813), one of Germany's most versatile and influential writers in the eighteenth century. He was, in fact, more influential than Goethe or Schiller. It is even debatable whether the German Classical Age would have matured so rapidly or would have blossomed so fully without Wieland, who did much to orchestrate the still somewhat harsh German language into subtle tones and harmonious rhythms.

A sign of Wieland's versatility is the manner in which he was variously known to his countrymen: the German Voltaire, the German Ariosto, or the German Shaftesbury. He also gave the Germans their first complete translation of Shakespeare's dramas, edited their first long-lived journal, and was author of the first modern German novel. All this, and more, was accomplished by a mild-mannered, pleasant individual who liked to refer to himself as a "cross between Socrates and Horace."[1] The comparison is not inappropriate, for, like Socrates, Wieland was small of stature and far from handsome, combining in himself a tendency to sober rationalism with deep religious conviction. These attitudes are accurately reflected in the poet's proclivity to writing dialogue and satire on the one hand, and in his lifelong preoccupation with the nature of enthusiasm on the other. Also like Socrates, Wieland believed that man's epistemological faculties are limited, that all man can know rationally is that he knows nothing. Just as Socrates had brought philosophy to the common man in the fifth century B.C., Wieland helped popularize the practical application of philosophy in the eighteenth century A.D.

The similarity between Wieland and Horace is no less striking. Horace was one of the most significant Roman poets, whose work chronicles his time and his personality. Just as Horace was an accomplished versifier who openly imitated the form and content of Greek masters, but succeeded in infusing the Greek forms and motifs with Roman character, so did Wieland succeed in imparting German character to the various literary models he used. Similarly, both the ironic tone adopted in the discussion of serious matters and the range of interest, further unite the two authors. Each intended to instruct *(docere)* while entertaining *(delectare)*. It is significant for their intellectual affinity that Wieland translated Horace's *Satires* and *Epistles* (1782), which are among the most stylistically mature and perfect works of the Roman poet.

Wieland has also been compared to Laurence Sterne (1713–1768), especially in light of his remark that Yorick (Sterne's spokesman in *Tristram Shandy* and *Sentimental Journey*) was his favorite character because he combined the qualities of both Socrates and Harlequin, whom Wieland also loved.[2] The reference to Yorick underscores the principal stylistic trait of Wieland's masterpieces: the intermingling of earnestness and humor. Sterne's comment in the preface to *Tristram Shandy* is valid for Wieland's major accomplishments as well: "—Here stands *wit*,—and there stands *judgment*, close beside it, . . . indubitably both [are] made and fitted to go together, in order . . .—*to answer one another.*"[3]

Despite these parallels to other great men, or perhaps because of them, Wieland was frequently misunderstood, even maligned, by his own and subsequent generations of writers. Rarely did he defend himself when unjustly attacked, and he did not leave behind an autobiographical *Dichtung und Wahrheit (Poetry and Truth)* as did his more famous contemporary, Goethe. To explain his own works and many literary masks autobiographically would have been to no avail, he thought. The prejudices against him were too strong. Once, however, under attack by the *Sturm und Drang* generation for presumed moral laxity, the author did respond indirectly in the fictive dialogue, "Unterredungen zwischen W[xx] und dem Pfarrer zu[xx]" ("Conversations Between W[xx] and the Vicar of [xx]") (1775). In this piece Wieland stated: "I do not have enough enduring enthusiasm to rise above all the judgments to which I would expose myself if I were to become my own biographer. The world in which we live would not tolerate such a high level of candor."[4]

I, on the other hand, as Wieland's biographer, can attempt to present his character and his works in a manner satisfying to both author and critic. Not that either the writer or his writings need be defended. Other biographers have done that. The present biographical-critical monograph, the first to be published in the United States, is designed to introduce a broad audience to one of Germany's most influential writers. My practice throughout has been to quote the author's works and correspondence in translation, making exceptions in the case of poetry, which is quoted in the original German. In such instances, however, English prose translations are offered in the notes. Unless otherwise stated, all translations are my own. Because of space restrictions, I have included renditions of prose passages in the original only when the style seemed to require it. Finally, all titles of works are cited in the original.

My research has been generously supported by a Jusserand Fellowship, a University of Pennsylvania Summer Research Fellowship and Grant-in-Aid, and by the American Philosophical Society, for which I am deeply appreciative. Last but not least I would like to thank my friends and colleagues, Professors Heinz Moenkemeyer and Frank Trommler, whose encouragement and advice were invaluable.

JAM

Philadelphia

Chronology

1766   Meeting in summer with Ludwig Gleim and Johann Georg
       Jacobi, who become his close friends.
1768   *Idris und Zenide*, a comic epic poem. *Musarion*, philosophi-
       cal verse narrative with comic overtones.
1769   Appointed privy councillor of Mainz and professor of
       philosophy in Erfurt.
1770   *Socrates Mainomenos, oder die Dialogen des Diogenes von
       Sinope (Socrates Gone Mad)*, a satirical-philosophical novel.
       Combabus, a verse narrative. *Die Grazien (The Graces)*, an
       idyllic poem with verse and prose elements. Beginning of
       friendship with Friedrich Heinrich Jacobi.
1771   *Der neue Amadis (The New Amadis)*, verse epic. Publishes
       Sophie La Roche's sentimental novel, *Geschichte des Fräu-
       leins von Sternheim (The History of Ms. Sternheim)*. May
       and June: journey to Koblenz, Düsseldorf, Mainz, and
       Darmstadt.
1772   *Der goldene Spiegel (The Golden Mirror)*, a political novel
       with progressive tendencies. Becomes tutor to the princes
       Karl August and Constantin in Weimar. Also named privy
       councillor of Saxony.
1773   *Alceste*, a "Singspiel" with music by Anton Schweitzer. Sec-
       ond edition of *Agathon*. Founds the *Teutscher Merkur (Ger-
       man Mercury*, 1773–1810).
1774– *Die Abderiten (The Republic of Fools*, first version, pub-
1781   lished as a serial in the *Teutscher Merkur*. *Titanomachia
       (War of the Titans)*, opens period of verse narratives that
       culminates in *Oberon* (1780).
1775   Duke Karl August comes of age, and Wieland is relieved of
       all pedagogical duties. Beginning of lifelong friendships with
       Goethe and with the Grand Duchess Anna Amalia of
       Weimar. *Geschichte des Philosophen Danischmend (History
       of Danischmend)*, a philosophical novel.
1776   February: Johann Gottfried Herder moves to Weimar. *Ein
       Wintermärchen (A Winter's Tale)* and *Liebe um Liebe (Love
       for Love*, later renamed *Gandalin)* continue the surge of
       verse narratives. *Rosemund* (operetta).
1777   *Geron der Adelich (Geron the Noble)*; *Das Sommermärchen
       (A Summer's Tale)*. Travels to Mannheim for the premiere of
       Rosemund.
1778   *Hann und Gulpenhee*; *Schach Lolo*; *Pervonte* (1778–1779),
       verse narratives.

Chronology

1780   *Oberon* appears in book form.

1781   Second version of the comic novel *Geschichte der Abderiten* published.

1782–   *Horazens Briefe (Horace's Letters); Briefe an einen jungen*
1784   *Dichter (Letters to a Young Poet)*.

1784   *Clelia und Sinnibald*, a verse narrative.

1786–   *Dschinnistan*. Three volume collection of fairy tales.
1789

1787   Nominated to the Berlin Academy of Sciences. Schiller arrives in Weimar.

1788–   *Lucians von Samosata Sämtliche Werke (Lucian's Collected*
1789   *Works)*.

1791   *Geheime Geschichte des Philosophen Peregrinus Proteus (Peregrinus Proteus)*, a novel in dialogue form. *Neue Göttergespräche (New Dialogues of the Gods)*, political essays on the French Revolution.

1794–   *Wielands Sämtliche Werke*, first luxury edition of a German
1802   author's collected works published during his lifetime. *Geschichte des Agathon*, third edition, appears as the first work in the collection.

1795   *Die Wasserkufe (The Water Trough)*, last of the "frivolous" verse narratives.

1796–   *Attisches Museum (Attic Museum)*, a journal dedicated to the
1803   study of antiquity. May to September: sojourn in Zurich with daughter Sophie and son-in-law Heinrich Gessner.

1797   Purchases the country estate Ossmannstedt, near Weimar, where he resides until 1803.

1799   *Gespräche unter vier Augen (Confidential Dialogues)*, dialogues on the human condition. *Agathodämon*, a novel. Sophie La Roche visits Ossmannstedt in the summer with her granddaughter, Sophie Brentano. July 26: Wieland meets Susette Gontard, Hölderlin's Diotima, Jean Paul (1763–1825) closes his "conjectural biography" with the words: "The sun is setting—my travels come to an end—and in a few moments, I'll be with a dear and cherished friend—you, immortal Wieland!" Beginning of Wilhelm August and Friedrich Schlegel's *auto-da-fé* of Wieland in their journal, *Athenaeum* (cf. Volume I, p. 919).

1800   Sophie Brentano returns to Ossmannstedt to spend the summer and dies suddenly on September 19. She is buried at Ossmannstedt.

1801   Wieland's wife, Dorothea, dies on November 8. Her final resting place is also Ossmannstedt, next to Sophie Brentano. *Aristipp* (1801–1802), an epistolary novel.

1803   Heinrich von Kleist last visitor at Ossmannstedt. Wieland sells the estate, which has become too expensive, and moves back to Weimar.

1804   *Menander und Glycerion*, an epistolary novel.

1805   *Krates und Hipparchia*, epistolary novel. *Das Hexameron von Rosenhain*, a collection of three fairy tales and three novellas.

1807   February 18: Sophie La Roche dies. April 10: Grand Duchess Anna Amalia dies.

1808   Interview with Napoleon; Wieland decorated with the Cross of the Legion of Honor.

1808–   Translation and annotation of M. Tullius Cicero's *Sämtliche*
1812   *Briefe* (*Collected Letters*) in five volumes (Volume six completed by Friedrich David Gräter; Zurich, 1818).

1809   Induction into the Masonic Lodge "Amalia."

1813   January 20: Wieland dies in Weimar. Final resting place with Sophie Brentano and his wife Dorothea in Ossmannstedt. February 18: Goethe delivers eulogy and first appreciation of Wieland's literary significance, "Zum Gedenken des edlen Dichters, Bruders und Freundes" ("In Memory of our Distinguished Poet, Brother and Friend"), at the memorial service in the masonic lodge.

CHAPTER 1

The Formative Years
(1733–1752)

I Early Influences

CHRISTOPH Martin Wieland was born on September 5, 1733, one of five children of Regina Katharina (née Kick, 1715–1789) and Thomas Adam Wieland (1704–1772), pastor in Oberholzheim near Biberach, an old city republic about one hundred kilometers southeast of Stuttgart. Three of the five children died in infancy, and only a younger brother, Thomas Adam (1735–1764), survived to adulthood. Christoph Martin was a precocious child. As was customary in many middle and upper class families, instruction began very early, so that by the time Wieland was eight, he was already reading Cornelius Nepos in the original Latin, and at thirteen, he understood Horace and Vergil better than his teacher.[1] He also displayed an unusual love of literature at an early age, beginning his study of Gottsched's *Versuch einer critischen Dichtkunst* (*Essay on a Critical Art of Poetry*, 1730) at age eleven and imitating Hinrich Brockes' poetry by age twelve. These early poetic attempts were not limited to German, for the youth also composed in Latin. His juvenilia include both shorter and longer poems, even a heroic one treating the destruction of Jerusalem. However, the quality of these works was not high, and the young poet destroyed them soon afterwards. Nevertheless, Wieland's early devotion to letters is further evident in his practice of rising with the sun in order to write poetry because his pietistic father disapproved of his penchant for poetry and did not allow him to compose during the day.

Wieland's precociousness in matters of learning and literature is borne out by his experience at the boarding school in Klosterbergen near Magdeburg, where the boy studied from 1747 to 1749. There he continued his intensive study of the Roman authors of the

15

Golden and Silver Ages, especially Livius, Terence, Vergil, Horace, and Cicero. Wieland's interest in Horace and Cicero was later to culminate in a translation of the former's epistles (1782–1784) and satires (1784) and the latter's collected letters (1808–1812). But neither was contemporary literature neglected. He studied Breitinger's *Kritische Dichtkunst* (*Critical Art of Poetry*, 1740), Albrecht von Haller's poems, and especially Klopstock's *Messias* (the first three cantos, which Wieland greeted enthusiastically, had appeared by 1748).

Young Wieland's development was strongly influenced by Xenophon's *Cyropaedia* and *Memorabilia* (recollections of Socrates). The latter he liked to refer to as "the gospel of the Greek salvation of the world,"[2] and eventually adopted Xenophon's ideal of kalokagathia as his own. He refined and expanded the ideal eight years later with the help of Shaftesbury's concept of the virtuoso. The ideas found in Xenophon were, like those of Horace and Cicero, a lifelong influence. Gottsched's adaptions of the English moral weeklies, *The Spectator, The Guardian*, and *The Tatler*, aided Wieland in developing the ideas found in the ancient authors.

Not all of the youth's intellectual endeavors were looked upon with favor. A philosophical essay—written at age fifteen—is a matter in point; in it he tried to show how Venus could have been born without the help of a god—indeed how the entire universe could have evolved without God. The work inadvertently fell into the hands of his teachers and caused quite an uproar. No wonder! Such free thinking was anathema in Klosterbergen, a citadel of Pietistic learning. But for his otherwise exemplary conduct he would have been expelled. However, the youth's desire for truth was not stemmed, and he continued to question all viewpoints to the end of his life. In fact, this intellectual skepticism is one of his major characteristics and was given its first major impetus by Pierre Bayle's *Dictionnaire historique et critique* (*Historical-Critical Dictionary*, 1695–1697), which proved to be a lifelong companion. Other philosophical influences during these years were exerted by Gottfried Wilhelm Leibniz, Christian Wolff, Bernhard le Bovier de Fontenelle, and Voltaire.

Despite the very serious religious and philosophical side of his nature, the youth was by no means without mischief. Once the high-pitched voice of his athletic-looking French teacher so amused him that he broke out in loud, merry laughter, which he tried to stifle when the teacher shot him an angry look. When the teacher continued the instruction in his falsetto voice, the contrast between the appearance and the reality was such that young Wieland could not contain himself and once again broke out in boisterous laughter. This impertinence earned him a box on the ear. The blow notwithstanding, Wieland continued, throughout his life, to be struck by the often amusing contrast between appearance and reality. He was also impertinent enough to repeatedly box the ears of his readers in a figurative and playful sense by offering them the unexpected.

In 1749, Wieland concluded his studies at Klosterbergen and started the journey home. On the way, he stopped at Erfurt to visit a relative, Johann Wilhelm Baumer, a surgeon and later professor of medicine and chemistry at Giessen. The "stopover" was to last a year. Wieland's attitude to this interlude in his life was distinctly ambivalent. The reason for remaining with Baumer was ostensibly to perfect himself in philosophy, but he did not seem to be very edified by his relative's philosophical views, which were based for the most part on Wolff, for Wieland later characterized them as "intellectual flatulencies."[3] And, even though the growing boy did not get much sustenance for his body either (he complains of going hungry at Baumer's table), the extended visit was redeemed by a tutorial on Cervantes' *Don Quixote*. Baumer saw Don Quixote and his companion as true representatives of mankind, not just as satirical reflections of Spanish chivalry, and used the novel to acquaint Wieland with the ways of men and the world.[4] We know from Wieland's numerous subsequent references to Cervantes and the novel that this initiation to *Don Quixote* made an indelible impression on him. Throughtout his career, Wieland strove for the same balance of sympathy and humor in his writings, and even contributed one of the best imitations to the tradition created by the Spanish novel, namely *Don Sylvio von Rosalva* (1764).

II *Wieland and Sophie Gutermann*

In 1750, young Wieland returned to Biberach to spend the summer with his family before commencing law studies in Tübingen. These few months were to prove momentous for him. Although Wieland was intellectually advanced well beyond his years, he lacked an experience equally important to human development: a close friendship. As a child he had no close friends, as a pupil in

Klosterbergen he was mostly alone, and in Erfurt he found no one he could warm up to. Thus his education up to this point had been entirely one sided. His head was filled with diverse and frequently conflicting ideas: with Wolff's dogmatism, Bayle's skepticism, Voltaire's mockery, Cervantes' irony, and the mystical leanings of Pietism. But his heart had not been touched. The summer of 1750 changed all that—or at least it initiated the change which took more than ten years to complete. It was during that summer that Wieland met and fell in love with Sophie Gutermann, a distant cousin who, if we can believe his correspondence, effected a radical change in him. To Riedel he wrote that his love for Sophie "suddenly transformed" him and that without her he would have been lost in his mental meanderings.[5] His love for Sophie injected a new spirit into his life; it helped him order his chaotic thoughts on the nature of man and the world according to a unifying principle and gave rise to his first major work, *Die Natur der Dinge* (*On the Nature of Things*), a didactic poem. However, the nature of his love has been so often viewed as a purely Platonic experience that the eroticism which erupted during the 1760s was seen as being out of character for him. We cannot deny that Wieland claimed to be enthralled by Sophie's virtuous and reserved character and that he delighted in intellectualizing with her, for she was just as precocious and as shy as he. What better friend could he have wished for! Yet, while the relationship was predominantly Platonic, there was a definite, albeit mostly suppressed, erotic side to it. To cite but one example in evidence of this contention, the enraptured youth writes in an ode to his Doris (i.e., Sophie):

> O ! wie liebt dich dein Freund ? o wie
> beglückst du ihn ! Wenn dein Hyblischer Mund
>   sich seinen Küssen beut,
>   Und die Sanftzitternde Lippe
>   Gleich der Rose in Knospen schwellt.[6]

The obligatory static flower metaphor of the rhetorical tradition is here expanded into a dynamic one: quivering lips are likened to swelling rosebuds. This passage not only reveals Wieland's acquaintance with Linnaeus' view of plants as dynamic and sexual[7] but is also in keeping with the mood of a seventeen year old in love for the first time with a beautiful girl!

What, then, is the explanation for the largely suppressed eroticism in the relationship between Wieland and his cousin? We need not look too far for a likely one. Wieland was, and remained throughout his long life, sensitive to and considerate of the psychological and emotional needs of others. He knew very well that Sophie was recovering from a broken engagement to Dr. Biancini of Augsburg, whom she had sincerely loved. However, her father had the engagement annuled in anger over Biancini's insistence that the children be raised in the Catholic faith. Sophie acquiesced in her father's wishes but was sullen, so that her trip to Biberach in 1750 was designed to distract her. After having been so recently and severely hurt by love, she is likely to have wanted only a Platonic relationship. This interpretation seems borne out by Wieland's remarks to Bodmer in 1752 concerning Sophie:

> I praised her beauty little; in the beginning I didn't speak much of my love either. Instead I endeavored to entertain her and uplift her spirits, and let her see that this was the most noble proof of my love. . . . I don't think it is possible to be more tender than I was. My love for her was the purest desire to make her happy for all time and to make myself happy through her. I saw how much true happiness she would lack without the love of such a friend.[8]

He played the role of Platonic lover because otherwise he would have run the risk of losing her friendship altogether. How else explain his explicit remark to his friend Schinz on May 25, 1752: "If I may speak frankly, I consider Platonic love, which wants to see us as mere cerebral beings, as the greatest of all chimeras.[9]

III   *In Tübingen: Rapprochement with Bodmer (1750–1752)*

In October, Wieland departed for Tübingen to take up his law studies, which, however, he dropped almost immediately for lack of real interest. Instead, he withdrew from all society to devote himself exclusively to the reading of literature and the writing of poetry. The poetry of the Tübingen period (1750–1752) was mostly inspired by his love for Sophie. This is particularly true of his Odes to Doris and *Die Natur der Dinge*. Wieland noted the importance of this affair for his poetic inspiration fifty-five years later, in 1805, when he wrote to Sophie: "Nothing is more certain than that I would not have become a poet if fate had not brought us together in the year 1750."[10]

Wieland's correspondence during these months mirrors the intensity of his emotion—he assures his mother that his love is no passing fancy and that he could not live without Sophie—and might
help explain his indifference toward law studies. Yet the seventeen
year old youth knew perfectly well that he could not marry until he
had established himself professionally. A clerical career was out of
the question because of his frail health, and he also had no stomach
for the rigors of a medical career. If we further consider that Wieland's father did not condone his son's literary endeavors, so that his
son felt compelled to conceal the extent of his poetic activities in
Tübingen from him, we can't help but wonder why it was that young
Wieland neglected everything for the sake of literature. How could
he hope to lay the firm financial base for his longed for union with
Sophie, when very few literary men had at that point succeeded in
earning a decent living from their trade?

When we look closely at Wieland's early productions, we can see
that they fall roughly into two categories: the one more or less directly expressing his love for Sophie and therefore of a more private
nature, the other more or less designed to further his literary career
and therefore of a more public nature. The second category can be
explained by young Wieland's attempt to attract Bodmer's attention
and thus secure an invitation to join the master in Zurich. It is quite
apparent from his correspondence and his writings from the summer of 1751 on that Wieland saw Bodmer as the key to his literary
future and the solution of his present dilemma. Through Bodmer,
who was renowned throughout the German-speaking countries,
Wieland hoped to establish himself as a man of letters or at least to
obtain a teaching post. For this reason, Wieland sent Bodmer the
first four cantos of his epic, *Hermann*, composed in hexameters, apparently to show that he could accomplish the task which Klopstock
had failed to accomplish in Bodmer's view: to write a national epic
worthy of Milton's *Paradise Lost*. (After the electrifying experience
of reading the first cantos of the *Messias* in 1748, Bodmer had invited Klopstock to Zurich to complete the epic as his guest. That was
in 1750. However, Bodmer was quickly disillusioned by Klopstock's
vanity and worldly ways, which clashed with the sublime sentiment
of the *Messias*. Klopstock and Bodmer eventually broke with one
another in early 1751.)

Hermann was followed by *Zwölf moralische Briefe in Versen*
(*Twelve Edifying Letters in Verse* Winter 1751-1752), which

reflect the poet's views on moral philosophy and which might also be interpreted as an attempt to assure Bodmer of his virtuous character. These and similar writings, as well as his letters to Bodmer from August 1751 on, ultimately persuaded Bodmer to invite Wieland to be his guest in Zurich. After having seen Sophie for only a few days in Biberach, Wieland departed in October 1752 for Switzerland. Neither she nor her family seemed to place much stock in his budding literary career.[11]

Of the works written for Sophie, *Die Natur der Dinge* (spring, 1752) is the most noteworthy, for it virtually launched Wieland's literary career. It is a didactic piece in Alexandrines, encompassing four thousand lines divided into six books. Modeled on Lucretius' *de rerum natura*, it was inspired by Thomas Adam Wieland's sermon "Was ist die Liebe?" ("What is Love?") and earned Wieland the title of "the German Lucretius."[12] The seventeen year old youth endeavored here to refute the materialism of Epicurus, Lucretius, Zoroaster, and as Wieland saw him, Leibniz by developing his own view of man and the world and his own moral philosophy. He tried to demonstrate that God infuses all aspects of the world, which is nothing but an elaborate hierarchy ascending to God (Great Chain of Being). According to Wieland, the universe is filled with spiritual entities ("Geistigkeiten") which differ from Leibniz's monads in that they have bodily components.[13] This is a major point, since it demonstrates that Wieland never divorced mind from body in his thinking as has been widely assumed by proponents of the "grand metamorphosis" theory, which will be discussed later. That young Wieland subscribed to the necessary and inseparable union of the sensual and spiritual is evident in such verses as:

> Kein Platon, was er auch für Ur-Ideen dichtet,
> Schied je den Geist vom Stoff . . . .
> Gott ist der Quell der Lust. Denn aus Vollkommenheiten
> Strömt alle Wollust aus in alle Geistigkeiten,
> Und beyder Quell ist Gott.[14]

To be sure, the sensual is expressed more explicitly in the Odes to Doris and in the *Anti-Ovid* (1752), yet it is not absent in *Die Natur der Dinge* or even in the *Zwölf moralische Briefe,* which exhort man to moderation, not to complete self-denial.[15] Perhaps the cause of this judicious balance was Wieland's love for Sophie Gutermann, which made a poet of Wieland and helped to mute the philosophical abstractness of the poem. Wieland intimated this influence when he characterized *Die Natur der Dinge* as "such a strange hybrid of metaphysical school twaddle and of the best poetry the god of love ever imbued in a young man of seventeen."[16] In the ensuing years in Switzerland, this more or less balanced dualism of the spiritual and sensual seemed—at least initially—to be lost.

The artistic quality of these early works is far below what the poet was later to achieve. He included most of them in the supplemental volumes of the 1794 definitive edition of his works, almost solely for their historical value in documenting his emergence as a writer. Yet, although uneven in quality, they are not without some poetic merit.

CHAPTER 2

The Swiss Years (1752–1760)

I *In Bodmer's House (1752–1754)*

IN mid-October 1752 Wieland arrived in Zurich, a city where he was to remain for the next six years. In accepting Bodmer's invitation to live in his house under his tutelage, he realized that he would have to accomodate the older man to some degree if he wanted to draw the greatest benefit for his own literary and journalistic career from the association. The concessions he made were not out of character; they merely tended to exaggerate certain traits. Thus, when Wieland wrote that he did not like large social gatherings and didn't smoke, he was speaking the truth. However, when he wrote that he was an "avid water drinker" ("grosser Wassertrinker"), he stretched the truth.[1] Wieland stressed what Bodmer wanted to hear, even going so far as to apologize for the somewhat pronounced eroticism in his love poetry.[2] It is undeniable that Wieland sincerely respected Bodmer and thus was not abusing the trust placed in him by stressing or "playing down" certain traits. He never "used" anyone in an insulting or demeaning fashion, but rather knew how to draw out the best in others while at the same time furthering his own cause. Wieland knew that Bodmer was still smarting from the severe disappointment which Klopstock had caused him and he wanted to avoid offending the older man. Perhaps, as has been recently argued, he even saw in Bodmer a father figure. For his part, the older man sought in the youth (as he had in Klopstock) a substitute for his own son, who had died.[3]

In Bodmer's house, Wieland enjoyed a quiet retreat on the outskirts of Zurich with a commanding view of the lake. In this idyllic setting, where he could study and write undisturbed, we note a pattern which evolved in Tübingen and was to continue in Biberach and much later in Ossmannstedt near Weimar. In these garden or country retreats, we can see Wieland's attempts to realize his own little *Sabinum* or *Tusculum* in the manner of Cicero or Horace. Of

23

course, this type of living implied a freedom from financial cares that made possible complete devotion to intellectual pursuits. Life in Bodmer's house foreshadowed this ideal, which Wieland later described to Zimmermann: "The only advantageous position for me would be one which would free me from all kinds of public business and social obligations; one which would afford me lifelong independence, ease and freedom to pursue in all things my own tastes."[4]

The period under Bodmer's guidance was a rewarding one. Wieland had at his disposal Bodmer's excellent library, which he used fully. In fact, he read so much that he got sick of reading. In Biberach he had learned Latin; in Klosterbergen, French; in Erfurt, Italian; and now, in Bodmer's house, he added Greek and English. To his favorite authors, Xenophon and Horace, Wieland added Plutarch and Shaftesbury during these early Swiss years, so that we can see how he continued to lay the foundation for the vast erudition evident in his later works. A second boon for the developing writer was the access to Bodmer's circle of friends with their contacts throughout the German-speaking nations. In association with them, and in conjunction with Bodmer's continuing battle with Gottsched, Wieland gained valuable journalistic and political experience. He eagerly joined his patron's cause because it offered him the opportunity to gain exposure while testing his writing abilities and intellectual acumen. The series of works written expressly or implicitly in support of Bodmer's camp was initiated in 1752 with the *Abhandlung von den Schönheiten des Epischen Gedichts Der Noah"* (*A Treatise on the Beauties of the Epic "Noah,"* completed in 1753), a favorable interpretation of Bodmer's attempt to rival Milton's *Paradise Lost*. At his patron's behest, Wieland also edited a collection of polemical essays attacking Gottsched (1753) and started his own religious epic, *Der gepryfte Abraham* (*Abraham Tested*, 1753).[5] Perhaps the most vociferous attacks in Bodmer's service occurred after the youth had moved out of the literary magnate's house. They would express Wieland's desire to remain on good terms with Bodmer, both out of a sense of gratitude and for diplomatic reasons.[6] The most infamous of these later attacks is found in the dedication to *Empfindungen eines Christen* (*Views of a Good Christian*, 1755), where Wieland harshly denounced Johann Peter Uz (1720–1796) as an immoral writer.

Yet not all the works written under Bodmer's influence were composed solely for the master. The dichotomy of the private and public purpose in the Tübingen works is still apparent in the Zurich ones, albeit not as pronouncedly. Wieland's plan seemed to be to profit as much, and as quickly, as possible from his association with Bodmer and then to strike out on his own, so as to be able to marry Sophie. Perhaps he discouraged her from visiting him in Zurich for fear that her presence would upset the delicate emotional balance necessary for him to persist in his "apprenticeship" with the master. The "Plan von einer neuen Art, von Privat-Unterweisung" ("Plan for a New Manner of Private Instruction," 1753; later expanded to "Plan for an Academy," 1756) was conceived with Sophie in mind, for he hoped by means of his pedagogical philosophy to obtain a teaching position and thus to take the first step toward independence. Eventually his plan bore fruit, but unfortunately too late for a union with Sophie; she abruptly broke off their engagement in December 1753, apparently as a result of a misunderstanding, and announced her imminent betrothal to Georg Michael von LaRoche (1720–1788), the bastard son of Count Friedrich von Warthausen.[7]

The youth was stunned by the news, but did his best to hide his pain by sublimating his very real love into a purely Platonic relationship.[8] In March 1754 Sophie married; and in June Wieland left Bodmer in order to take a position as tutor. The proximity of these two actions is so striking that we cannot help but wonder whether the loss of Sophie was not a direct cause of Wieland's distancing himself from Bodmer. The youth had been motivated by her love to write Ovidian poetry; and her love had driven him to establish himself as a national literary figure. Now that he had no hope of marrying Sophie, he no longer needed Bodmer or immediate recognition. Seemingly as a result, he began to experiment with other styles and forms, for Bodmer's hexameters no longer sufficed. Although striking out on his own, he remained conscious of how much he owed to Bodmer's generosity, speaking many years later of his former mentor with respect and gratitude.[9]

II *Tutor in Zurich (1754–1759)*

Wieland's life style in Zurich changed radically. For example, he mingled with others and even began to attend the meetings of the Tuesday Society, a group he had formerly scorned because of its anacreontic leanings.[10] Now he was frequently seen in the company of several more mature women, one of whom—a not unattractive widow of fourty-four. Frau Grebel-Lochmann—particularly impressed the young man with her intelligence, wit, and charm. He came to refer jokingly to the group as his "seraglio" and to himself as the "Grand Turk." These pietistic ladies were entertained by his rhapsodic works which foreshadowed a future, better world where kindred souls would be united. The works written in this vein include the meditative *Empfindungen eines Christen* and *Sympathien* (*Sympathies*), both composed in 1755. They capture the author's predominantly mystical and Platonic mood in the years following his loss of Sophie. He tended to avoid girls of his own age because he felt that they were too flighty and coquettish (he called them "papillons").[11] In addition to the Serena and Doris figures (Sophie) of his earlier poetry, a bevy of ethereal women figures appears: Selima, Diotima, Melissa, Cyane, Ismene, Arete, Eulalia, and Sacharissa. This new seraphic phase is undoubtedly tied in with Wieland's conviction that Sophie was the only woman he really wanted, and since he could not have her, all women with an aura of sensuality must be renounced.

This situation was aggravated by Wieland's total lack of confidence in his outward appearance, for which he was very apologetic in the years to come.[12] He was, to put it mildly, not very attractive. His slight build, spindly legs, and pockmarked face would make life difficult for any young man. Gruber suspects that Wieland was only disdainful of the sweet young girls because he felt he had no chance with them and thus concentrated on intellectual qualities.[13] Regardless of the role which his physical appearance played in his return to a sublime kind of love in 1754–1756, the youth took Sophie's loss as a sign from Heaven that he was not destined to enjoy the pleasures of this world. In June 1756 he wrote to Zimmermann: "Two and a half years ago I saw the most beautiful prospects dissipate in front of my eyes, the fondest hopes which a true-blooded man ("ein menschlicher Mensch") can have in this life. I took this to be a clear sign that the Creator wants me completely free and requires blind obedience of me, as one dedicated to him.[14] That Wieland meant these words seriously is attested to by his mystical way of life at that time, during which he condemned not only Ovid, but also Anacreon, Tibullus, John Gay, and Matthew Prior. He rejected the art of worldly poetry as "the devil's brew" by means of which unsuspecting souls are intoxicated and turned into mindless beasts.[15]

His literary tastes reflected this changed attitude; he was now reading the works of Augustinus, of Young and Klopstock, and the lives of the saints, especially of St. Theresa of Avila. But, above all, he turned to Plato again and neglected the more down-to-earth Xenophon. For approximately two years after leaving Bodmer's house, Wieland nurtured this seraphic mood, which reached its peak in 1756. By the middle of that year, however, his fervor began to subside, and he gradually became more keenly aware of the real world around him. Perhaps the change was brought on by psychological factors, for Wieland wrote to Zimmermann in the letter just quoted that he slept most of the time and seemed overcome by lethargy; furthermore, his eyes were bothering him, and he couldn't even seem to think a straight thought. About this time he began to read Shaftesbury, d'Alembert, Diderot, Hartley and the French materialists. His purely Platonic relationship with Frau Grebel-Lochmann gradually degenerated into a more sensual love.[16] As with Sophie, it was again the woman who forced Wieland to restrain his sensuality. Frau Grebel-Lochmann acted as she did probably because she was to marry a wealthy Zurich businessman and no longer "needed" Wieland's affections. Fortunately for Wieland, he had at that time (October 1758) met another woman who was in the process of capturing his heart, Fräulein Schulthess. She was young, charming, and witty, but her father prevented a greater rapprochement between the two.[17]

We can assume that the gradual weakening of Wieland's extreme mystical mood had to do with the natural healing power of passing time and with his growing affections for these women. As a result, he once again took a more reasonable attitude toward the things of this world, appreciating again secular poets and natural philosophers. That he was totally aware of this duality of the sublime and the mundane in his character, and in human nature in general, is evident from a letter to Zimmermann, written in December 1758.[18]

In tracing the main stages of Wieland's early formative years, which are so important for understanding his later works as well, we note that he was already aware of his duality in Klosterbergen, where as a youth he had experienced both pietistic effusions and rational doubt. In Erfurt, he became even more of a skeptic, only to return to a view of the divinely infused world in *Die Natur der Dinge* in Biberach under Sophie Gutermann's influence. In his love for Sophie he experienced sensual longing ("Doris-Oden," *Anti-Ovid*) as well as yearning for a mystical union of souls (*Zwölf moralische*

Briefe). In Bodmer's house, the Platonic-religious element seemed to dominate (*Der geprüfte Abraham*) so that the loss of the girl he loved caused the progression to the mystical phase of the mid-1750s (*Empfindungen eines Christen*). Nevertheless, his contemporaries, even his good friend Zimmermann, knew him so little that they expressed astonishment at the "change." What is striking is the consistency with which Wieland portrayed the chameleon like creature called man who was born with his feet on the ground and his head in the clouds. Even in connection with *Empfindungen eines Christen*, a copy of which he sent to Zimmermann in November 1756, he urged his friend: "Don't make me out anew to be a seraph, a saint, or a sylph. I am by all means a human being and not ashamed of that in the least."[19]

In *Die Natur der Dinge*, Wieland had spoken of the dichotomy of sensual and spiritual pleasures having the same source in God; in *Das Rätsel* (*The Enigma*, 1735), the first of four planned cantos dealing with the nature of man,[20] he noted the vain efforts of thinkers through the ages to classify the creature known as man "who constantly changes color like the chameleon," and concluded: "But for this being no suitable rung on the ladder of existence can be found."[21] The image of the chameleon appeared frequently during these years as a simile for the deceptiveness of appearances, as well as for the psychological malleability of man. What seemed to fascinate Wieland most in his inquiries into man's (=his own) nature was the catalytic role of love, which struck him as being both a positive and a negative force.[22]

III   Araspes und Panthea *and* Cyrus: *"The Psychological Element"*

Perhaps the work best documenting these concerns in the mid-1750s is *Araspes und Panthea* (*Araspes and Panthea*), begun in the fall of 1756 but not finished until 1760. Martini rightly points out the affinity of style and tone between this work and Goethe's *Werther*.[23] The story relates in dialogue form an episode from Xenophon's *Cyropaedia*, according to which Araspes is entrusted with the safety of Cyrus' wife, Queen Panthea. Cyrus is absent on a military campaign. The assignment is not an easy one, for Panthea's beauty is irresistible. In his naiveté (he has known only Platonic love), Araspes is confident that his virtue will stand the test. Needless to say, the Platonic lover turns quickly into a more earthly one who violates his lofty moral code. Although he does not violate Panthea, he loses face because of his passion and is ashamed and confused by the conflicting emotions in his breast. In terms predating Goethe's *Faust* by about twenty years, Araspes laments:

> Oh! At this moment I recognize that I have two very different souls in my breast. It is impossible to believe that, if I had only one soul, it could be simultaneously disposed to good and evil, to such contradictory things as virtue and vice. No! There must of necessity be two. When the good one is dominant, we act nobly: when the evil one has the upper hand, we act despicably and shamefully. Experience has taught me this truth at the expense of my tranquillity and honor.[24]

Cyrus, however, the representative of Wieland's true ideal, is much calmer about the whole matter. He succinctly remarks: "What happened to you was nothing other than the natural consequence of the effects of beauty and love."[25] Thus Wieland draws the lesson that it is sometimes necessary to flee temptation in order to preserve virtue. These are concepts which recur in modulated form throughout his later work.

The completion of *Araspes und Panthea* was delayed, perhaps due to the complicated nature of the problem and to the fact that Wieland himself was not yet sure of how to resolve the dilemma. When he began work on this love story, the ideal of the completely virtuous and steadfast woman modeled after Sophie seemed to be the focus.[26] However, under the influence of his emerging passion for Frau Grebel-Lochmann and his attraction to young Ms. Schulthess, the problematic nature of the view that true virtue is unassailable underwent a change. The focus seemed to shift from Panthea, who does remain true to virtue, to Araspes, whose virtue is threatened by a forbidden passion. Wieland thus explicitly stated that in Part V, Araspes was not to appear as a remorseful sinner, but rather as a "patient,"[27] a highly unusual designation for the hero of any eighteenth century tale, as Paulsen[28] has rightly pointed out. The term "patient" would indicate that the hero is no longer viewed in the religiously idealistic terms characteristic of Bodmer's circle, but rather in purely human terms. Man cannot be so confident in the power of virtue that he could unnecessarily expose himself to danger. Just as he should take precautions to protect his physical health, so he must take precautions to preserve his virtue. This is

the signficance of the work's motto: "amare et sapere vix Diis con-
cessum esse," ("it is hardly given to gods to love and to know.") The
image of Araspes, a symbol of man per se, was one which had hov-
ered before Wieland's mind's eye six years earlier, when he wrote
in *Das Rätsel*: "A cripple deserves only sympathy, not mockery or
loathing. It is of this, my fellow man, that I sing, myself a man."[29]

Another work of the same period, the verse epic *Cyrus* (only the
first five of the planned eighteen cantos were completed), is distinctly related to *Araspes und Panthea*. In fact, Wieland seems to
have gotten the idea for this heroic epic in hexameters while working
on the latter piece.[30] In a sense, it is a pendant to *Araspes und
Panthea*, for whereas the latter tended to concentrate on the hero's
"development"—namely the recognition of his limits and the vul-
nerability of virtue—Cyrus represents the accomplished ideal of
kalokagathia Wieland had adopted from Xenophon and Shaftesbury.[31] Wieland strove to create in Cyrus the ideal man who combines in his character the state of perfected virtue with an enthusiastic yearning to achieve even higher perfection. That is to say, Cyrus
is unlike Araspes in that he knows he must be on constant guard if
he is to maintain inviolate his perfect virtue, because perfection for
man implies not so much a static condition as it does a dynamic one.
In Araspes the static aspect dominates, in Cyrus the dynamic. Even
more important for Wieland is the religious, rather than the merely
ethical, nature of Cyrus' virtue. By stressing the divine moment instead of the human factor which dominates in Xenophon's
Cyropaedia, Wieland reveals that he is still more indebted to the
Plato-Plotinus line of thought than to the Socrates-Xenophon line,[32]
despite the author's own claim that "Plato was formerly my favorite,
now it is Xenophon."[33]

Araspes und Panthea and *Cyrus* are important milestones in the
development of Wieland's mature view of man and in his artistic
evolution. They document the continuity of Wieland's thought from
his early ideas to his later views, for, as we shall see, Araspes and
Cyrus are prototypes for Wieland's later heroes: Agathon, Archytas,
Peregrinus, Agathodämon, and Aristipp. The female figures, Panthea and Aspasia (in *Theages order Unterredungen von Schönheit
und Liebe* [*Theages or Discourses on Beauty and Love*], a work
thematically related to these two and written simultaneously), pre-
figure as well the women of later works, such as Psyche, Danae, and
Lais. Artistically speaking, Wieland considered *Cyrus* to be the best

of his early works, praising especially its hexameters.[34] No wonder, since, in contrast to *Araspes und Panthea*, he had devoted his best hours to it.

IV Tutor in Berne (1759–1760)

By the beginning of 1759, Wieland had to look for new employment, for his charges had grown up and no longer needed his tutelage. As a result of his early "Plan einer Akademie," he received offers of employment from various places in Germany and from as far away as Marseilles. However, the poet ultimately decided to become private tutor in the home of Cantonal Magistrate Sinner in Berne, because he had been assured that he would be treated as a friend rather than as a servant and also because he would have time to write. Before leaving for Berne in mid-June 1759, he polished off the five canto fragment, *Cyrus*, and sent it to press in May. When he left Zurich, he took with him a *Welt*- and *Menschenanschauung* that remained virtually intact for the rest of his life.

The young man who had worried whether he would cut a ridiculous figure in Berne if he dressed in black or wore black trousers with a white vest was surprised by the totally different way of life in that city. The many parties, visits, and excursions in which he was expected to participate struck him as an endless round of tedious amusements. Wieland was far from being a fraternity brother and often thought back with joy on the peace and quiet of Zurich. Among the people he met early on during his stay in Berne was a certain Julie von Bondely, a young woman with truly exceptional intellectual qualities. She later gained notoriety through her friendship with Jean Jacques Rousseau. Wieland was not initially taken with her, finding her vexatious and loquacious. His first encounter with her elicited the following reaction: "Long live dumb broads!"[35] Not exactly flattering. Several weeks later he again wrote of her: "To be sure, she has her merits, but she is not my type. I don't feel at ease with her."[36] In addition, Julie was as ugly as sin, so that it is astonishing that Wieland could fall in love with her; but that is exactly what happened. Unfortunately for him, she also turned out to be a *prude par principes* who insisted upon a purely Platonic relationship. Again Wieland was restrained by the woman.[37]

How in the world could he fall in love with this woman? If we read between the lines in his correspondence with Zimmermann during July, August, and September of 1759, we seem to detect signs of a psychological explanation, which has to do with his proclivity to peace and quiet. As early as 1756, he had expressed his preference for a "Schneckenhaus" (literally: snail house) existence; but in view of the incessant social activities, he more frequently expressed his desire for tranquillity.[38] Thus, although Julie's physical appeal was negligible, she had much to offer the poet intellectually, and they became engaged. The tone of their relationship is summed up in Wieland's remark to Zimmermann: "She wants *friends*; she considers friendship to be a more reasonable and enduring love; and because she doesn't want to be loved in any other way, she loathes everything which has the semblance of an overwrought fanatical passion."[39]

Wieland was role playing and fully aware that role playing was a necessary part of life. If it got him what he wanted without compromising his integrity, he was willing to do it. What he wanted was a more serious relationship than Bernese society provided. Without Julie he would not have been able to "stick it out" in Berne, for he was bitterly disappointed in his rather immature charges, in his employer's lack of genius, and in the lack of freedom to write. His engagement to Julie provided him with a way out. Yet now he had to find a suitable position which would allow him to marry. As chance would have it, on April 30, 1760, the poet was elected senator in his home town of Biberach, an honor he could scarcely reject, although he feared that the office would allow little time for his writing. In June of that year, he left Switzerland to return to Biberach. Julie was to follow after he had become established there.

Aside from *Araspes und Panthea*, the only work of note to be completed in Berne was the prose drama *Clementina von Porretta* (1760). The play was modeled on a chapter in Richardson's sentimental novel, *Sir Charles Grandison*, and written in the manner of Diderot's bourgeois *drame*. The piece is not one of the poet's better works, and he knew it. Like his earlier play, *Lady Johanna Gray* (1758), a martyr drama adopted from Nicholas Rowe and best noted for its use of blank verse (it opened the blank verse tradition in German drama), this new play was written at fever pitch. What fascinated Wieland most was the inscrutability of man's destiny. Despite it's cursory style, *Clementina von Porretta* was an even greater hit in Switzerland than *Lady Johanna Gray* had been. However, the North German critics took little notice of this last of Wieland's sentimental works. In the "Neuer Vorbericht" ("New Preface," 1770) to

Clementina, the aspiring playwright later remarked that he was "almost adulated at the one end of Germany and at the other end mistreated like the worst pen pusher."

The Swiss years were very important for Wieland's development as a writer. He had been in touch with great men of letters; had gained an invaluable friend and confidant in Dr. Johann Georg Zimmermann, whom he often called his alter ego; had further developed his creative and critical abilities; had intensely experienced the loss of Sohie; and had learned what "society" was. His years of apprenticeship and journeymanship now over, he was about to launch an astounding career as a public figure and internationally renowned writer. It is fitting that the literary products of these formative years were published in a three volume edition, *Poetische Schriften des Herrn Wieland (The Poetic Works of Mr. Wieland*, 1759–1761) as the crowning touch. The "Allgemeiner Vorbericht zu den *Poetischen Schriften*" ("*General Introduction to the Poetic Works*") is a valuable document for an appreciation of the significance these early works have not only for the author's personal development but also for the general evolution of German literature and aesthetic thought at mid century.

CHAPTER 3

In Biberach: Municipal Administrator and Court Poet (1760–1769)

I Political and Personal Turmoil (1760–1764)

SHORTLY after his arrival in Biberach, Wieland discovered the harsh realities of politics. His quick advancement to chancery administrator was the immediate cause of his enduring political fight with the tiny republic. According to an agreement subsequent to the Peace Treaty of Westphalia (1648), the governing body of Biberach had to reflect the religious make up of the city state. Thus there had to be two magistrates—one Catholic and one Protestant—and all offices had to alternate between the two factions. Wieland's predecessors as director of the chancellery had been predominantly Catholic, so that there should have been no problem when he was named successor to the Protestant von Hillern, who had been appointed Bürgermeister. The Catholic party did not attack the succession itself; rather, they argued that the director had either to be of noble extraction or to possess a *doctor juris*. Obtaining the law degree would have been easy enough for Wieland, but he considered it a waste of time and refused to do so, thus irritating his own party. The struggle had finally to be settled by imperial edict from Vienna; however, that didn't happen until 1764. The fight for his office was but one of many incidents—often very petty and ridiculous—aggravated by the faction system in Biberach. This peculiar situation later bore much literary fruit in the hilarious satire, *Die Geschichte der Abderiten* (*The Republic of Fools*, 1774–1780).

Not only was Wieland peeved by the constant petty infighting; he also felt the onus of pedestrian administrative work. He sought relief from these political and professional tensions in his poetry and in flirtations. We will want to scrutinize the works of these years because they signal Wieland's first mastery of prose and verse form and because they, together with Lessing's dramas, mark the coming of age of German literature. But before we look at the works themselves, let us first examine further experiences which form their backdrop. Wieland had scarcely arrived in Biberach when he renewed his acquaintance with Sophie's younger, more beautiful, and coquettish sister, Cateau, who, as von Hillern's wife, had been influential in bringing Wieland back to Biberach. If we were to believe that Wieland truly loved Julie Bondely in distant Berne, we would be amazed that he could become so quickly enflamed with Cateau. He went so far as to pay court to her openly, so that von Hillern forbade him his house, and a minor scandal ensued.

However, we have seen that the philosophic and mystical turn which Wieland's love had taken previously was, at least in part, determined by the attitudes of the women he loved. He never really wanted to disassociate mind and body. What he needed was a natural woman without the usual sexual inhibitions who could show him how the two needs of the spiritual and the sensual could be balanced. Cateau seemed to be that woman. But she was married, and to the most respected man in town: the mayor. His flirtation with Cateau, therefore, had certain limits which could not be overstepped. Fortunately, the twenty-eight year old poet and senator finally found the woman who could and did respond to him on the desired level. This woman was a twenty year old girl, simple and uncomplicated. She first caught Wieland's eye on the Feast of St. Cecilia, November 12, 1761, and he was immediately attracted to her. She also had a beautiful singing voice, a talent which had already charmed him in Ms. Schulthess, whom he had delighted in accompanying on the pianoforte. Wieland's courting of the girl, Christine ("Bibi") Hagel, culminated in her moving in with him and having his baby. Their love was genuine and passionate, but was nonetheless incapable of overcoming all the obstacles placed in its way from all sides. Wieland wanted to marry Bibi; her family wanted him to convert to Catholicism, his father wanted him to marry—if at all— Protestant; and neither solution was acceptable to the two politica¹ factions. Furthermore, Wieland's friends felt that Bibi was below his station.

The story of their affair reads like a dime novel. Bibi's parents had, of course, observed the senator's interest in their daughter and, although flattered by it, felt it better to avoid undesirable consequences by sending the girl off to a neighboring estate as a lady's maid. However, Christine ran off a few days later to move in with Wieland, where she remained from December 1762 to September 1763. When he learned that she was carrying his child, he was overjoyed and even decided to write a book about child-rearing! He also requested Sophie's aid in locating a private girl's school so that Bibi could acquire the education necessary for his new position in life, for he fully intended to marry her. She was also to await her child's birth there. The cloister of the "Englische Fräulein" in Augsburg was selected. At this point, their affair took a turn for the worse. Wieland had decided to marry in the Lutheran church in order to appease his father, the town's pastor, and to placate the Lutheran faction. However, Christine's mother was convinced that all Protestants went to Hell and wanted to save her daughter from this fate. Wieland sensed trouble, so he sent off a friend, Schmelz, to retrieve Bibi from Augsburg; bring her back to Biberach, where he could marry her secretly; and hide her in his apartment until things calmed down. His preparations included covering the windows of his apartment with paper so that neighbors would notice nothing. Only the old woman Floriane, who kept house for Wieland, would be admitted, and she was sworn to secrecy.

Unfortunately, Christine's mother had arrived in Augsburg before Schmelz, had taken Bibi out of the cloister with threats of legal action, and had had her brought to the monastery at Roth, south of Nuremberg where Bibi's brother was a monk and the abbot a trusted family friend. There was nothing left for Schmelz to do but return to Biberach with the bad news. Irate, Wieland went to see Mrs. Hagel, assured her of his intentions to raise the children in the Catholic faith, and allayed her fears that he would run off with her daughter to a life of want in Switzerland. He was able to get her to agree to do what the abbot of the monastery at Roth advised. Thereupon, Wieland went to Roth, requested an audience with the abbot, and was able to get him to agree to the marriage. Back in Biberach he learned that the situation had changed again; the town was in an uproar. The Protestants were angered that their chancery director was going to marry a Catholic; they threatened to remove him from office—or at least not to support his petition in Vienna—if he went through with the marriage. Mrs. Hagel had changed her mind about following the abbot's advice because she did not want her daughter tied to a deposed director with no decent income nor the prospect of one.

In despair, Wieland returned to Roth to seek the abbot's advice on the new turn of events—in the middle of the night! The abbot had apparently gained Wieland's trust. To his dismay, Wieland had to hear from the monk exactly what he did not want to admit to himself. By marrying Bibi in the Catholic Church, he would most surely lose his position as senator and chancery administrator and most likely lose his citizenship in the city-republic as well. A Protestant marriage was out of the question, because of the mother's opposition. Thus Wieland had to resign himself to fate and renounce Christine. He knew the abbot was right, yet it was extremely difficult for the young man so desperately in love to follow the advice. For over a year he had been working too hard, days in the chancery, nights at his writing desk. In consequence of the excitement of the previous days and the difficult decision to renounce his love, Wieland collapsed, defeated. He became depressed, melancholy, and even began to think of death. Only once more did he see Christine, who seems to have returned to Biberach earlier than her parents expected in order to spend a night with her beloved. They were never to see each other again. Wieland even thought of giving up his post voluntarily, fantasizing about landing a professorship in Catholic Erfurt or retreating to a small farm in the country. But these were mere dreams, not viable alternatives. Soon afterward, Christine was removed from Biberach.

The intensity of his love for Bibi, combined with the impossibility of living his love to the fullest, persuaded Wieland never again to allow himself to become so deeply involved with a woman. It hurt too much. He returned to a more Platonic type of love, yet not the kind evident in Julie's case. Bibi and he had fathomed the depths of true love, and the experience had had a purifying, liberating effect on the poet. His sensual nature had been fully acknowledged; his affair with Bibi complemented his philosophical view of man as a hybrid of body and spirit, and gave it real meaning. From now on Wieland could be much more confident of himself and uninhibited in his writing and behavior. At the same time, he had acquired an indelible impression of the inscrutability of fate and of man's powerlessness in the face of it. To be sure, these were prominent themes in *Cyrus* and *Araspes und Panthea*, even in *Lady Johanna Gray* and *Clementina von Porretta*, but now they were more than

mere concepts. Yet Wieland was too much a child of the Enlightenment to give himself up to an all-encompassing cynicism. His
private and public affairs in Biberach taught him to temper his
excessive optimism and idealism with a dose of skepticism. It was
safer that way, for the disappointment could not be so great. Besides, it was more realistic. Yet Wieland did not abandon his fundamental idealism.

Throughout the Bibi affair, Wieland had sought the aid and advice
of Sophie LaRoche, who had moved with her husband to Warthausen, a country retreat located a short distance from Biberach.
Wieland required a trusted friend and a woman like Sophie, who
was acquainted with the ways of the world, to help him handle the
delicate situation with Christine. We detect in Sophie's correspondence a note of irritation; perhaps she did not want to see herself
replaced in the poet's affections.[1] Be that as it may, she did what she
could to help Wieland. She also informed Julie of the whole "sordid"
affair, although it was not necessary, since the author had never kept
his feelings for Bibi a secret from her. Under the circumstances, we
can't help but wonder how he could continue to maintain that he
loved Julie. Julie, for her part, did not believe him and broke off the
engagement, disappointed at not finding in Wieland what she
thought she had seen. Later she became even more incensed over
the erotic turn Wieland's poetry took in these years.

II *Warthausen*

The Bibi affair represents an important stage in the poet's
psychological and literary development, even as Sophie's love had
done earlier. The liberating influence of Bibi's love was complemented by the freer, more enlightened atmosphere of the Warthausen circle of literary connoisseurs. The estate belonged to
Count Friedrich von Stadion (1691–1768), LaRoche's father, who
had retired there in 1761, after a long and successful diplomatic
career in Mainz and England.[2] By the end of 1761, Wieland had
become a kind of court poet at Warthausen and enjoyed Count
Stadion's patronage. The count was elated to find a poet of Wieland's calibre in provincial Biberach; never had he heard or read
such supple, titillating verses in German. In order to stimulate the
poet's creativity, the elderly patron of the arts set aside a room for
him with a view of the surrounding gardens. This was an idyllic
setting, which approximated Wieland's ideal of Horace's *Sabinum*

and which he duplicated in typically Rococo miniature in the garden house he later acquired outside the town walls. There still exists today at Warthausen the shaded linden arbor where the pensive poet penned many a scintillating verse. The witty verse tales which were produced under these favorable conditions found an appreciative audience in the "Musenhof" of Warthausen.

The aristocratic circle at Warthausen was important for Wieland's development as a poet because he found there for the first time a public marked by culture, wit, and an agreeable lifestyle. In addition, he had at his disposal the only library in the vicinity, stocked extensively with the latest works of English, French, and German literature. Without such a library, Wieland might have been unable to create as he did. Life was carefree, the conversations were stimulating, and the meals were exquisite, served with genuine Tokay wine. Here Wieland once again learned to appreciate openly the pleasures of this world. In so doing, he did not become an "epicurean pig," as his detractors began to claim.[3] Like the anacreontic poets Friedrich Hagedorn, Johann Peter Uz, and Ludwig Gleim, Wieland lived the life of a "Biedermann." In view of the quiet pleasure afforded at Warthausen,[4] it is no wonder that he "fled" from stuffy, tense Biberach at every opportunity (i.e., except for the period when he was living with Christine). The combination of the Warthausen and Bibi experiences excited his poetic verve, with the result that a veritable torrent of verse and prose ensued.

III *The Shakespeare Translations*

Just after his return to Biberach in 1760, Wieland had embarked on a project which proved to be one of his first major contributions to German letters: the translation of Shakespeare's complete plays. The first play translated was, appropriately, *A Midsummer Night's Dream*, "appropriate" because of the young author's penchant for the fairytale atmosphere. The wondrous figures as a major element in many of Wieland's subsequent works. The play was the only Shakespearian one he translated into verse. Together with a prose translation of *King Lear*, *A Midsummer Night's Dream* was published in 1762; twenty additional plays in translation appeared over the next four years. There is a marked decline in the quality of the translations which is due no doubt to the rapid sequence in which they appeared. When we bear in mind that Wieland simultaneously held a public office, waged a lengthy legal battle, was involved in a turbulent love affair, composed two major novels, and penned several comic verse tales—the feat of translating twenty-two Shakespearean plays is amazing. Later Wieland came under attack by the Stürmer und Dränger, who found his understanding of Shakespeare's spirit insipid and his translations inadequate.[5] The criticisms leveled at him are not without foundation, for, as Gundolf has pointed out, Wieland translated with the reading public and its ability to understand the Briton in mind. Regardless of the faults these translations may have, it is indisputable that they introduced subsequent generations of writers such as Heinrich Wilhelm von Gerstenberg, Goethe, Schiller, the Schlegel brothers, and Ludwig Tieck, to the English genius. That in itself would have earned Wieland a place in the history of German literature.

Wieland probably got the idea for the translation project from Wolfgang Dietrich Sulzer, to whom he had given an English edition of Shakespeare. In January 1759, Sulzer had written to Wieland: "If only a clever person wanted to take on the task of summarizing these plays in German as Pere Brumoy has done for Greek drama. As far as I can tell, there isn't one drama worth translating completely. One could just make an outline of the play, while stressing the scenes and passages which are really beautiful, and then carefully arrange everything. I think such a translator would merit great acclaim."[6] Although Wieland's translations tend to be free ones, he is a much better judge of Shakespeare's worth then Sulzer shows himself to be in the cited passage. True, the poet's guiding principle was to telescope and expand where necessary in order to bring Shakespeare as close as possible to his German audience. Thus he even allowed some Swabian dialect to slip in. He did this not to "improve" on Shakespeare, but rather to transmit a feeling for the quality of the Englishman's work. It was the content, not the form, which attracted Wieland.

A recent study of Wieland's earlier, little known, "Theorie und Geschichte der Red-Kunst und Dicht-Kunst. Anno 1757" ("A History and Theory of Rhetoric and Poetry," which is really a collection of lectures) has convincingly argued that Wieland's attitude is "characterized by great admiration and uninhibited enthusiasm for Shakespeare which in language and content clearly anticipates the rhapsodic praise of the *Sturm und Drang* generation by a good fifteen years, be it Herder's "Shakespeare" (1773) . . . or Lenz' . . . *Anmerkungen übers Theater [Observations on the Theater,* 1774]."[7]

Furthermore, the authors were able to show that Wieland had called for greater recognition of poetic genius even before Young's *Conjectures* (1759), that he had advocated less strict adherence to classical literary rules before Lessing, and that he had demanded more realism in literature before the *Sturm und Drang*. This Shakespeare appreciation of 1757 was not without significance for the translations of the 1760s. The explanation for the use of prose and the sometimes careless work is to be sought in the state of the German language (which at that time was not yet capable of duplicating Shakespeare's mastery) and in the pressure Wieland felt to earn money to support himself and Christine during those critical years. The inadequacies of the translations are due less to a faulty understanding of Shakespeare's texts. Also, toward the end Wieland was devoting his most creative hours to his novel, *Agathon*, so that little time or energy was left for the Shakespeare project. In a sense, it had become a task to finish just for the sake of finishing, so that subsequent translations of Shakespeare's works by August Wilhelm Schlegel and Johann Joachim Eschenburg surpass Wieland's original endeavor in artistic quality. Nevertheless, Lessing acknowledged the value of Wieland's feat, perhaps seeing in it a fulfillment of what he called a proper understanding of Shakespeare's characters as hybrids of noble and base sentiment. Goethe later maintained that he preferred Wieland's translation when all he wanted was to amuse himself, because Wieland had best captured Shakespeare's naturalness. Long afterwards, Wieland expressed amazement that he had ever undertaken such a demanding task.[8] All in all, the significance of these translations for German literature is still underrated.

IV   *Comic Tales*

A.   *"Nadine"*

Also in 1762, a work of a very different kind came into being. It was the brief, so-called "lascivious," verse tale "Nadine," which is perhaps the first product of the combined Warthausen and Bibi experiences. It is the first in a series of capricious verse tales which became Wieland's trademark. Like the vast majority of his previous—and subsequent—poetic works, "Nadine" is not an original piece, for Wieland was convinced that the proof of a genuine poet was not originality in subject matter but originality in execution.

42   CHRISTOPH MARTIN WIELAND

Thus he made no secret of his literary debts.[9] "Nadine" is modeled on Matthew Prior's "The Dove," and the girl who teases her lover is probably an image of Bibi.[10] The dove appears as a winged god of love, "Scherz," who leads Amunt, the lover, to ever higher stages of ecstasy. The poem is quite explicit. It was just the kind of piece Count Stadion and his Rococo circle especially valued. Wieland, now fully liberated by Bibi, discovered in himself a tantalizing, erotic vein. To later tales he added a stronger ironic tone and often a moralizing one. The more poems he composed in this frivolous fashion, the more he mastered their technical aspects. In composing the rhymed verse narratives of the 1760s' he was motivated, no doubt, in part by the idea of competing with such masters of the genre as Boccaccio and Jean de Lafontaine, Ariosto and Prior.[11] What seemed to attract him most was the naturalistic element, which had, despite Julie Bondeli's prudish influence, already emerged in 1759 in *Lucian des Jüngeren wahrhafte Geschichte (The True History of Lucian the Younger)*. However, Julie had objected to the risqué note and had apparently caused the author to destroy the manuscript.

Julie's objection on moralistic grounds is symptomatic of the general reaction of Wieland's stuffy contemporaries, who identified the poet with the persona. For them the poet actually thought and acted like his fictive characters. Wieland was, nevertheless, instrumental in teaching his middle class readers to differentiate not only between the poet's point of view and that of the persona, but also to distinguish various add differing perspectives in the work. In the beginning, however, he suffered dearly because of his readers' ignorance. He was accused of immoral behavior, of leading the young astray, and he saw many of his works censored.

B. Komische Erzählungen

The work to cause the first public outcry of indignation was the collection *Komische Erzählungen (Comic Tales,* 1765), and not "Nadine," which was not published until 1770. The verse tales included in the volume were written between 1762 and 1765: "Das Urteil des Paris" ("Paris' Choice"), "Diana und Endymion," "Juno und Ganymed," and "Aurora und Cephalus." Of these, Wieland considered "Das Urteil des Paris" to be the least and "Aurora und Cephalus" the most successful effort. The source for all these verse narratives was suggested by his Lucian studies.[12] It is noteworthy that the Greeks are portrayed here as vain, petty, and frail at a time when Greece was exerting its "tyranny over Germany" through its idealization by such men as Winckelmann and Lessing. Perhaps the inclusion of the introductory excerpt from Gajus Plinius Secundus' letter to Ariston was to stress the anthropomorphic view of the legendary heroes.

The theme of each tale—in fact the predominant theme in all of Wieland's original works of the 1760s—is the nature of love and its effect on the lover. We have seen that as early as 1752 Wieland had distinguished two kinds of love, the sensual and the Platonic, which were strangely interrelated. This is a view which can be traced through *Araspes und Panthea* to the *Komische Erzählungen*.[13] It is clear from a letter written to Riedel in Erfurt on August 10, 1768, that this twofold kind of love was active in Wieland's consciousness in the early 1750s. Those years are referred to as a time "when Plato's cupid and Coypel's cupid (which, by the way, just between you and me, are two very different cupids) exerted their greatest influence on me."[14] Most significant in this regard is the poem "Psyche," conceived in 1758, planned as a large-scale work in the mid-1760s, but not published until 1767, and then as a fragment. The mythological Psyche is the representative of the human soul; in Wieland's poetry, the name usually refers to Sophie Gutermann (LaRoche). In the "Bruchstücke," the two kinds of love are called "half brothers," although they seem to be "exact opposites in origin, shape, and inclination" (AA, ser. 1, VII, 216). In conjunction with the *Komische Erzählungen*, Wieland had planned an extensive work dealing with this theme.

Even though the "Psyche" poem, in its fragmentary form, did not appear until two years after the *Komische Erzählungen* had been published, traces of the conception of the two cupids as "half brothers" are clearly observable in these frivolous tales. In 1766, Wieland had written his friend and publisher, Salomon Gessner, that he was convinced that his *Komische Erzählungen* could be defended on moral grounds, for they were "true and satirical portraits of the prevailing moral values of the upper classes."[15] Sengle questions the appropriateness of this defense, whereas Kurth-Voigt more recently concludes that Wieland meant what he said. Gruber's argument that these works were clandestinely intended as "Warnungstafeln" (danger notices) seems convincing and dovetails nicely with Wieland's own distinction of the two kinds of love.[16]

"Diana und Endymion" (1762), "Juno und Ganymed" (1765), and "Aurora und Cephalus" (1764) treat either the theme of fragile Platonic love or mawkish prudishness or both. Only the first of the four comic tales, "Urteil des Paris," does not deal with either of these themes, although Wieland did state that in this poem he attempted to combine the ideally beautiful with the burlesque.[17] Nevertheless, the burlesque dominates here as in "Nadine," and the reason for the lack of any moralizing or idealizing tendencies is to be sought no doubt in Wieland's erotic intimacy with Bibi. Both poems were written in 1762. Of the four comic tales included in the *Komische Erzählungen*, "Das Urteil des Paris" was the only one the author did not defend after he had come under attack. The explanation is to be found in a letter to Gessner of 1767: " 'Das Urteil des Paris' is the only [poem] not to my liking; but I do confess that I would rather have forfeited my entire authorship than not to have written the other three."[18]

In "Diana und Endymion," Diana is mocked for her fickleness, for despite her alleged virtue, she gives in to her sensual nature at the first temptation when she thinks that she is unobserved. However, she was not alone with the sleeping Endymion, but was observed by a lustful faun, who forces her to sleep with him in return for his silence. The moral intention of the "frivolous" work is summed up in the lines: "The eye is not sated by seeing, as a wise man did note, and Luna's example here can teach us how true he spoke."[19] We could argue that these verses are ambiguous, at best, that they might only be meant to tantalize and amuse the open-minded listeners at Warthausen. But then again, they might also be designed to satisfy other readers' needs for moral instruction. The two aspects of the dual intent are not mutually exclusive, as is borne out by the closing remark of a later comic verse tale, "Aspasia," which was conceived together with the *Komische Erzählungen*, but not published until 1773: "We could easily draw many more fine moral lessons from the story. But we gladly grant the reader some freedom. He who has a nose will surely scent them out; the others can do without them."[20] Under the prevailing influence of the Rococo atmosphere at Warthausen and at home, Wieland obviously felt no need to justify his frivolous works on moral grounds. Yet inherent in the theme of the two cupids is a natural source of justification, for Plato's cupid stands higher than Coypel's. This qualitative relationship between the two seems to lurk behind the indecorous facade of "Juno und Ganymed," which Wieland deleted from the 1769 edition of the *Komische Erzählungen* because of the incessant attacks upon its "bordello character."

In the course of the tale, prudish Juno is converted to sensual pleasures, whereas her lascivious husband, Zeus, converts to Platonic love. Zeus has turned his attentions from women to young Ganymed; Juno's frigidity and steadfastness have also given way to Ganymed's beauty. The conclusion is typically ambivalent: Zeus maintains that he loves the boy's beautiful soul and is following the wise Socrates' example in this homoerotic relationship. Juno's reply is impudent and to the point: "Very good, fine sir, it is your prerogative to dally to your heart's content with their souls; I do not begrudge you this noble impulse. As for myself, as you see, I am modest and make do with their baser part."[21]

The allusion to Socrates' wise example could, of course, be entirely ironic. Yet when we consider the extent and the intensity of the influence which the Greek philosopher exerted on Wieland otherwise, it is difficult to believe that this paragon of wisdom and virtue would be totally ironicized. In addition, the impact on Wieland of Diotima's concept of love as elucidated in the *Symposium* was so great that we could see its effect even here. For example, Juno loves Ganymed's physical beauty, while Zeus is attracted to his noble qualities, so that Ganymed could be taken as a representative of beauty per se, and the love relationships could very well reflect the first two stages of Diotima's love concept: love of the physical leads to love of the spiritual, which, in turn, was to lead the lover to a love of the source of all beauty. Juno seems to echo this hierarchical relationship in her use of the adjectives *edel* (noble) and *gröber* (baser). Nevertheless, such subtleties were missed by Wieland's readers, and the tale was rejected outright as immoral. The reception of "Juno und Ganymed" is a classic example of an author being only half understood.

The comic tale widely acclaimed as the best of the *Komische Erzählungen* is "Aurora und Cephalus."[22] The last of the four tales to be written, it was understandably more masterfully executed than the preceding ones. Like "Juno und Ganymed," it evinced another major theme in Wieland's work: the deceptiveness of appearances. The goddess Aurora abducts the hunter Cephalus, who is happily married to Procris, and attempts to seduce him. They fall in love, but in doing so, deceive themselves, for Cephalus believes that he is

loving his wife Procris in Aurora, whereas Aurora loves not
Cephalus himself but her own husband, Tithan, who, as a young
man, is reflected in Cephalus. Before he actually becomes unfaithful
to his wife, Cephalus gets hold of himself. Yet the close call was
enough to cause guilt feelings. In order to ameliorate these un-
justified feelings, he calls Procris' staunch fidelity to mind. However, Aurora, a bit piqued at her failure, makes him suspicious of
Procris' virtue, with the result that Cephalus decides to test his
wife's fidelity. To this end, he receives from Aurora a magic ring
with the power to make him unrecognizable. After several attempts
at seducing his wife in the form of other men, Cephalus ultimately
succeeds in making Procris waver in her constancy. The hesita-
tion—that is, the merest indication that she would become unfaithful to him—suffices to justify his (unfounded) suspicions.
Cephalus reveals his identity and accuses Procris of infidelity. Procris is understandably enraged at her husband's deception and tells
him that she had not loved the stranger himself, but rather
Cephalus' traits in him. Thereupon she leaves him, and he tries to
commit suicide in despair. It is interesting to note that no one in the
tale actually sleeps with anyone else, so that there is little justification for calling the tale immoral. The lesson to be learned from this
comic tale is clear and certainly not new to us: since virtue is such a
fragile thing, it is unwise to unnecessarily endanger it. Furthermore, the motivation for an action is not always what we take it to
be; thus we should be more tolerant of others, bearing in mind that
a changed perspective might cause us to alter our views.[23] Wieland
has profited greatly from his study of human nature, which began in
the early 1750s. We have here an example of how he shows us the
internal workings of his characters, how he "throws light . . . directly on their thinking, emotions and striving."[24]

A stylistic feature related to point of view is the topos of ignorance, of "je ne sais quoi." Wieland frequently uses this topos as a
ploy to induce the reader into active participation. For example, in
"Juno und Ganymed," the poet writes:

> Doch hörten sie (denn Götter hören fein)
> Ich weiss nicht was, das sie zum Schluss bewogen,
> Die Dame sei im Bade nicht allein.[25]

Hundreds of examples of the titillating use of feigned ignorance
could be found easily, yet this one will suffice to transmit a sense of

its effect. However, the "je ne sais quoi" is not restricted to a purely stylistic function. It also has definite philosophic connotations. For example, Wieland uses it to refer to the inscrutability of the human soul. In a very telling letter addressed to Sophie in 1767, Wieland speaks of his plan for the large-scale "Psyche" poem mentioned earlier. To all appearances, the poem would just be fanciful (*blau*); in reality, however, it would entail "true philosophy" and a "critical . . . somewhat comical natural history of our soul, this incomprehensible *je ne sais quoi*, whose contradictions Pascal had known so well and whose grandeur and weakness he had demonstrated by his own example."[26] The "je ne sais quoi" therefore has a philosophic as well as a stylistic aspect. Wieland was so taken with the plan that he intended to make it his opus magnum, by which he wanted to be remembered. The idea is an echo of a suggestion made in 1758 to collaborate with Zimmermann on a work dealing with the nature and kinds of human love.[27] Although the grand plan was never realized, all the works written in the sixties and seventies reflect what would have gone into it. This is particularly true of *Die Geschichte des Agathons* (*The History of Agathon* 1766–1767), the novel which did become Wieland's opus magnum.

C.   *The Comic Verse Epic*: Idris und Zenide

Perhaps the most original—and bizarre—of the verse compositions of these years is the fragment *Idris*, later entitled *Idris und Zenide*. Of the ten cantos planned for the narration of Idris' wild and fabulous adventures, only five were completed and published in 1768. Critics disagree on the reason for the work's remaining a fragment. Sengle, for example, presents an aesthetic argument: the Rococo atmosphere which provided the stimulus for such creations was beginning to dissipate, meaning that there was no longer a complete world picture to justify a rounded epos. Besides, the fragment form was already fashionable. Wieland was probably thinking of Sterne's *Tristram Shandy*, which he had been studying assiduously since 1767. Arguing in this fashion, Sengle moves Wieland closer to the generation of Romantic poets, one of whom, Tieck, owed more to Wieland's capricious genius than he cared to admit. Sengle cites the historicoliterary significance of the work as "the point of juncture between Rococo and Romanticism."[28] Gruber, on the other hand, is less academic and more psychological in his approach. In 1765, Wieland had quietly married the simple girl his family and friends had chosen for him, Dorothea Hillebrand of Augsburg. The marriage proved to be a very happy one; in fact, the first years proved to be especially idyllic for the poet. His position as town clerk had been secured in 1764 by imperial decree so that he had no more professional worries. His young wife (she was twenty, he thirty-two) cared lovingly for all his needs at home. Under the influence of these circumstances, his poetic spirit expressed itself in voracious, giddy activity. *Idris und Zenide* is the "product of the honeymoon months of his marriage." His "Schneckenhaus" existence was well-established, and he was looking forward to the birth of their first child in late 1767. The baby, however, was stillborn. This sobering event robbed the author of the capricious mood necessary to continue such a whimsical work.[29] There is, perhaps, a kernel of truth in both views. Although *Idris und Zenide* was never completed, certain of its traits can be easily observed in the verse epic *Der neue Amadis* (1771).

According to Wieland's own words, the plot of *Idris und Zenide* is unimportant. What seemed to interest the poet most was the Italian verse form, *ottava rima*, which had gained wide recognition in Tasso's epic *Gerusalemme liberata*, and Ariosto's *Orlando Furioso*. The poet openly admits that his *Idris* is an attempt to match his talents with those of Tasso and Ariosto and to show that the less supple German tongue could be molded to this verse form as well as Italian. In doing so, however, Wieland discovered that he had to loosen the Italian syllabic and rhyme scheme somewhat to avoid the monotony of strict regularity and to provide a greater musicality to the stanza. The lines in *Idris* vary from eight to thirteen syllables, the rhymes can be either feminine or masculine, and the rhyme scheme is not fixed. Wieland was the first poet to attempt *ottava rima* in German literature and was justifiably proud of his innovation. Introducing this verse form into German cost him great effort, as is evident from his complaint to Riedel in 1767. He assured Riedel that, contrary to what the critic in *Die allgemeine Bibliothek* thought, he did not work rapidly or superficially. Rather, he spent hours painstakingly polishing his verse until he achieved a musical flow of words. The motivation behind such effort was not the desire for critical acclaim, but an inner artistic need to create verses that were as perfect as is humanly possible.[30] This statement is one of the first and clearest concerning the author's approach to creative work, a method already hinted at in reference to *Cyrus* (1759). Nevertheless, the image of Wieland as ruled effortlessly by a spirit of fanciful-ness, churning out verse after verse without much consideration, prevailed for two centuries, until Beissner demonstrated on the basis of newly discovered manuscripts how words, phrases, even whole lines were continually revised, until perfection was achieved. This method of writing is known as "Poesie des Stils."[31]

Although Wieland emphasized the poem's form, he was very excited about the plot, too, as can be seen from his effusions to Gessner:

Imagine a story in the manner of Hamilton's *Four Flasks (Quatre Facardins)* or *Bélier*. Imagine a story unequaled by any produced by a sound mind ["gesunder Kopf"], one which is the quintessence of all the adventures of your Amadises and your fairy tales. And imagine embedded in this plot, behind the frivolous facade, metaphysics, morality, and the unfolding of the most secret urge of the human heart. Imagine it filled further with criticism, satire, real characters, scenes, passions, reflections, sentiments—in brief, with everything you could possibly want. And all wonderfully combined with magic, ghost stories, duels, centaurs, hydras, dragons and "Amfisbä-nen!" "[32]

The plot is so bizarre and confusing that the reader himself is not sure what happens. Yet the contours are familiar and its theme is well known to us by now. The hero, Idris, is a knight errant in search of a fairy queen. He is not only a Don Quixote figure but also a Platonic enthusiast whose fairy queen is obviously symbolic of a highly idealistic goal. Opposed to the Platonic Idris is Ithyphall, a man of the world and a paramour. He too is constantly on the move and is basically a Don Quixote himself—but the fixation is different. Ithyphall is Greek for "erect penis," a word play which surely caused eyebrows to be raised. Between the extremes of the Platonic and the phallic, Wieland has posited an exemplary pair, Lila and Zerbin, who live in idyllic tranquillity on an island. Idris' (and Ithyphall's) goal is evidently this golden mean of calm between the restless extremes, a goal which was to have been achieved in the second half of the epic. The structure recalls that of many medieval epics, for example, of *Erec*, *Iwein*, and most notably, the dualism of Parzival and Gawain in *Parzival*. Wieland was, of course, exposed to these medieval romances and to the Minnesingers through Bodmer, who, together with Gottsched, initiated medieval literary studies. The theme of *Idris* is again the kinds of human love, and this epic seems to have been intended as a kind of philosophy of love, a partial ersatz for the incomplete "Psyche" poem. The work is, therefore, an integral part thematically and stylistically of all the verse endeavors of the Biberach years.

The capricious mood of *Idris* is continued in the epic, *Der neue Amadis*, begun in 1768 under the influence of Sterne's *Tristram Shandy* and concluded in Erfurt in 1771. *Der neue Amadis* is also written in *ottava rima* and deals with the idealistic and materialistic concepts of love. But this work takes us beyond the verse productions completed during the author's nine year stay in Biberach.

D. Musarion: *Rococo Mastery*

The crowning achievement of Wieland's verse narratives in the 1760s is *Musarion, oder die Philosophie der Grazien (Musarion, or The Philosophy of the Graces*, 1768). It too demonstrates the author's innovative vein. Wieland himself called it "a new kind of poem which holds the middle between the didactic poem, comedy and narrative," while Sengle credits Wieland with the ability to create new genres long before the Romanticists came upon the scene.[33] The metric form is free verse, predominantly dithyrambic, with an occasional Alexandrine to underscore the didactic intent, despite the whimsical mood. This pastoral work spread Wieland's fame even further, from Switzerland to central Germany. Adam Friedrich Oeser was so enthused by the poem that he brought it to the attention of his student, Johann Wolfgang Goethe, in Leipzig. Goethe too was quite taken with the poem, seeing in it a genuine expression of Greek antiquity. In Book Seven of his *Dichtung und Wahrheit (Poetry and Truth)*, he later wrote of his first encounter with *Musarion:* "It was here that I believed to see antiquity alive and fresh again. Everything plastic about Wieland's genius was evident here in the most perfect manner."[34] Another contemporary, George Christoph Lichtenberg, was enthralled by its "rose color and silver," the silver referring to its pristine coolness, which is enlivened by the rose-colored glow of love.[35] These terms describe *in nuce* the qualities of the narrative which has come to represent the best of the Rococo movement in German literature and which is, above all, striking for the harmony it achieves between aesthetic and didactic intent.

In her excellent study of *Musarion's* place in Rococo literature, Elizabeth Boa speaks of the Rococo poet's view of man in anthropomorphic rather than religious terms. The human view stresses equally man's rationality and sensuality—the latter with a decided proclivity for curving shapes such as bosoms and buttocks, preferably enshrouded in shifting colors, fluid movement, and decorative detail. These qualities are designed to appeal to man's rational as well as to his sensual nature. Boa sums up this situation as follows:

"Rococo style, then, is the blending of an intellectual, an emotional and a sensual element into a unified, elegant form. Where intellectuality becomes too strong, the mode approaches the rationalism of the Enlightenment; where emotion is untempered by wit, and sensuous beauty, the mode tends towards *Empfindsamkeit* or the cult of sentiment; where sensuality runs riot, unbounded by formal control and enlightened by humour, Rococo will tend to degenerate into overdecorative *Kitsch* or pornography . . . . Everything must be subject to elegant form, which is the product of a balanced mingling of appeal to the senses, the mind and the emotions."[36]

Wieland achieves that harmony of formal expression and sensual appeal admirably in *Musarion* and, in doing so, becomes the "first significant German poet in modern times to infuse poetry with a decidedly worldly atmosphere."[37]

The central idea of the poem is that of moderation. The extremes of "enthusiasm and indifference" (Wieland in the preface to the second edition of 1769) are to be avoided, while both the mind and the body receive their just due. The tripartite structure of the narrative is not only reminiscent of the three acts of a comedy but also reflects Musarion's middle course between the extremes of the stoic, Kleanth, and the Pythagorean, Theophon. Her student in this comic lesson of the golden mean is Phanias, her Platonic lover who ran off into the wilderness to join these two philosophers because he was disappointed by Musarion's physical interest in the dandy Bathyll. Musarion decides that she really loves Phanias and goes off in search of him, hoping to cure him of his extremism. Book One shows Phanias in the country under the influence of Theophon and Kleanth. Of a mind to reject the world entirely, he spurns the beautiful Musarion. Book Two deals with the exposure of Kleanth and Theophon as mere men. The power of wine induces Kleanth to reject his stoic principles; Theophon reveals the flatulous nature of his moral enthusiasm through his infatuation with the seductive Chloe, and Phanias' passion for Musarion is rekindled. Book Three presents us with a characteristic Rococo motif, that of the impatient lover and the reluctant but finally yielding beauty. Following the banquet in Book Two, Phanias pays Musarion a nocturnal visit, while Theophon goes off with Chloe and Kleanth sleeps off his drunken stupor. After first assuring herself of his genuine love, Musarion succumbs to Phanias' advances, now certain that he has learned how inappropriate either extreme represented by the two philosophers is.

As Boa has pointed out, each of the three parts of *Musarion* forms a Rococo tableau: Phanias with the two philosophers in front of an Arcadian hut, a candlelight banquet, and a moonlit bedroom scene. Rococo motifs abound: bowls of fruit, wreaths of flowers, jugs of nectar, dew on the grass, butterflies, nightingales, breezes and honey — all of which help to convey a sense of the joys and pains of love. Yet through the use of irony, Wieland prevents his reader from entering this idyllic world entirely. In the opening lines, when Phanias is placed in the stereotyped Arcadian scene, Wieland points out expressly that he is not wearing the prerequisite wreath of roses.[38] At another point, the poet depicts the two awe inspiring philosophers wrestling like schoolboys in the dirt in front of their pastoral abode. There are countless allusions to classical philosophy and literature, rendered in an easy conversational manner. The erudition is not introduced for its own sake, but in order to enhance the aesthetic and philosophic content of the poem. Other aspects of Wieland's style and technique are the narrator's ironic stance toward the characters and the readers, and the rhythmic and syntactical effects designed to heighten the irony and the narrative suspense. The urbane tone presupposes a cultivated reading public.

The all-pervasive irony of the poem is intended not only to keep us at a distance so that we can admire the aesthetic construct, but also to allow us time for reflection on the didactic content. It is a means of speaking "beneficial truths in a joking manner, truths which one normally would not speak."[39] The stoic's extreme asceticism is thus totally discounted: Kleanth spends his last night in a pig sty, never to be seen again. The Pythagorean's excessive spirituality is chided, but not his ideals as such. Musarion states: "The man [is ridiculed], not his teachings, not Truth, although (in the manner of all fantasts) his inflamed brain couples it with chimeras. My ridicule is aimed only at the chimeras." And a few lines later she says of the Pythagorean dreams: "Who can say that we don't see more clearly in dreams?" At this point, the poet seems to have sensed that the tone was becoming too earnest and has Phanias remind Musarion (and the reader) of the situation at hand: his presence in her bedchamber after midnight. Phanias sanguinely asks: "Musarion, why put off that which makes us like gods?"[40] Thereupon her resistance to his insistence fades, and they do what comes naturally. Like Phanias in Musarion's arms, so Theophon discovers in Chloe's arms what it means to be human and alters his philosophy accordingly. Man must get to know and accept the duality of his nature, with its penchant for extreme rationality and idealism on the one hand and extreme materialism on the other.

The famous inscription at the temple in Delphi, *gnothi seauton*, (know yourself) is cited at the poem's conclusion as the best formula for the lesson to be learned. Self-knowledge is the ultimate source of human happiness and therefore the fitting goal of man's striving; and the knowledge gained from self-study is also a guard against all kinds of excess. Phanias learns how necessary it is to know one's weaknesses (as well as one's strengths) and as a reward is united with Musarion. Health, self-knowledge, and the "philosophy of the Graces" are the prerequisites of human happiness: "Healthy blood, a clear head, a tranquil heart, and a happy face. How rich he is! Consider, Musarion, what more can the gods give him, and better, for a happy life?"[41] These lines are an echo of a vision Wieland had in 1754 when he wrote to Bodmer concerning his ultimate goal in life: "I want to be happy, and indeed to be happy according to my own view of happiness. I also want to be of service to the greatest extent possible. May I lose the esteem of all honest men if I ever fail to achieve my destiny."[42] The most obvious models for this ideal, to which Wieland remained true for the rest of his life, are the ironic mirth of Laurence Sterne and the psychological honesty of the third Earl of Shaftesbury. The latter's vision of the virtuoso combining in himself physical and moral grace, beauty of body and beauty of mind, are descriptive of Musarion, who teaches Phanias (i.e., us) the art of life, yes, the art of loving life in a calm and temperate way, but nevertheless sincerely and joyfully.

As the subtitle openly announces, *Musarion* presents us with the philosophy of the Graces and with that the direct Greek influence. In order to understand *Musarion* more fully, we should also consider Wieland's poem *Die Grazien (The Graces,* 1770), which was conceived about the same time and which defines more specifically what Wieland intended to connote with the phrase "philosophy of the Graces." The Graces (Aglaja, Euphrosyne, and Thalia) contribute significantly to the perfection of man. If we see them as goddesses of sensual beauty we misunderstand them, for they are rather divinities of charm (*Liebreiz*), which is closely associated with the sensation of spiritual love and with gracefulness. The spring of the Graces is the soul itself, and the love inspired by them is therefore more spiritual in tone. The morality they teach is neither the stern virtue of the Enlightenment's moral philosophy nor of Christianity's. The Graces do not deny the body and its charms but integrate them with spiritual beauties to create a whole. In this sense they create the foundation for true humanity and point the way to Schiller's concept of *Anmut* (grace). The Graces are motivated by noble love to please and to be sensitive to the needs of others. Wieland sums up the significance which the Graces have for man's quest for perfection with the words: "Only in the hands of the Graces do the wisdom and virtue of mortals lose their exaggerated and inflated side effects, their tartness, their stiffness and angularity, which are just so many defects through which wisdom and virtue cease to be wisdom and virtue."[43]

That is precisely the lesson Wieland intended to teach with his *Musarion*. Unfortunately, he was all too frequently misunderstood by his contemporaries. A major reason for the misjudging was the tendency to see him as the seraphic poet in Bodmer's house and to remember only his strong attack on Uz's alleged licentiousness, which, as we have seen, was less the result of conviction than of concern for Bodmer. The image of Wieland as a pious bigot lingered the longest in Northern Germany, where he was regularly "attacked" in Nicolai's *Bibliothek der schönen Wissenschaften* for his alleged scurillity. Wieland felt that he was especially unfairly treated by Thomas Abbt, Heinrich Wilhelm von Gerstenberg, and Johann Gottfried Herder. Yet Friedrich Nicolai was astute enough to recognize in the 1750s that Wieland's muse was unbefittingly dressed as a devotee: "Wieland's muse is a young girl, who, like Bodmer's, wants to play the devotee too. In order to please the old widow, she puts on an old-fashioned bonnet, which does not suit her well. She tries to put on a prudent, experienced expression, but reveals only too clearly her youthful remissness. It would be a strange spectacle if this young teacher of piety were to change into a vivacious, popular beauty."[44] Of course, Nicolai's vision came true as soon as Wieland had had time to develop further. His religious fervor, however, was not feigned. His pietistic vein dates back to Klosterbergen, where he reportedly got himself worked up into a state of "holy contrition and ecstasy."[45] Life in Bodmer's shadow was conducive to such enthusiasm.

Wieland did not like being misunderstood, complaining on one occasion that "nothing seems less understood than my true character and my literary production," a state of affairs to which he could not remain indifferent.[46] At least he undertook to convince his friends that his new works did not signify a changed attitude toward true virtue. A letter to Julie Bondely of 1764 contains a lengthy defense of himself and an explanation of his so-called metamorphosis, which Lessing had noted as early as 1759:

Formerly I was an enthusiast in religious, metaphysical and moral matters; and I was completely sincere. Enthusiasm was then my way of life, or rather, the result of 100,000 physical and spiritual causes. Even though I might have ceased to be an enthusiast in one sense of the word, and although I no longer believe in the preexistence of the soul and am no longer enthralled at the sight of a rose-colored seraph with wings of gold and azure, I am no less an advocate of truth and do not find virtue less attractive . . . . In my enthusiastic and Platonic period I was rash, quick to anger, capricious, grumpy, and sullen; since beginning to write about Biribinkers and Endymions, I have learned to moderate my passions. I hope to convince you that I have consistently maintained the character of a sincere man, which is basic to me, even when I erred. I have never presented myself as a paragon of virtue. My critics will find that my head was sometimes foolish, but my heart was always well-intentioned . . . . Since I was seventeen, I have, thank God, loved at least a dozen charming women. All of them have caused me grief; all my loves were of the kind one calls *passions*, all my beloved were goddesses whom I adored. I even practiced Platonic love to an heroic extreme on several occasions; I no longer feel myself capable of such love . . . . Why can't one forget these spiritual quixotisms of my youth, why can't I be judged by the general standard, and why can't I be allowed the same freedom which the most esteemed writers of the past and present enjoyed and which went unopposed in them? ! . . . If somber and devout persons wonder at my being the author of these latest works, I am to be pitied. They can reproach me, but they should not go so far as to think badly of my morals or my character.[47]

Wieland suffered a long time from his chameleonlike appearance, for apparently very few people ever really understood him. It was the rare critic who, for example, saw the comic element in the

Komische Erzählungen and judged them on aesthetic rather than moral grounds. This practice was due no doubt to the continued association in the public mind of Wieland with Bodmer and his circle, particularly with Johann Georg Sulzer (1720–1779), who subjugated aesthetic concerns to moral ones in his aesthetic theory, which he popularized from the mid 1750s on. It is strange that Wieland was seldom judged by the standards applied to others; it happened again in the 1770s and the 1790s, when he came under attack first by the *Stürmer und Dränger* and then the Romanticists. His reaction in each case is surprising because he persisted along the path he considered right. Had he been as spineless as some critics have argued, he would have acceded to public opinion. Apparently Wieland was much more self-reliant in personal and professional matters than has often been thought.

The fact that Wieland's virtuoso in *Musarion* (and elsewhere) was a woman should not be surprising. Judging by his letter to Julie, the role women have played in his life is evidently central. Love is at least *a* major theme in Wieland's opus, not only in the works of the 1760s. Therefore, it is the woman who, time and again, leads the errant male to the golden path of happiness by teaching him moderation. This is the lesson learned from the Bibi affair, which was a necessary prelude to the marital contentment he found with Dorothea Hillebrand from 1765 onwards. Musarion is a type of "schöne Seele" (beautiful soul) and, as such, in a class with Panthea, Psyche, Danae, Aspasia, and Lais. Musarion—and this is psychologically striking, for it means that the figure of Musarion was working on the author's subconscious—is in fact the fictional mother of Psyche and Agathon in the novel *Agathon,* and she is Lais' foster-daughter in the epistolary novel *Aristipp,* who subsequently marries Aristipp's best friend, Kleonidas. The Musarions of *Agathon* and *Aristipp* both have in common that they are mothers, which might provide fuel for Gruber's argument that *Musarion* reflects essentially Wieland's marital joy and contentment. His *Sturm und Drang* period behind him, the poet could now look forward to the role of *pater familias* and created for himself a utopian vision of the future. The hint of an idyllic conjugal existence at the conclusion of *Musarion* seems to support Gruber's contention. At least in the author's subconscious, the characteristics of Plato's cupid and Coypel's cupid are united in Musarion's person, so that she might be seen as a kind of madonna-harlot figure.[48]

In all his jovial, ironic verse narratives of the 1760s, Wieland saw a greater educational value than in the traditional straight-faced somber exhortations to a virtuous life. He once wrote that works in the manner of "Swift, Rabelais and Sterne have a much greater educative value than the works of most serious writers"; and he quite obviously combined the humor and burlesque of these writers with the sensuality of a Hamilton, LaFontaine, or Prior.[49] Quickly attaining mastery over form and rhyming technique, Wieland emerged in these years as a powerful poetic force.

CHAPTER 4

The Modern Novel in Germany

I.   Die Abenteuer des Don Sylvio von Rosalva *(1764)*

T HE innovativeness evident in the structure and style of the
verse productions of the Biberach years is also characteristic of
the two major novels Wieland composed between 1761 and 1767.
Although the *Komische Erzählungen* and *Musarion* were unique,
they belonged to a short-lived genre and thus did not have the later
impact that the novels had. The phenomenal rise in the popularity
of the novel in the last third of the eighteenth century was accompanied by a corresponding decrease in the interest in verse narratives. Bluntly stated, the prose novel was the art form of the rising
middle classes, while the verse form was the domain of aristocratic
circles.

Don Sylvio has been hailed as the first modern German novel.[1]
whereas *Die Geschichte des Agathon (The History of Agathon)* has
been lauded as the first novel for the thinking reader.[2] *Don Sylvio* is
one of the first successful attempts at writing a comic tale in prose,[3]
while *Agathon* opens the series of "Bildungsromane" prominent in
the late eighteenth and throughout the nineteenth century. Although the latter novel was begun in 1761, Wieland interrupted
work on it in June 1763, in order to write the former. One rainy day,
as he sat at his desk looking out of the window, depressed with no
desire to continue with that arduous undertaking, he suddenly felt
the urge to write something in a lighter vein to cheer himself up.
The result was *Don Sylvio.* On August 5, 1963, he wrote to Gessner:

A couple of months ago, on a rainy day, I hit upon the idea of writing a little
novel in which both clever people and fools would find much to laugh at and
which would amuse me without costing me the least effort. I prepared my
outline and began to write without further ado. This divertissement amused
me so much that I began to take it seriously and decided to create out of my

basic idea, which in itself is crazy enough, the cleverest thing I was capable of. It is a kind of satirical novel, philosophic enough behind its frivolous façade. I like to think that no reader, except for devotees, will find it boring.[4]

Wieland was not wrong in his estimation, for the novel was an immediate success. As a first introduction to Wieland, *Don Sylvio* is ideal for the modern reader because it acquaints him with the author's essential ideas and style in a highly entertaining fashion. Wieland had stated that *Don Sylvio* would reveal another side of himself, and so it did. For example, we find here, for the first time, the same frivolous tone of the later verse narratives. Many readers took offense at the novel's frivolity and apparent sexual levity, condemning it loudly. One such critic was Julie Bondely, who most adamantly rejected the interpolated Biribinker episode, a section dating back in concept to Wieland's manuscript, "Die wahre Geschichte Lucian des Jüngeren" (*The True Story of Lucian the Younger*). In 1759, Julie had caused him to destroy that manuscript because she had objected at that time to its frivolous tone.[5]

Unfortunately, the novel was widely misunderstood, even attacked. The attacks on *Don Sylvio* proved, however, to be but a prelude to the more intense reaction to the *Komische Erzählungen,* which appeared one year later. Since *Don Sylvio* had appeared anonymously, only the initiated knew who the author was. In order to counterbalance a view of the novel as irreverent, the author emphasized in his correspondence its philosophic and satiric intent. Thus, he assured Gessner:

If the question is whether *Don Sylvio von Rosalva* is a composition worthy of teaching virtue, then I think—presumably because of paternal blindness toward the youngest child of my wit—that I should win my case handily. Sometimes one appears to make merry and have fun, but instead philosophizes better than Crantor and Chrysippus. I doubt very much that you (if you could overcome your prejudice) would find confirmed, at a second reading, your idea that the author of *Don Sylvio* had no higher intention than to amuse . . . a predisposed public. The more I have gotten to know man and men in various lights and in various circumstances, both in history and in my own experience, the more I find my view confirmed that the nuclei of superstition and enthusiasm . . . have always wrought, and continue to exert, tremendous havoc on sound reason and on human society."[6]

It is revealing that Wieland twice refers to subjective views in this passage. First, he admits that he is probably prejudiced in favor of *Don Sylvio*; after all, he wrote it. Second, he questions whether his friend Gessner could reread the novel with sufficient detachment to recognize another point of view. We are left with the impression that Wieland was fully aware of the need for detachment and a multiplicity of views in order to get to the heart of the matter. This, at any rate, seems to be the upshot of his study of man. Shakespeare's insights into the complexity of the human personality have obviously affected his German translator, who was equally strongly influenced by his study of ancient and modern skeptics, such as Crantor and Chrysippus or Bayle and Locke.[7] In addition, Wieland always had before his mind's eye Socrates' assertion that the only thing he knew was that he knew nothing.

The letter to Gessner cited above accurately describes the tone and intent of *Don Sylvio*. Its apparent foolishness is highly instructive because it shows the reader the dangers of excessive myopia and suggests ways of reducing prejudice. Basically, then, this first novel deals with the subjective way in which we perceive things. What better model than Cervantes' *Don Quixote* could Wieland have chosen for his "perspective portrayal of man"?[8]

Because of the double thrust of the novel—satire and philosophy—the adventures of Don Sylvio seem to be two dimensional. The narrator himself speaks of the "twofold nature of reality," which consists of empirical reality and the individual's subjective perception thereof. Wieland, in fact, attempts to show how everyone perceives the external world more or less prejudicially and fashions, on the basis of his own particular bias, an internal reality which can diverge radically from the external one. Man's task is to try to attune his inner reality as closely as possible to the outer one, since the latter is the common denominator of social interaction. The two dimensions are further evident in the stylistic consequences of Wieland's satiric and philosophic intentions. While the satirical vein destroys, that is shows vice and/or folly to be what they are through ridicule and reprobation, the philosophic vein attempts to establish the guidelines for human action and interaction. In order to better understand how Wieland fulfills his double purpose, it is advisable to briefly outline the novel's plot.

The hero of this wondrous tale is Don Sylvio, a youth of eighteen, who had been raised by his spinster aunt, Donna Mencia, on their isolated country estate of Rosalva in Spain. The boy had lost his mother at an early age, and his father died when he was ten. His only sister had vanished without a trace. His aunt attempted to raise her nephew according to chivalric ideas which she had gleaned from adventurous tales of knight-errantry and pseudohistorical Baroque novels, such as the saga of King Arthur's Round Table, La Calprenède's *Pharamond*, and Madame de Scudéri's *Clelia* and *Cyrus*. Donna Mencia firmly believed in the actuality of these adventures; it never occurred to her that they were fictional. Just as empirical reality had been altered in his aunt's mind by her love of adventure stories, so was Don Sylvio's perception of the real world strongly affected by his voracious reading of fairy tales. Fairies, nymphs, sylphs, and a host of other supernatural creatures are just as much a part of his reality as the force of gravity. Considering the youth's almost total isolation in the country and the influence of his aunt's unusual convictions, Don Sylvio's naïvete is understandable. In a remote corner of the garden, he erects a cozy arbor where he spends hours dreaming of heroic feats. His favorite dream is that of liberating a beautiful fairy enchanted by a wicked witch.

One day, while strolling through the woods, he spots a beautiful butterfly, which seems to look at him melancholically. To his inflamed imagination, however, this is no ordinary butterfly, but a lovely princess enchanted by the witch Fanfürlüsch. For the hero, the look expresses a longing for release. Without further thought, he sets off to capture the butterfly and release his princess. Although he loses the butterfly in the chase, he does discover a medallion in the grass with a miniature portrait of an angelic young woman on it. For him, this medallion is concrete evidence that his assumption is correct, and he sets about secretly organizing a search for his enchanted princess. In the dark of the night soon after, this new Don Quixote sets out on his adventures with his servant, Pedrillo, who shares many traits with Sancho Panza (also with Fielding's Slipslop and Partridge). Don Sylvio and Pedrillo undergo several quixotic experiences involving a frog and some crude farmhands, but none of these adventures causes Don Sylvio to admit his delusions. At one point, the two adventurers aid in the rescue of a young woman, Donna Jacinte. They meet her beau, Don Eugenio, and his friend, Don Gabriel. We later learn that Donna Jacinte is Don Sylvio's long-lost sister, who had been kidnapped years before by a gypsy. Don Eugenio turns out to be the brother of Donna Felicia, who had lost the miniature portrait found by our hero. The painting, in fact, is apparently an exact image of her. Shortly thereafter, the quixotic adventurers stumble upon Donna Felicia's summer villa at Lirias, where Don Sylvio discovers his love for the young mistress. In effect, then, the search for an imaginary princess leads him to true love and a recognition of his folly. He learns that the world of fantasy is separate from the real world. At the novel's conclusion, Don Sylvio sets off on the prerequisite grand tour before returning to marry Donna Felicia. In short, the novel traces the hero's transition from profound naïveté to a budding cosmopolitanism.

Don Sylvio's subjective view of reality is paralleled not only by his aunt's belief in chivalric romances, but also by the differing, equally subjective, views of reality embraced by Pedrillo and Donna Felicia. Although Pedrillo does not believe in his master's fairies, magicians, and nymphs, he is firmly convinced that ghosts and giants exist. Donna Felicia, for her part, sees the world through the eyes of the poets who envision Arcadian idylls and tender love stories.[9] Thus, although Don Sylvio is the main character, his subjectivism is not the only one to be mocked. The author, not content with drawing character parallels to the protagonist, introduces into the narration of Sylvio's adventures two lengthy episodes which parody in toto the fictive reality of the young hero. These two episodes are "Dïe Geschichte des Prinzen Biribinker" and "Die Geschichte der Donna Jacinte." Each is completely logical and probable within its own individual framework, and each is a further example of how subjective realities function. Both can therefore be seen as further elucidations of the intent expressed in the second part of the original title: "A Story in which Everything Wondrous Occurs Naturally." One might take the word "naturally" to mean simply that Don Sylvio's "adventures" occurred according to the laws of nature and ordinary probability and that it was his false perception that made them seem wondrous to him. The first part of the subtitle, "The Victory of Nature over Fanaticism," tends to substantiate such an interpretation. Yet such a view speaks more to the author's satiric than to his philosophic intent, and it just does not extend far enough to include the structural function of the two other histories contained in the novel. Wolfgang Preisendanz's judgment seems to me to be more inclusive of the philosophic intent. He suggests that neither "the adventures of Don Sylvio as such nor the nexus of events in themselves are substantive; they are worth telling only in as far as a subjective view of reality is manifested in them."[10] If this statement is true of Don Sylvio's framework, then it would also be true of Biribinker's and Jacinte's, which constitute parodistic parallels.

Compared to each other, the Hyacinthe (Jacinte's name in the first edition) and the Biribinker stories represent the extremes of Don Sylvio's experiences and reflect the polarity of fantasy and reality which determines the novel's structure. Donna Jacinte is a noble-minded girl of sixteen who has been surrounded by bad company for as long as she can remember. Raised by a gypsy woman who claimed that she was her daughter, the girl was placed in a bordello, where her face and figure promised to earn the gypsy a fortune. However, Jacinte feels out of place in these lascivious surroundings and is told by an inner instinct that she is meant for a better lot in life. She resists repeated assaults on her virtue and ultimately escapes her predicament with the aid of the noble Eugenio, who has fallen in love with her. Since her virtue is rewarded at the novel's conclusion with the announcement that she and Eugenio are to marry, we might speak of a parallel to Richardson's *Clarissa*.[11] In contrast to Don Sylvio, Donna Jacinte was fully aware that her world contradicted her ideal. All of her contacts with the world should have persuaded her that she was deluding herself in thinking that the external world, rather than her inner world of imagination, was out of sorts. In Don Sylvio's case, of course, there was never any awareness that the inner and outer worlds did not coincide. Whereas Jacinte's ultimate experience of the world validates her intuitive perception of herself, her brother is forced to recognize his folly.

Unlike Jacinte, Biribinker exists in a purely illusory and exceedingly fantastic world, of which a fiery, invisible castle, dry water, a sylph transformed into a chamber pot, a whale's belly complete with sun and moon, and a talking pumpkin are part and parcel. None of this is astounding in Biribinker's fantastic realm because everything is consistent with the accepted rules. All sham of intercourse with the "real" world is rejected. As Eugenio comments: "in this story . . . nature is turned upside down."[12] Nevertheless, the exotic story is logical and plausible when viewed from Biribinker's standpoint. Within the framework of the novel, this unbelievable tale is narrated by Don Gabriel to surreptitiously demonstrate to Don Sylvio how ludicrous his own fairy tale perception is. Don

Sylvio, however, accepts the logic of the story, arguing that the credibility of the historian, of the eyewitness, is the ultimate test of authenticity. The youth is stunned when he learns that Don Gabriel made up the story as he went along. Furthermore, Don Gabriel questions even the reliability of an historian or eyewitness. What guarantee do we have that they are not deceiving us or were not themselves deceived? Pressed, Don Sylvio cites the authenticity of his own experience as guarantee for the veracity of such unusual occurrences, whereupon Gabriel cites the need to examine each unusual occurrence in the light of reason. Sylvio is led by these arguments to accept the adventures of Prince Biribinker as not necessarily genuine "natural events."[13]

Don Sylvio's belief in the nature of his own experiences, however, had not been completely shaken. Furthermore, Sylvio's own adventures are presumably authenticated by an old Spanish manuscript authored by Don Ramiro of Z***. Yet we have not one, but three distinct voices in the novel, for both the German translator and the German editor interpolate their own views into the manuscript. Thus three separate voices are used to satirize and comment on the characters and on the novel itself. Despite the many indications throughout that the manuscript is fictitious, Don Sylvio's escapades remain the reference point for all other kinds of reality. On the one hand, the narrator wants the reader to believe that Don Sylvio's world is the real one. On the other hand, he is motivated to reveal this "real" world as equally fictitious.

At the moment when Donna Felicia and Don Gabriel (the spokesman of reason) cure Sylvio of his naive beliefs and introduce him to the real world, that "real" world is poignantly exposed as genuine fiction. The country estate at Lirias proves to be the former estate of Gil Blas of Santillana (Lésage's famous fictional hero). Felicia is none other than the granddaughter of Gil Blas and Dorothea of Jutella, whose image is on the medallion found by Don Sylvio. Felicia and Jutella are look-alikes, a fact which—once discovered—causes Sylvio to understand why he was irresistibly attracted to both Felicia and the woman portrayed on the locket. (Because he had lost the locket, he could not compare Felicia with the image.) The true to life atmosphere of Don Sylvio's setting is therefore exposed for what it is—a literary setting—and the victory of nature over aberration is seemingly called into question.[14] It forces us to look more carefully at the cause of the hero's salubrious "return" from the realm of fairy tales.

We would do well to consider the connotations of "nature." Whenever the term is used to denote one particular set of characteristics, it is accompanied by a limiting adjective, such as "human" nature or "animal" nature, "his" or "her" nature. Otherwise, the term implies the general concept of the laws of gravity, attraction, repulsion, organic growth, which we derive from our study of the phenomenal world. Basic tenets of Wieland's epistemology are that all perception is subjective and that man gains insight into himself and into his environment from two sources: the intellect (head) and the intuition (heart). Although the insights of the mind are more distinct and those of intuition at best vague, the intellect is initially dependent upon the mediation of the five senses, whereas intuitive insight is immediate. Because of the fallibility of sense perception and—in Wieland's "system"—the infallibility of intuitive perception, the latter is a more reliable guide in man's search for truth. Human intuition is attuned to a natural force which Wieland labels *Sympathie*. It is a concept which he formulated early on. His earnestness concerning the phenomenon is revealed not only by the fact that he devoted an entire essay to it (*Sympathien*, 1755), but also by repeated references to that force in many of his works.

In *Don Sylvio*, for example, we encounter, in Book III, Chapter 10, the term *Sympathie* used to explain the immediate and inexplicable attraction between two people:

As poetical, mystical, or magical as the word *Sympathie* might sound to the ears of many of our modern sages, we know of no other word to designate a certain kind of attraction which we (i.e., all the children of Adam and Eve) feel on occasion at first sight for strangers, and which, in origin as well as in effect, is vastly different from all other types of attraction, friendship or love.

In the next paragraph, the author conjectures on the possible sources of this sensation and in so doing reveals his intimate knowledge of Platonic concepts and materialistic philosophies:

To determine what could be the actual cause of such a wondrous effect, and of all those effects which distinguish sympathetic love from all other kinds of

love, would require an analysis which would take us too far afield. Therefore, we will allow our readers to select that hypothesis which strikes them
as being the most proper. It could be that the souls of such sympathetic
beings knew and loved one another in a previous life or that there is a
natural affinity between souls and that there are sister-souls, as an English
poet calls them. It is also possible that their spirits stand in a special relationship to one another, or that a musical accord of their filaments and
fibrils produces this effect mechanically. Let it suffice to say that this *Sympathie* is as much a part of nature as gravity, attraction, elasticity, or the
magnetic force. . . .[15]

Despite the bantering tone in which the author concludes these
deliberations in the next paragraph (he anticipates that future com-
mentators will try to research his true opinion on these matters!),
there is sufficient evidence even in this satiric novel to assume
sincerity on his part. For example, Don Sylvio is ultimately convinced by his love for Donna Felicia that his perception is false. As
soon as he has determined that the twofold object of his love was, for
all intents and purposes, one and the same (i.e., that the portrait
was of Felicia), all of Don Gabriel's logical arguments are acceptable
to him. What prevented these rational explanations from taking full
effect previously was Don Sylvio's conviction that the outer world
deviated from his innermost, intense experience of love for the
portrayed woman. It is this experience of sympathetic love which
reestablishes the proper perspective. All in all, there are four occurrences of "love at first sight" in the novel. In each instance, like
is unerringly drawn to like. Sylvio is attracted to Felicia, who also
suffers from delusions; noble-minded Eugenio is irresistibly drawn
to the virtuous Jacinte; Pedrillo is immediately attracted to his
feminine counterpart, Laura; and Biribinker instantly falls in love
with the princess destined to be his wife, although he is unaware
that she is a princess. Each time, *Sympathie* is presented as the
cause of the mutual attraction. In Wieland's subsequent works, the
functioning of this phenomenon is devoid of all traces of any comic
effect which the reader might discern in it here.

The many subjective perspectives and shifting points of view in
the novel have affected even its syntax and style. The following
example of this shifting perspective, with its frequent ironic or
satiric undercurrent, is characteristic of any number of passages. It
is taken from the opening paragraphs of the work: "Several years ago
in an old crumbling castle in the Spanish province of Valencia there

lived a woman of station. At the time when she played her role in the following story, she had, under the name of Donna Mencia of Rosalva, made for over sixty years—no mark on the world." In the original German, this opening paragraph consists of one sentence and is so constructed that the concluding negative remark catches the reader totally by surprise. Equally interesting is the manner in which the narrator implies a parallel between the crumbling castle and the aging woman, who several years *earlier* had *already* reached sixty. This initial irony is mild compared to what follows in the next paragraph:

Ever since the War of Succession, this woman had given up all hope of distinguishing herself by her personal charms. To be sure, in those days she was young and not disinclined to make a worthy admirer happy. However, she had experienced such grievous mortification from male indifference that she had been tempted more than once to sacrifice her heart of which the world had shown itself so unworthy in the seclusion of a convent. . . . She became a *prude*, determined to avenge her affronted charms on all those unfortunate men whom she considered to be like clouds which had absorbed and debilitated her personal luster. She publicly declared herself the sworn enemy of *beauty* and *love* and established herself as the protectress of all those venerable vestals who were endowed by nature with the gift of *transcendental* chastity and the mere sight of whom was sufficient to—disarm the most spirited faun.[16]

When read closely, this description of Don Sylvio's aunt can be seen as a web of interrelated views from different perspectives. The terms "personal charms," "worthy," "make happy," "grievous mortification," "indifference," and "to sacrifice" all reflect Donna Mencia's opinion. Other terms, such as "prude," "transcendental chastity," and "to disarm the most spirited faun" reflect the author's view in his role as a satirical *vir bonus*. In this capacity the author functions as an ironic commentator who is more interested in suggesting universally valid explanations for individual human conduct. Another mask assumed here by the author is that of *ingenu*—that is, the role of a straightforward storyteller who is not particularly interested in ironic commentary. The *ingenu* is, if you will, a type of "fall guy" who unwittingly sets himself and his narration up for the *vir bonus'* ironic wit.[17] The presence of these personae is further evidence of the far-reaching influence of point of view. The subtle irony which pervades the characterization of Donna Mencia affords a more plausible view of the facts, and the psychological depiction of that frustrated woman is more complete. In addition, the reader feels himself more closely aligned with the narrator than with the fictional character because of the knowledge which only he and the narrator share. What we have here is an early instance of the personal narrator in German literature, that is, the type of narrator who draws the reader into a dialogue with himself. By means of the rapprochement between narrator and reader, Wieland hopes to influence the reader to recognize the all-pervasive subjectivity of perception in the novel and, by extension, his own biased way of viewing things. Once the reader has fully grasped this significance of the Terentian adage cited at the beginning of Chapter 7, Book V, "tu sic esses, aliter sentias" ("If you were here, you would think otherwise"), he will be able to appreciate the need for tolerance and forbearance. In fact, this line from Terence's *Andria* (Act II, sc. 1) could easily serve as the motto for the novel. In view of these brief considerations of *Don Sylvio,* we can see how well Wieland has succeeded in fulfilling his dual intent of satirizing and philosophizing. His method is best summed up by the lines from *Idris und Zenide* (1768): "Ergetzen ist der Musen erste Pflicht, Doch spielend geben sie den besten Unterricht."[18] Wieland's mastery of prose in his first novel is such that *Don Sylvio* can stand as a stylistic accomplishment comparable to Cervantes', Fielding's, and Sterne's best works.

II   Die Geschichte des Agathon

Wieland's actual "first" novel was not published until 1766–1767. After writing *Don Sylvio* in six months in 1763–1764, the author did not immediately return to *Agathon,* but rather continued in the comic vein in several verse narratives. Nevertheless, *Agathon* was never far from his mind. In fact, *Don Sylvio* can be seen as that novel's forerunner, for they have several traits in common.[19] In *Agathon,* Wieland examines more closely the phenomenon of *Schwärmerei*—subjective perception. In this second novel, *Schwärmerei* is expressed as idealism in philosophical and moral terms, whereas in *Don Sylvio* it was identified with an excessive concern for the world of fantasy. Agathon, however, is not a naive fantast like Don Sylvio; when we first meet him, he has already experienced disillusionment and is fully aware of the discrepancy between his inner world and external reality. The belief in his inner reality, however, is unshaken. In *Don Sylvio*, the dissonance between the two worlds is resolved when the protagonist realizes that the wondrous is not inherent in external reality but belongs to the inner world of imagination. This solution was adequate for a novel meant primarily as an entertaining intermezzo, as a "comedy in novelistic form" which draws upon the unperturbed optimism of preestablished harmony.[20] However, for the more philosophically aware Agathon, the real problem had scarcely been touched upon, for the recognition of the subjectivity of perception raises a more basic question. Don Sylvio erred in believing that the wondrous was an element of nature itself rather than of the individual's inner world.[21] If this is true for the poetically wondrous, would it not also hold true for the philosophically and the religiously ideal, both of which are related to the wondrous? If they are purely subjective, what function can they serve in a real world framework? Is there any external justification for projecting philosophic (or religious) idealism onto the world or will it ever remain purely subjective, a matter of the individual, not of the group?

Thus, what interested Wieland most in writing *Agathon* was the contrast between the mellifluous idealism of the Swiss years and the crass political realities of Biberach. He got the idea for the novel from Euripides' play, *Ion*, whose protagonist combines in his character boyish simplicity and innocence with an instinctive premonition of man's nobler nature. Invariably, Wieland saw in this hero a reflection of himself; he could not resist imagining how this youth, who had been raised in the protective shadow of Delphi, would develop in society.[22] He consciously transferred his own and Ion's youthful idealism to Agathon, a little-known poet of Greek antiquity who is mentioned in Plato's dialogues. Agathon's relative obscurity allowed Wieland to depict him with poetic license and so develop his more or less vague ideas concerning the nature of man. They reflect the recurrent encroachment of external reality upon the individual's subjective idealism, a process which invariably leads to conflict. On January 5, 1962, he wrote to Zimmermann: "several months ago I began a novel, which I call *Die Geschichte des Agathon*. I am depicting myself in it as I would like to be."[23] In the fairy tale atmosphere of *Agathon*'s pendant, *Don Sylvio*, Wieland found it much easier to depict the hero's ultimate happiness; but in the real world framework of *Agathon*, the author found that happy ends are much harder to come by.

The novel opens in medias res and recounts in anticipatory as well as retrospective fashion the experiences of the hero through various stages of psychological, sociological, political, and intellectual development. The action is placed in the fourth century B.C. for several reasons. The heroic, Homeric, and Periclean ages did not suit his purposes nearly as well as the later stage of Greek culture with its moral softness and decay, for only an indulgent consumer society could provide the necessary contrast to his hero's moral idealism. Wieland rightly saw in the fourth century B.C. many intellectual and cultural parallels to his own Rococo Age. Although he has been criticized for having failed to achieve the realism of *Tom Jones* or *Tristram Shandy*, it must not be overlooked that he gained the necessary critical and ironic distance from which to analyze his own century without fear of reprisal or rejection. More important, however, was the possibility for exposure to a greater variety of cultural and social influences than would have been possible in an eighteenth century German setting. This was essential because he had come to appreciate the determining influence of milieu. Furthermore, he cared more for the exemplary character of any given epoch than for its uniqueness. Thus, despite the novel's strong autobiographical overtones, Wieland focused his attention on Agathon as a representative of mankind, not as an individual. For this reason, his depiction of Greece is stylized. All this means that *Agathon* is not to be judged by the criteria of the nineteenth century realistic novel.[24]

The fact that *Agathon* begins in medias res not only places the novel in a time-honored literary tradition, but also reflects—in this case—its autobiographical nature. The idealistic goal was known, but the meandering path of the author's own future was unclear. The frequent interrupting of the narrative by the narrator and the editor reflecting upon the psychological, sociological, philosophical, religious, and even literary implications of the events creates the impression that one is reading a series of essays rather than a novel. (This is particularly true of the third and final version of the novel published in 1794.) Furthermore, the reader is continuously exhorted to actively participate in the creative process by imagining what is to happen next or to wonder what the cause of a particular event might have been. Chapter I, Book 11, offers a prime example of this cooperative effort.

When we first make the hero's acquaintance, he is alone and

without friends, without means. Unwittingly he becomes involved in a bacchanal; is captured, along with some Thracian maenads, by a group of Cilician pirates; and is sold as a slave in Smyrna to the sophist, Hippias. Because of his intellectual abilities, he soon attains a favored position in Hippias' household, eventually even gaining his freedom; but not before the Epicurean philosopher repeatedly attempts to demonstrate logically the inaneness of Agathon's Platonic idealism. In a last effort to convince the hero of the fallacy of his views, the materialist introduces him to the lovely hetaera, Danae, who has been instructed to seduce him. Agathon and Danae, however, fall in love, and Agathon tells her the story of his life, how his father had sent him at an early age to be educated at Delphi, after his mother, Musarion, had died. There his Platonic enthusiasm was nurtured until it reached such a pitch that he even considered it possible to communicate with the gods. After several disillusioning experiences, Agathon left Delphi, found his father in Corinth, and ultimately launched a political career in the republic of Athens. His rise to power and popularity was quick; but he had enemies who brought about his fall and banished him from Athens.

Danae's and Agathon's happiness in Smyrna is short-lived, for Agathon soon learns from Hippias that Danae is "nothing" but a high class prostitute, with whom he, Hippias, has also had dealings. Without questioning Danae about Hippias' insinuations, our hero abruptly leaves Smyrna, sorely disappointed and with a sense of guilt for his supposed moral transgressions. His ship takes him to Syracuse, where he reenters politics, this time as adviser to Dionysius, the tyrant of Syracuse. Again Agathon rises to power and fame; again he is deposed by jealous enemies and even imprisoned. Following his release, he leaves Sicily for the republic of Tarentum, which is renowned for the wisdom and benevolence of its ruler, Archytas. In Archytas, Agathon finds his spiritual father, whose philosophy of life reflects the perfection he has been striving for. The hero is accepted into the sage's family, where he reencounters his first love, Psyche, whom he had first met at Delphi and whom he had last seen on the pirate ship on the way to Smyrna. He discovers in her his long-lost sister. In a country house not far from Tarentum, he also reencounters Danae, and the old passion is rekindled, but Danae—now called Chariklea—insists upon a Platonic relationship, having been changed by her genuine love for Agathon into a full-fledged "schöne Seele," (that is, one who exudes a sense of grace and harmony and who inspires the love of virtue). Danae now tells her life story (added in the second version of 1773), which demonstrates that she would have become a second Psyche had the circumstances of her youth been different. The significance of sociological factors in the determination of human conduct is thus pronounced. The conclusion of the novel caused Wieland so much difficulty that the work remained unfinished until 1794. The ending of the second version of 1773 is little altered from the first. Neither the 1773 nor the 1794 version fully realizes Wieland's intent, expressed to Zimmermann, to make Agathon as happy as the author himself would have liked to be.

For the outline it contains of the story's further evolution, the final chapter of the original version is rather interesting. It announces that, contingent upon public demand, other portions of the Greek manuscript which allegedly underlies the *Geshichte des Agathon* could be published. Thus, for example, the editor suggests that the reader might be interested in hearing Danae's own story up to the point where she meets Agathon. Or, perhaps the reader would like to have an exposition of Archytas' philosophy. Third, he might be curious to learn what Agathon thought about human existence at age fifty.[25] The success of the 1766–1767 version justified its reissuance.

In the second version, Wieland added the announced "History of Danae"—ostensibly to attract more female readers—and the prefatory essay "Concerning the Historical in *Agathon*." Although Wieland's reader is expected to be educated, the plethora of allusions to characters and events of Greek antiquity proved to be so confusing that the preface is designed in part to explain the historical framework of the novel. Wieland simultaneously clarifies here why *Agathon* is more like *Tom Jones* than like Xenophon's *Cyropaedia*. In Fielding's work, the historical truth is built into the poetic fiction so that Tom Jones' world seems real. In Xenophon's epic, on the other hand, historical fact is distorted by introducing poetic elements as if they were historically true. Wieland did not intend to idealize his hero as Xenophon had apotheosized Cyrus as the ideal ruler. Rather, he wanted to depict the protagonist as a real man striving to realize his human ideals but falling short because of human frailty.[26] This explanation is reminiscent of the author's attitude eight years earlier, toward his Araspes, who can now be seen as a forerunner of Agathon. The depiction of flawed Greek heroes and gods in the *Komische Erzählungen* is repeated in *Agathon*—quite a daring undertaking in the wake of Winckelmann's and Lessing's well nigh uncritical praise of the originators of "humanitas."

The newly added preface on the use of history in the novel reiterates an essential idea broached as early as 1754 and sounded again in the preface to the original version—the concept of probability. The test of truth is not historicity, but psychological and sociological verisimilitude. The main thing is that characters be depicted in accordance with "the nature of the human heart" and maintain "the essence of every passion with the particular colors and shades which each acquires through the individuality and environment of each separate person. . . ."[27] Yet the effects of time, climate, and ethnic culture must also be taken into account. These views strike us as being very modern. And they are when we consider that the materialistic and deterministic theories dominant in modern psychology and sociology were much discussed in Wieland's time by such men as Charles Bonnet, David Hartley, Claude Adrien Helvétius, and Voltaire.[28] Wieland was one of the first writers to consciously apply these theories to a poetic creation. His view that the approximation of truth is best achieved through observance of the "inner and relative possibility" of psychogenesis rather than by a projection of ideals onto history tells us a lot about his concept of reality. In the guise of editor, he can ridicule the idea that the *Geschichte des Agathon* must be based on an old Greek manuscript (which is defective in places because rats have gotten to it!) because the historian's view of man and the events is no less subjective than the poet's. The only guarantee of truth is for the individual perception to coincide with the accepted view of human nature. Man's attention should not be directed solely toward the external world but also inwardly toward the essence of human nature. Shaftesbury's influence is obvious here, and there is no more fitting summation of this attitude than Pope's couplet: "Know then thyself, presume not God to scan, The proper study of mankind is man."[29]

In order to get to know man's nature one must study it "in a multifarious light and from all sides."[30] This means that "the test case" must be placed in a variety of conflicting situations. Not by chance is Agathon raised in the shadow of the Delphic exhortation, "Know thyself." The original preface and the newly added essay on historical elements in the novel, therefore, both expose the polarity of the inner and outer worlds (the two-fold reality) which create a magnetic field of opposing forces exerted on Agathon as he tries to bring the extremes of human nature—body and spirit, intuition and reason—into balance. Hippias represents the materialistic side of human nature and is the spokesman of the contemporary eighteenth century materialists, whereas Archytas symbolizes the spiritual side and presents a more Kantian approach.

The multiple influences on the protagonist reflect the basic philosophical positions of the one or the other of these two men. For example, the biographical (but not narrative) order of the hero's major experiences is: Delphi, Athens, Smyrna, Syracuse, and Tarentum. In Delphi and Smyrna, Agathon's contact with the world is strictly limited, and he is primarily acted upon, while the irrational impulses of the heart dominate. In Athens and Syracuse, however, the situation is reversed: under the guidance of reason, Agathon actively strives to control his environment. To be sure, in each theater of action, the hero's idealism is thwarted by the real situations, so that one might feel justified in concluding that "Agathon's idealism is disabused by reality, contradicted, condemned to miscarry" and, further, "that his idealism [even] turns against itself," thereby causing the hero's world view to rupture.[31] Yet the nature of the disillusionment in the passive and active spheres seems to belie that conclusion. In Delphi, the youth's naive belief in the possibility of a theophany is pungently dispelled by Theogiton, the priest who stages a theophany for Agathon, with himself as Apollo, so that he might find it easier to seduce the youth. The priestess Pythia's later onslaught on his virtue opens the boy's eyes a little more to the frailty of even those who have dedicated their lives to the gods. Although he no longer believes in theophanies when he leaves Delphi, Agathon has not lost his basic faith in man's nobility. Only the excesses of his enthusiasm have been purged.

In Athens, Agathon assumes that all citizens of the republic desire what is best for everyone, and therefore his faith in his fellow citizens is sorely disillusioned when selfish aims replace the common good. Here the essence of Agathon's view of man is seemingly contradicted. It is in his depressed state following this severe disappointment that we first meet him. It is significant for the Platonic core of the novel that the picture of the broken hero concludes with his dreaming of his beloved Psyche. He dreams that he has found her again after having lost sight of her since Delphi. Psyche (the

human soul incarnate, as her name implies) is proof that his encounter with crass reality has not yet succeeded in loosening the
hold Delphi has on the hero.[32] Significantly, he finds Psyche on the
ship to Smyrna, only to lose her again.

The experiences in Smyrna are of two types: philosophical (Hippias) and erotic (Danae). Neither of these encounters destroys
Agathon's basic enthusiasm. He arrives in Smyrna as a fantast and
departs as a fantast. Why? Because he traveled to Syracuse with the
idea of reforming Dionysius into a somewhat less despotic ruler. He
deceived himself in thinking that he could achieve what Plato had
failed to do. Neither Hippias' arguments nor Danae's sensual love
had been able to weaken his idealistic view of man, but in Syracuse
he does observe the new maxim of not expecting more of others than
they can give, demanding perfection only of himself. However, the
use of this double standard proves to be a mistake, because others
doubt that he truly observes a higher moral standard than they. For
example, Dionysius endeavors to control his licentious desires as
long as he feels Agathon expects it of him. When Agathon informs
him that the extramarital affairs of a ruler would be judged lightly,
however, he automatically assumes that Agathon is just as lax in his
own moral life. The result is that Dionysius spurns all of Agathon's
subsequent exhortations, and our hero loses all influence over the
tyrant. There is a double deception here, for Dionysius thinks that
his minister is hypocritical, while Agathon assumes that he can retain his influence by encouraging the affair with the harmless girl,
Bacchidion. The point to be made is that even Dionysius' moral
behavior improves under the impression that Agathon expects it of
him. In this we have a parallel to Danae's moral improvement resulting from Agathon's view of her. In her case, the irony of the false
perception is just the reverse: Agathon changes his view of Danae
after Hippias reveals her past and, in so doing, switches from a true
perception to an erroneous one. His intuitively correct view of her
as a *schöne Seele* gives way to a logical but false one of her as a
hetaera.

In Chapter I, Book 11, of the first version, Wieland, in the guise
of a Greek author and in the role of editor, draws the reader into
deliberations of how to end Agathon's quest for happiness, which
was supposed to express itself in harmony of the soul and the world.
Aside from the fact that this narrative technique was new in German
literature, it was also an expression of honesty on Wieland's part, for

he truly did not know what to do with his hero. Critics have argued that the solution chosen—placing Agathon in Archytas' Tarentum—is highly utopian. Yet this authorial action does affirm Agathon's fundamental idealism and does reject Hippias' sophism and epicureanism. Not only is Psyche found again, she is also revealed as Agathon's sister, a fact which stresses the correctness of his idealistic view of man. Danae, too, is rediscovered. As a *schöne Seele*, she too is now (i.e., in the third and final version) a spiritual sister to the hero. The significance of Tarentum for Wieland's view of man is further underscored by the meaning of Agathon's name. "Agathos" means "morally good" and is part of the Socratic ideal of *kalokagathia* ("kalos kai agathos"), which Wieland defines in the *Neuer Amadis* as the "habitual nexus of the morally beautiful and good in the soul of man and in his social behavior."[32] Finally, the section dealing with Tarentum also contains the Agathon-Archytas dialogue (composed is 1794) which the preface to the final version calls "the crown" of the entire work. It is, to a large extent, the result of Wieland's exposure to Kant. All of this would seem to affirm the validity of Agathon's subjective perception of man's higher moral nature, which should determine all of his actions. Agathon has not parted completely from the enthusiasm of his youth; and he is far from being a Hippias. But this was not immediately clear to Wieland's contemporaries.

At first, readers thought that Wieland was advocating Hippias' epicureanism, and the author came under attack from many sides. The self-righteous were all too ready to see only coarse pleasure-seeking in Hippias' Smyrna. The enlightened readers, on the other hand, objected to the poor figure that Agathon cuts in his discussions with Hippias, who argues so eloquently. Wieland anticipated the reaction of the close-minded and bigoted when he wrote to Gessner in November 1763, while still composing the work: "I know already that I and my works will require a defense in a few years. Agathon, who is in all respects more disconcerting than Sylvio, will arouse enough grumblings and outcries."[34] However, the negative criticism from informed circles was much less anticipated. After a number of reviews had appeared which did little justice to the novel and demonstrated that even literary critics were incapable of judging *Agathon* as an entity, Wieland let off steam in a letter, again addressed to his friend, Gessner: "In the meantime, the German critics are judging my works as if I, like most of them, had nothing better to do than to make the presses turn. Poor *Agathon* in particular is praised so abominably and criticized so stupidly that one doesn't know whether to laugh, cry or grab the switch [i.e., to chastise them] . . . . The funniest thing is that absolutely no one has discovered the intent and plan of the whole."[35] He was so angry that he contemplated writing his own analyses.

Only one critic apparently understood *Agathon* the way Wieland had intended it; it was Lessing, the most perspicacious and most feared critic of the time, who had consistently judged Wieland's works harshly. Because of his high standards, Lessing's recognition of *Agathon* must have been all the sweeter for Wieland. In the sixty-ninth installment of the *Hamburgische Dramaturgie (Hamburg Dramaturgy*, 1767), Lessing proclaimed that *Agathon* "is indisputably one of the finest works of our century but seems to have been written much too early for the German reading public. In France and England it would have caused the greatest stir, the author's name would be in all the papers. But Germany? We have it, and that is enough. . . . It is the first and only novel for the thinking person and in the classical style. Novel? Let us call it that, so that it might gain a few more readers. The few readers one might lose by calling it a novel are unimportant." The novel's audience was perhaps larger than one would think after the above. In fact, *Agathon* was apparently the first German novel to be equally successful with both the upper and middle classes.[36] Years later, Lessing's view was elaborated in a detailed study of the *Geschichte des Agathon* by Friedrich von Blanckenburg (1744–1796) in his *Versuch über den Roman (Essay on the Novel*, 1774). In this treatise, *Agathon* serves as an exemplary model for the novel form and the depiction of character. Yet it wasn't until the reading public's taste had so improved (Wieland himself played no small part in this development) that the novel finally gained its deserved acclaim. A sign of this increased recognition is the fact that Wieland opened his *Sämmtliche Werke (Collected Works*, 1794) with it. Ever since, this work has engendered more critical interest than any of his others.

The ambiguity and relativism which critics have seen, and continue to see, in Wieland's moral and philosophical positions mirrored in the novel are only partially justified. The author's intention to observe Agathon in manifold circumstances and shifting perspectives and his desire to show the influence of milieu, time and climate on the formation of ideas tended to obscure his own philosophical position. On the advice of his good friend, Friedrich Heinrich Jacobi (1743–1819), Wieland added two additional footnotes in the second version.[37] They were intended to bolster Agathon's argument. Stylistic changes were also made in the Hippias-Agathon dialogue to strengthen the hero's hand and to demonstrate that Wieland's sympathies were really with Agathon. Jacobi had perceived that Agathon's "rebuttal" of Hippias' reasoning was disarmingly a-rational. The opponents were, in fact, arguing on two different levels, Hippias using logic to show that Agathon's universal values of the good and the beautiful were not absolute but relativistic, and Agathon arguing that the good and the beautiful rise above mere ultilarianism. For Hippias (and the Enlightenment), salubrious reason is man's only guide to happiness; but for Agathon, reason becomes a secondary guide. His primary guide for perceiving the good and the beautiful is intuition, which (unlike reason) is independent of logical factors.

Agathon thus does not attempt to refute Hippias' argument; instead, he calmly asserts that his "experiences and sentiments contradict Hippias' rational conclusions."[38] When Agathon goes on to say that he would still be convinced of the truth that he has intensely felt, even if the whole world were to speak against it, we have an unmistakable echo of Sylvio's claim for the subjective perception of truth. For Agathon, the heart fulfills a vastly more important function than the mind in the perception of ultimate truth. He declares that even if Hippias were able to demonstrate the fallacy of his experiences and sentiments, the sophist would only be able to prove that he is Hippias and not Agathon. But he would not have proven Agathon wrong. It is the same "tu si hic esses, aliter sentias" argument of Don Sylvio. Because his sentiments are caused by the unmitigated impact of the wonder of nature on his heart, Agathon is certain that his perception of the good and the beautiful is not erroneous. Although nature is the touchstone of truth for Hippias too, he sees it only mechanically and intellectually. Thus Agathon concludes that it is not Hippias' head, but his heart that is awry; otherwise he would sense that there must be some intangible cause of the wonder which man experiences when confronted with nature. Agathon exclaims: "I need only to open my eyes, only to be aware of myself, in order to perceive in all of nature and in the innermost recesses of my own soul the originator, this most sublime, beneficient spirit. I recognize his existence not just via rational inferences. I *sense* it, just as I feel that the sun exists, just as I feel that *I myself exist.*" The concluding remark is a piquant variation of Descartes' "cogito ergo sum."[39] Agathon pities Hippias because nature has apparently denied him this sixth sense, this inner sensitivity to the transcendental effect of the outer world.[40] The sentence "I know his existence not just through rational inferences" is one of the later additions to the novel. Apparently, the chief objection raised by critics was that Agathon did not employ rational arguments as well as Hippias. In the Age of Reason, this objection was well understood; in the following Romantic period it was no stumbling block. Thus *Agathon* could serve well as a model both for the extroverted *Wilhelm Meister*, which the Romanticists praised profusely, and for the introverted *Heinrich von Ofterdingen*.

Agathon's argument in the newly added encounter (third version) with Hippias in the Syracusan prison adds nothing to the protagonist's basic argument of man's inner voice being attuned to the deity. The hero has landed in prison after having been caught in a conspiracy to overthrow Dionysius. There he has time to reflect upon the recent past, which seems to substantiate Hippias' *Weltanschauung*, and is on the verge of capitulating when the sophist unexpectedly visits him. Hippias has come to finally win Agathon over to his viewpoint, but his presence only alerts Agathon to two important facts which he, in his despondency, had overlooked. First, the protagonist realizes that he had been beguiled by his vanity, not by his Platonic philosophy. He trusted too much in his own powers to achieve political reform "with zither in hand." This vanity made him incautious. Second, Agathon suddenly realizes that his own heart does not reproach him, for he had been morally lenient only toward others, not toward himself. So, instead of joining Hippias, Agathon rejects him a second time: "Your [Hippias'] presence suddenly reestablished our proper relationship. I felt myself to be again the person I used to be."[41] Hippias' visit ironically helps Agathon to again hear his inner voice, which has been drowned out by adverse circumstances, after which his mind can reattain the proper perspective. The skeptic has to be reintroduced at this time, so that Agathon can once again consider his exalted ideals as universally binding. Hippias' visit is, therefore, structurally and philosophically a necessary prelude to the normative significance of Archytas' philosophy of life, for the notion that Agathon's views are relativistic must be dispelled before a detailed exposition of Archytas' system can be presented. [42]

The presentation of Archytas' *Lebensphilosophie* in Book XVI, Chapter 3, is the crowning event of the novel, for it provides the Kantian basis for Agathon's exalted idealism, which until then "was based more on feeling and intuition than on logical conviction and clearly conceived concepts." Although Archytas explains in detail the active and passive functions of the mind in the quest for truth, he acknowledges that analysis of sensual perceptions and ratiocination based on them are insufficient. Study of the phenomenal world and its laws is not enough. Man must also study himself, look into his own "feelings, thoughts, presentiments, instincts, and aspirations" for truth. Both mind and heart are necessary. The intellect can take man to the brink of recognizing that the phenomenal world is merely a reflection of the noumenal one and that the physical world is in the process of perfecting itself, but the goal toward which it is advancing is intuited by the heart. The mind by its very nature is incapable of taking this irrational step. [43] The key to Archytas' philosophy is, therefore, still man's intuition. The difference between his and Agathon's views is that the sage's idealism is based as far as possible on a rational substructure. Thus, Agathon's basic position throughout the novel is maintained, while a major attempt is made in the third version to meet Hippias on his own rational ground.

Wieland's first biographer, Gruber, saw that the harmony of head and heart in Archytas' system was necessary to demonstrate that man's felicity is not dependent only on the sylvan glades of Delphi, which are so conducive to sweet enthusiasm. He correctly judges "that truth lies between Hippias' system and Plato's, but [that it] is closer to the latter than to the former." [44] Perhaps Gruber had taken note of the author's own statement in the preface to the original edition that he considered a detailed rebuttal to Hippias' materialistic theory superfluous because "Agathon refutes Hippias almost in the same way as Diogenes refuted the sophist who denied that movement exists: Diogenes allowed the sophist to prattle on as long as he wanted. And when he had finished, Diogenes contented himself with walking up and down before his eyes. Surely, this was the only rebuttal worthy of the sophist." [45]

Agathon's fidelity to the essence of his idealism was, in Wieland's eyes, the only necessary and worthy rebuttal to Hippias' seductive sophistry. The common sense attitude of Diogenes is equated with the protagonist's inherent enthusiasm. Curious in this connection is the author's comment to Zimmermann, in December 1762, that "Agathon, after he has undergone all the experiences which still await him, is to be led back to the very point from which he had departed."[46] What all this amounts to is that the novel, when read as an autobiographical piece, reveals that Wieland's "metamorphosis" was not as radical as is sometimes thought, that he has not turned his back on the ideals of his youth; excesses have been pared, and the idealism purified of extraneous elements. The senses·and the intellect are still less trusted than the imagination in conjunction with intuition.

Wieland's depiction of Danae underscores this process. It has been stated that Danae's predilection for becoming a *schöne Seele* was nurtured to full fruition by Agathon's love. But what of her significance for him? How is she able to fill his whole life in Smryna and make him forget Psyche? It is possible because Psyche's nature has coalesced with her own.[47] The pantomime representing the story of Apollo and Daphne, presented in Book IV, Chapter 5, prefigures this merging. The role of Daphne is first danced by a girl named Psyche whose name reminds Agathon of his own Psyche, and his criticism of the dance further reveals his bias for Platonic virtue. It is then that Danae slips away, returns dressed as Daphne, and interprets the pantomime exactly as Agathon prefers it. In the ensuing chapter, "Geheime Nachrichten" ("Private Information"), the narrator affords us psychological insight into Agathon's state, explaining that Agathon saw his Psyche in Danae, who was dancing the role of Daphne. The traits of the three individuals have fused into one. Thus, for all intents and purposes, Danae succeeds in making Agathon fall in love with her by assuming Psyche's traits.

Shortly afterwards, Agathon has a dream which is psychoanalytically significant for this development. Agathon sees Psyche on the other shore of a raging river; with difficulty he crosses the river and pursues Psyche's image, which recedes before him. Psyche runs to the statue of virtue, which stands alone but undamaged among the temple ruins in what appears to be Delphi. Before disappearing, she casts a meaningful look at him. The dream can be interpreted as follows: the ruins represent the lost idyll of Delphi, the untouched statue reflects Agathon's uncompromised virtue, and Psyche's disappearance signifies that her purely spiritual kind of love has given way to a new type. The narrator concludes: "Psyche now appeared to him to have been destined to nothing other than to nurturing the sensitivity of his heart, in order to make him capable of appreciating Danae's incomparable talents." In the author's view, there is no doubt that this is the case. That is the reason why he entitles the chapter "Dass Träume nicht allemal Schäume sind" ("Evidence that Dreams are not Always Empty"). For Agathon, however, a modicum of doubt still remains. He cannot get the image of Psyche pointing to the sylvan glades of Delphi—an image which reflects the purity of their love—out of his mind. Yet Danae's impact on him is so strong that he cannot turn away from her and justifies his love for her by citing her many virtues. Finally, he achieves peace of mind by thinking of his love for Psyche as "the love of a brother for a sister, a mere love of souls," whereas what he feels for Danae is love in the truer sense. This discovery—as the narrator notes—"seemed to him to be indisputable after comparing the symptoms of *these two kinds of love*."[48] Nevertheless, the effect of the dream is enduring because Agathon still identified the image of Psyche with the image of virtue. He has not yet learned that virtue can also appear in the shape of a Danae. The identification of virtue with only his first love creates the predisposition necessary for Agathon to reject Danae outright when he learns that she is a hetaera. In both instances, he is deluded by appearances and would have done better to follow the impulses of his heart rather than the fallacious conclusions of his head. The stature which Danae enjoys together with Psyche at the novel's conclusion sufficiently demonstrates how wrong Agathon was to identify virtue only with Psyche.

The analytic, polyperspective style of the novel is apparent everywhere and mirrors the nexus of fantasy and reality. As in *Don Sylvio*, so too in *Agathon* the reader is invited to actively participate in the creative process together with author and editor, so that a type of dialogue arises. Wieland's sentence structure is characteristically elaborate, frequently consisting of several hypotactical constructions. The author himself asserted that this highly Baroque style represents, in fact, an attempt to be very precise:[49] it reflects a desire to study a question from various psychological and sociological angles in order to get to the truth of the matter. Dialogue is one of the primary methods employed to achieve a multiple perspective, and Wieland's use of the technique is marked by urbane graciousness, tolérance, and wit. Whole sections of the novel are given over to dialogue, and even when the author or one of the characters soliloquizes, the reader has the distinct impression of an *erlebte Rede*. Contrasting ideas, and even sentiments, are presented in dialogue form. Agathon's solitary ruminations are, in effect, soliloquies. So frequently is this trait encountered that it has become a hallmark of Wieland's style.[50] At the conclusion of *Agathon*, the reader is left with the impression of having been witness to and participant in an uninterrupted series of conversations. So effective is his use of rhetorical forms and techniques that we might contend that his style represents a high point of the rhetorical tradition in literature.[51]

If rhetoric provided many of the linguistic techniques used to involve the reader in the narration, the tradition of the "Reiseroman" provided the model for the exposure to different cultures and situations which enhances the multiplicity of perspective. We know, for example, that Wieland had read François de Fenélon's *Les aventures de Telémaque* (1699) and André Michael Ramsay's *Voyages de Cyrus* (1727). Furthermore, the tradition of the Baroque novel made itself felt in the various tests to which the hero's virtue is put, in the abrupt changes of fortune, in the theme of life as a dream, and in the view of the world as a theater. Wieland combined these various traditions with the relatively new art of the psychological novel *(Tom Jones)* to create the first modern psychological novel in Germany.[52] Regardless of how the novel is viewed, its content and style give it a special place in German literature. Together with its companion piece, *Don Sylvio*, *Agathon* marks the emergence of both German Classicism and Romanticism. With these two works, Wieland's reputation in Europe as one of Germany's leading authors was firmly established.

CHAPTER 5

In Erfurt (1769–1772)

I Rising Popularity

BY the author's own admission, the works preceding *Agathon* were written for an exclusive audience: his "seraglio" in Zurich, theatergoers in Berne, a Rococo salon in Biberach.[1] The works were, of course, read by persons other than the original addressees. Nevertheless, Wieland's literary star did not begin to shine luminously over Europe until after the publication of the aforementioned novel, a literary form, by the way, which was rapidly gaining ascendancy among readers of all classes. Only at that point did *Musarion, Idris und Zenide*, and subsequent works begin to reach a more broadly based audience. One sign of the author's growing fame abroad is the rapidity with which his works were translated into French and English. An anecdote illustrates the recognition Wieland was beginning to receive in the highest German aristocratic circles. A courtier in imperial Vienna, the Marquis Boufflers, entertained his guests with a translation of *Die Grazien* (*The Graces*, 1770). The ladies and gentlemen were rather impressed with the quality and wit of the French verses; but how surprised they were to learn that these were but translations of an inimitable German original! The marquis rebuked them for their prejudice against German poets. Had they been tolerant, they could have been enjoying all along the far superior verses of Wieland's original German! The report tells us two things about the author's principal audience around 1770, first, that he wrote for the upper social circles who were refined enough to appreciate the many literary and mythologic allusions in his works, and second, that there existed a bias against German literature. Excellence in literature was expected in French, but not in German. We need only think of Frederick the Great's *De littérature d'Allemagne* (1780) and the

84

ignorance of the contemporary state of German letters which it betrays. Voltaire could enjoy the monarch's patronage, but Lessing could not.

Although the ideal of a free-lance existence was coming closer to reality, German authors still required, by and large, patronage to survive. In his correspondence with his publisher Gessner during the 1760s, Wieland lamented the fact that he was unable to purchase a country estate (his *Sabinum*) like Pope because German writers are not properly remunerated. He also complained about the format and the limited sales of his books (average about seven hundred), so that he eventually changed publishers in an effort to increase both sales and income.[2] His move from Biberach to Erfurt in June 1769 can be seen as an "outreaching toward society."[3] It was not only a change of social position but also one of audience. Erfurt offered Wieland the opportunity to bring his nascent ideal of a free-lance existence closer to realization, because his new position paid well and left him much free time for his writing. He took advantage of the opportunity by trying to broaden the appeal of his style. These efforts met with such success that his works began to find acceptance not only in the gracious upper classes but also in the diligent upward-striving middle classes.[4] Consequently, the poet's writings began to appear in editions in excess of two thousand copies—an unusually large number for 1770!

The enthusiasm with which Wieland was greeted by nobility and bourgeoisie alike during his "sentimental journey" to Koblenz, Düsseldorf, Mainz, and Darmstadt in 1771 gives ample evidence of his rising popularity. Everywhere he was fêted, but especially in Ehrenbreistein, where he saw Sophie LaRoche and other friends. Friedrich Heinrich Jacobi describes this meeting and its excitement in a letter dated June 16, 1771. In the same letter, Jacobi also provides us with one of the most detailed descriptions of Wieland's appearance and personality. The author did not cut an impressive figure. On the contrary, as we have seen, he was of medium, delicate build and had a severely pockmarked face, which made his eyes seem even smaller then they were. Yet his expressions and movements revealed an inner liveliness that communicated itself to others, and he exuded a sense of openness and warmth which inspired confidence.[5] These were the same inner qualities which were later to turn such *Sturm und Drang* opponents as Goethe and Jakob M.R. Lenz into admirers.

II *Professor of Philosophy*

The call to Erfurt was occasioned by an upper class admirer of
Agathon: Baron Grosschlag, prime minister at Mainz, whom Wieland had met at Warthausen. Through this minister's intervention,
the archbishop and electoral prince of Mainz, Emmerich Joseph,
offered Wieland a professorship in philosophy at the Catholic university in Erfurt.[6] Erfurt was then under Mainz' jurisdiction, and
Emmerich Joseph was in the process of upgrading the faculty in an
effort to regain the prestige the university had enjoyed as a citadel of
humanistic thought in the fifteenth and sixteenth centuries. It was
felt that Wieland's presence would contribute greatly to the reform
and attract more students. Although the poet was flattered by the
prospect of playing a major role in a university town, it was not easy
for him to give up his well-ordered, relatively comfortable existence
in his home town, his "womb" as he called it in a letter to the
electoral prince.[7] Ever since he had won his case against the
Catholic faction to retain his chancery position, he had gotten along
well with both the Protestants and the Catholics. Through his administrative efficiency, he had gained respect and had also been
able to free most summer afternoons for his writing. For this purpose he had acquired a miniature *Tusculum*, a tiny garden house
just outside the town walls, ideally suited for his rococo muse. Furthermore, Wieland presumed he would meet with difficulties in
Erfurt because he lacked an academic degree. Eventually, all of his
objections were overcome, and in the process, he had negotiated a
good contract, for he would receive five hundred and fifty
Reichsthaler (roughly sixty-nine hundred dollars) per annum in addition to three hundred liters of grain, three hundred of barley, and
four cords of wood. All this amounted to more than he was earning
in Biberach. Economically, he was raised from the master craftsman
class to the upper class.[8] In return, all Wieland had to do was to be
physically present in Erfurt; he did not have to teach. Thus, in May
1769, he loaded his family (his daughter, Sophie, was twenty-three
weeks old) and belongings onto a wagon and left Biberach for Erfurt.
He was never to see Biberach again.

In Erfurt, Wieland did give courses because he was at heart a
pedagogue and enjoyed the contact with students. Besides, ever
since his early Zurich days he had often dreamed of being a professor. He took advantage of the opportunity, offering courses on a

wide range of topics—the history of the human race, the history of philosophy, the history and theory of fine arts, the comedies of Aristophanes, Horace's epistles, Cicero's concept of duty—and even gave surveys of the best Greek, Roman, Italian, English, and French writers. Most fitting, perhaps, was the seminar on Cervantes' *Don Quixote*, which Wieland had first encountered twenty years earlier in Erfurt. According to eyewitnesses, he was a capable, exciting lecturer, so that his presence did indeed tend to enhance the university's image and to attract hundreds of students.[9] One of his most devoted students, a man named Becker, tells us that Wieland would lecture using only a few notes. Of course there was a danger involved. Wieland later recalled that it was Becker who would provide the verb he had forgotten by the time he had reached the end of his involved sentence.[10]

The initial joy Wieland felt upon settling into his new profession did not last long, for he quickly learned the true state of intrigue at the university and found most of the professors disappointing. An exception was Friedrich Justus Riedel, with whom he had corresponded during the negotiations. In one another they found allies against the (ultimately triumphant) conservative resistance to reform. With his popularity with the students and his quick promotion to university professor of philosophy, Wieland had aroused the envy and ire of many colleagues from the start. When he was subsequently made privy councillor to the elector and named voting member of the steering committee by special decree, the resistance stiffened. In order to discredit Wieland, his student Becker was accused of blasphemy and brought to trial, but the poet eventually succeeded in clearing his protégé of the charges. Had he failed, his opponents would have attacked him personally. As the reform movement increasingly ran aground, the liberal professors left one by one, and after two short years, Wieland too began to look for a new job. He tried to keep out of the intrigues as much as possible, living a retiring life, devoting most of his energies to his writing, but not neglecting his growing family. Between June 1769 and October 1772, three more children were born to him, and he enjoyed nothing better than playing with them. Even this withdrawal into his *Schneckenhaus* aggravated many colleagues, who could not understand how the author of the *Komische Erzählungen* could find happiness in family life.

From Wilhelm Heinse, the future author of *Ardinghello* (1787) and Wieland's student, we have a description of the professor's way of life which provides us with a background for the political and social views reflected in his works. Heinse wrote to Gleim in 1770:

Wieland is almost completely without friends in Erfurt. Surely he would remain home for months on end if he didn't have to go to church on Sundays. . . . He has two daughters with whom he horses around, chit-chats and amuses himself. Oh, if only you could see him thus!. . . . Every babble, every little word, every look, expression and gesture is for this acuminous man a new discovery in this philosophy of the human heart and in the musicality of language. Once, just once, that citizen of Geneva, that author of the work on the inequality of man, should see this fatherly love. Surely he would then travel through all Europe stealing and burning [the copies of] his book!—at least he would revoke the statement that the vague love of the fatherless, wild state of mankind is the love which imparts happiness."[11]

It is surprising perhaps to see such a famous man enjoying the joys of family life. Yet these simple pleasures represented for Wieland the path to true contentment for all men. Heinse's allusion to Rousseau suggests that Wieland's personal, political, and social philosophy was based on the love and respect that he felt for his family and they for him. We have here an explanation for his tenacious support of monarchy.

III   The Poet-Philosopher

A.   Verse Productions

In Erfurt, Wieland completed several major works (from June 1769 to September 1772) which can be divided into two general categories: those conceived and begun in Biberach and those initiated in Erfurt. The former are in verse and have much of the Rococo flavor of the titillating *Komische Erzählungen;* the latter are didactic prose works which stress sociopolitical theory. To the first group belong *Die Grazien* (1770), *Combabus* (1770), and *Der neue Amadis* (1771). As can be expected, they attest most readily to the continuity of the author's Sternesque virtuosity regarding style. The second group reflects more obviously the altered social and intellectual circumstances in Erfurt and includes *Socrates Mainomenos oder die Dialogen* [sic] *des Diogenes von Sinope* (1770), *Beiträge zur Geheimen Geschichte des menschlichen Verstandes und Herzens*

(*Essays on the Private History of Human Understanding and Feeling*, 1770) and *Der goldene Spiegel* (*The Golden Mirror*, 1772). Yet each group reveals in its own way the consistency of Wieland's basic concerns.

Until very recently, the products of this period were generally neglected in Wieland research. Yet even in the present context their significance for the author's total oeuvre can be only briefly sketched. In the verse-prose poem *Die Grazien*, the continuity of Wieland's anthropological views is charmingly revealed. As mentioned earlier, it is to be seen in conjunction with Musarion's philosophy of the Graces. Since the Graces represent for Wieland the perfect harmony of body and spirit in human nature they are "very essential divinities." Wieland does not differentiate between Shaftesbury's moral graces and Homer's "profane" goddesses, for the two should not be separated. It is erroneous, he states, to consider the former to represent merely spiritual values and the latter to stand only for corporeal ones. Rather, the Graces signify a natural, more fulfilling unity of the opposing poles, spirituality and sensuality. For this reason Wieland affirms: "Never, with God's good will and the aid of my common sense, will I follow a philosophy other than that of the Graces."[12] Despite such unambiguous statements, Wieland's works continued to be misinterpreted by many of his contemporaries who could see only the eroticism and not its truly moral basis.

Thus, even *Agathon* was banned in Zurich and Vienna. Due to this bias, the true significance of the verse tale *Combabus* has been overlooked. Instead of viewing the titular hero's act of self-castration as an heroic sacrifice to virtue—as Wieland intended it—it has been seen as merely grotesque and repugnant.[13] *Der neue Amadis*, based on *Amadis de Gaule*, is written in the same vein as the earlier poem, *Idris und Zenide* and undoubtedly represents a major formal achievement. Begun in Biberach, it was completed in Erfurt in 1771. Wieland was very enthusiastic about this work, as can be seen from his long letter of October 2, 1769, to Gleim, where he calls it "something truly original, a hybrid of all other genres of epic poetry, because it has something of all of them. It is one of the most quixotic progenies of the Socratic satyr and one of the Graces, begot half voluntarily, half forcefully." Amadis himself is described as a "satyr, half faun, half Amor" who appears as a knight-errant in a magical world peopled by the Graces and nymphs in the form of errant princesses. With these descriptions, external parallels to works of the 1760s are readily apparent. Even more striking is the inner parallel to *Die Geschichte des Agathon* which Wieland draws at the end of this letter to Gleim: namely, that "Amadis is Agathon's half-brother."[14] The reference is presumably to the hero's search for his ideal and his repeated disappointments. As elsewhere Wieland applies to *Der neue Amadis* the principle of "ridendo dicere verum" ("to laughingly speak the truth") which he found so characteristic of Laurence Sterne's *Tristram Shandy*. To this end he created a new verse rhythm which allowed his *Geist Capriccio* (Capricious mood) full reign to choreograph what is called a *Silbentanz* (syllable dance) of ten line stanzas with alternating verses of six, five, and four feet in which trochees and dactyls predominate.[15] The opening stanza may stand as an example of the tone and quality of the entire poem:

> Von irrenden Rittern und wandernden Schönen
> Sing, komische Muse, in freier [sic]irrenden Tönen!
> Den Helden sing, der lange die Welt Berg auf Berg ab
> Durchzog, das Gegenbild von einer Schönen zu finden,
> Die aus dem Reich der Ideen herab
> Gestiegen war, sein junges Herz zu entzünden,
> Und der, es desto gewisser zu finden,
> Von einer zur andern sich unvermerkt allen ergab:
> Bis endlich dem stillen Verdienst der wenig scheinbaren Olinden
> Das Wunder gelang, den Schwärmer in ihren Armen zu binden.[16]

At the outset, the reader (or listener!) is aware that a basically serious problem—the desire to realize uncompromising ideals in a flawed empirical world—is going to be treated in a whimsical fashion. The Sternesque and Rabelaisian elements in Wieland's style are especially pronounced in this "last production inspired by the Biberachian cacodaemon."[17]

Sternesque implies, of course, the humorous disruption of the fiction and the narrator's witty addresses to the reader, while Rabelaisian refers to the satirical exaggeration of the characterizations and descriptions. Michel's term "cacodaemon" also underscores the sense of unrest and dissatisfaction with rigid rules which even Wieland felt on the eve of the *Sturm und Drang*. The poet remarked in a letter to Sophie LaRoche that his light style was aimed at a general audience interested more in entertainment than in erudition[18] and that it is for this reason that he also uses it in his more outspokenly philosophic works of the same period.

The truly innovative feature of *Der neue Amadis* is its form. It is a hybrid of narrative and epic and as such reflects the author's insight that the age of grand epics á la *Paradise Lost* is past, he himself having failed to complete the epic torsos of *Hermann, Cyrus,* and *Idris.* Thus, Wieland consciously sought to achieve an epic short form, unaware that he was recreating the epyllion of antiquity. That form is not to be confused with the shorter comic epic initiated by Nicolas Boileau and Alexander Pope because—for one thing—it does not even take itself seriously as parody. It is an experimentation with a form which points forward to the poet's own *Oberon,* to Johann Heinrich Voss' *Luise,* and to Goethe's *Hermann und Dorothea.* In other words, *Der neue Amadis* lays the cornerstone for the *Kleinepos* (epyllion).[19] This short epic was to be Wieland's last work in verse for several years, for the mounting pressures of his unstable position in Erfurt proved too distracting. Instead he turned to prose and to immediate professional concerns.

B.   *The Prose Works*

1.   Die Dialogen des Diogenes

Wieland's move to prose reflects, to a degree, the growing impact of the nascent *Sturm und Drang* atmosphere. Prose was the characteristic idiom of the new generation of writers seeking freedom from social and literary conventions, and Wieland's use of alternating prose and verse passages in *Die Grazien* was already a sign of this shift. The works conceived in Erfurt have a dual purpose. First, they can be seen as a justification of his professorship for philosophy (a term used broadly in the eighteenth century). In fact *Diogenes,* the *Beyträge,* and *Der goldene Spiegel* can be interpreted as contributions to Wieland's planned—but never executed—history of the human spirit. At the same time, the author tries to present his ideas in a more popularizing form than in the *Agathon* novel. Sengle's remark that Wieland was too much a storyteller to accomplish anything as intellectually rigorous as a history of philosophy is well taken.[20] Wieland was by nature incapable of producing systematic philosophy. Yet we should not see in the sociopolitical views of these Erfurt works mere "concessions" to academic demands. To do so would be to misjudge the ultimate nature of Wieland's concern for man's social condition.[21] The criticism that Wieland's ideas lack sharp focus and that he is too much a compromiser can be traced back to his philosophical skepticism, which began to evolve fairly early and which is intimately linked to his views on perception. The term "skepticism" must, however, be understood in the proper manner. To call Wieland a skeptic is not to assert that he doubted everything and therefore took no stand. The term refers only to epistemological concerns. Gruber wisely made this distinction: "Wieland had become a skeptic in the face of [the objects of metaphysics]; it was not as if he doubted the existence of the world, the soul, and the divinity. He doubted only the dogmatic claims of metaphysics and the sufficiency of man's faculty of perception in attaining genuine knowledge."[22]

Sokrates Mainomenos (or *Der Nachlass des Diogenes* [*Diogenes' Literary Estate*], as the work was later titled) reveals the continuing tension arising from conflicting perceptions of the real and the ideal which lie at the heart of *Agathon* and *Der neue Amadis*. Within this context, *Diogenes* (and the *Beyträge*, which were written more or less simultaneously) can be seen also as a response to Rousseau's perception of man's social and political environment. In a sense, they are a second response, because shortly after the appearance of the *Discours sur les sciences et les arts (Discourse on the Sciences and the Arts*, 1750) and the *Discours sur l'origine de l'inégalité (Discourse on the Origin of Inequality*, 1754), Wieland had made plans for a history of human understanding. The Erfurt prose works demonstrate his renewed interest in Rousseau's views on society and education caused by *Du Contrat social (The Social Contract*, 1762) and *Emile* (1762). However, Wieland does not take note of Rousseau's modified position on the question of man's sociability and continues to polemicize against the premises of the *Discours sur l'inégalité*.[23] *Diogenes* is a vindication of the titular hero told in the bantering style of *Tristram Shandy*. Although the work is not an "antinarrative" like the English work, there is little plot, only apparently random groupings into chapters of Diogenes' "experiences, observations, sensations, opinions, day dreams . . . foolishness—our own foolishness—and the wisdom . . . gleaned from all that."[24]

The unifying factor is the protagonist's character. The novel is thus marked by a formal openness which Wieland seems to have consciously striven for. It has been convincingly argued that this openness is appropriate for Wieland's particular manner of philosophizing since he is concerned only "with the depiction of an attitude toward the world," not with systematic exactness and comprehensiveness.[25] As Gruber had put it, Wieland was concerned with the art of living.[26] The conclusion of the novel contains a whimsically portrayed utopian state of nature ("Die Republik des Diogenes"), which suggests that the original state of nature is a phantom, the *beau savage* ("beautiful savage") a mental construct. The influence of flawed social realities prohibits the continuance of a naturally egalitarian state. In order for Diogenes' natural colonists to preserve their happiness, they would have to do without all the trappings of society (class distinctions, wealth, luxury, etc.). Since this is impossible, Diogenes causes his republic to disappear with a wave of his magic wand. A search for his enchanted island would be fruitless, for it does not exist.

Within the context of the novel, the parody of the impossible utopia is the "wise insight" drawn from Diogenes' various experiences and conversations. The main body of the work is peppered with striking philosophical, economic, and political criticisms which are made especially effective by being bound together with short allegorical narratives, a technique known as "philosophizing as narrative process."[27] One of the most memorable episodes has to do with the man in the moon, a hilarious indictment of speculative philosophy. Diogenes holds a public lecture on "The Man in the Moon" in which the speciousness of abstract reasoning is blatantly exposed in such arguments as: "the man in the moon is there, because how could he otherwise be the man in the moon?" This remark is, however, merely the beginning of the descent into "the metaphysical abyss," which becomes ever more ridiculous—and highly entertaining:[28] The man in the moon episode lucidly demonstrates the continuity of Wieland's thought concerning the theory of knowledge by stressing the inanity of speculative thinking and the blindness of dogmatic assertions. Another episode, Diogenes' rescue of a drowning maiden, further elucidates the nature of true knowledge by showing how one's perspective toward the incident is crucial to right perception. The several views of what Diogenes, naked, did with the bare-bosomed beauty on the beach vary with the perceiver's personal background and expectations. The reader is thus cautioned to tolerate other opinions and to question his own, a warning which is often repeated in subsequent works. In the preface, which treats ironically the manuscript and translator fictions so popular in the eighteenth century, Wieland directs his barbed wit at the closemindedness and self-righteousness of the monks in a certain monastery in B*** in the province of S***. This satire was probably inspired by the Catholic opposition in Erfurt, which made life difficult for the author.

Finally, Wieland's views expressed in the novel on the socioeconomic state of Europe at the time are worthy of mention. Noteworthy is the rejection of slavery on ethical grounds: no man has the right to deprive another human being of his innate freedom, for to do so is to violate his humanity. Especially caustic is the indictment of the rich minority, which squanders its resources on a lavish lifestyle while others go without food, shelter, and clothing. The pampering of personal whims, when others suffer extreme want, is a misuse of wealth. Furthermore, the ethical justification of wealth is based solely on the benefit it brings society as a whole. Unfortunately, wealth has a way of hardening man against his fellow man; the rich become concerned with preserving and increasing their possessions rather than with aiding others. They tend to be drones, who live off the laboring classes. With great insight, Wieland predicts a revolution from below once the oppressed learn to organize and dare to overthrow their exploiters.[29] However, Wieland is incapable of envisioning a complete social upheaval (such as was envisioned by Saint-Simon), which would do away entirely with ruling princes. The explanation for this is to be sought in the author's experience of man's incorrigble weakness and foolishness.[30] As will be seen more clearly in *Der goldene Spiegel*, Wieland sets his hope for the wise governance of the individual state in an enlightened, constitutional monarchy. Yet the ultimate, permanent safeguard of man's inalienable rights is the progression toward a *Weltbürgertum* (cosmopolitanism). Diogenes achieves his greatest significance in this regard. As an outsider, with only a barrel to his name, he symbolizes Wieland's ideal of independence from all involuntary action:

birth does not make me a citizen of any particular state, if I do not will it. Nature places her children in the world as free and independent, with equal rights and obligations and without any other connection to their fellow men than the natural bond with those through whom Nature gave us life or the bond of *das Sympathetische* by means of which she draws men to each other. The bourgeois conditions of my parents cannot rob me of my natural rights."[31]

Because Diogenes makes no claims on an individual state, no state can make claims on him. His demands are made rather on all mankind; thus his obligation is only to the whole. Diogenes foreshadows Democritus in *Die Abderiten* in his role as contemporary critic and guide to an envisioned utopian *Weltbürgertum*. The whimsical depiction of the "Republik des Diogenes" betrays how hopeless the ideal would appear to be. Nevertheless, Diogenes does not turn his back entirely on society. He remains in it, hoping to someday convert the powerful—if only one—to true humanity.[32] *Menschlichkeit*, expressed through the bond of sympathetic feeling, is the prerequisite for *Weltbürgertum*. Today we would say he believed in "working through the system." Like Goethe, Wieland rejected revolution in favor of evolution.

These are only some of the considerations which mark *Der Nachlass des Diogenes* as a major accomplishment; its formal achievement is no less formidable. Truly one can say with Sengle that the novel is one of Wieland's best works. The author's correspondence from the period attests to his satisfaction with the outcome, and—judging by the two thousand seven hundred and fifty copies printed and the acclaim it received from all sides—the work proved to be highly successful. Years later the author supposedly said: "This *Diogenes* is one of my best works. I don't know if I ever wrote anything better in prose."[33]

2. Der goldene Spiegel

Together with *Diogenes, Der goldene Spiegel* (1772) captures the mood of the Erfurt years and marks the beginning of a concerted effort on Wieland's part to reach a larger reading public. The novel was composed toward the end of Wieland's stay in Erfurt, when the professor's situation was becoming less and less tenable, so that the work was, in some respects, an ostentatious attempt to attract attention from elsewhere in hopes of obtaining a new position. Wieland had Emporer Franz Josef II most notably in mind. Although Franz Josef was flattered by the attention this now renowned poet was according him, his mother, Maria Theresa, still saw in Wieland a libertine. Perhaps for this reason the poet was not called to the

imperial court: however, the novel did attract the interest of the
Grand Duchess Anna Amalia of Saxe-Weimar, who eventually lured
the author to her provincial court.

Nevertheless, it would be fallacious to see the work as mere
"unverbindliches Salongespräch" ("noncommittal chit-chat") or as
an *Irrweg* ("wrong turn") which led the author away from his central
concerns *(Kern)*, views which have recently been corrected.[34] With
its ideal of an enlightened constitutional monarchy, the novel does
not break new ground regarding political theory, but it does reveal
the consistency of Wieland's anthropological views and does demonstrate his continued mastery of artistic form and syntax, a skill
which he has in common with Thomas Mann.

The novel is a story within a story which presupposes the reader's
acquaintance with the principal characters in *1001 Nights*. Again we
encounter the ironic fiction of manuscripts and translators and the
droll style of earlier works. Shah Gebal is a spoiled sultan who leaves
the governing of his country to the women around him while he
indulges his senses. In order to help him fall asleep at night, the
sultan requires that he be told bedtime stories which must be true,
morally decent, and historical. Above all, they may not contain
anything wondrous. These requirements lay the ground rules for
the ensuing interplay of fantasy and reality whereby it becomes
clear that each realm (the framework, the history of Scheschian, and
the interpolated utopias) is to be judged according to separate
criteria.[35] Thus it is that the sultan's favorite, Nurmahl, and the
court philosopher, Danischmend, relate the history of the
neighboring kingdom of Scheschian. Each evening a portion of the
history is read, until the sultan falls asleep. The translator presents
the work as a "faithful description of the errors and excesses of the
human mind and heart" from which many a lesson can be drawn.[36]
The very formulation evinces the novel's proximity to the *Beiträge*.
In fact, Shah Gebal does occasionally resolve to alter his rule in
accordance with the insights into poor and wise governance gained
from the readings. Unfortunately, the resolve is taken just before he
falls asleep, and the next morning he has forgotten it. The history of
Scheschian itself tells of the good and bad rulers of the nation and of
the rise and fall of its fortunes. In the process, the causes for success
or failure are discussed. In general, they concern the education and
person of the ruler. But other determining factors, such as climate,
economic conditions, and religion, are also taken into account. In

this delineation of natural order, the fruits of Wieland's study of Montesquieu, Bonnet, and others can be observed. The high point of Part One of the novel is reached with the description of Prince Azor's upbringing and a list of a ruler's moral obligations. The foremost of these is to treat everyone with respect and justice and to punish those injustices which cannot be prevented. Since King Isfandir, Azor's successor, does not follow these moral dictates, he is killed in a revolution which rocks the nation. Interpolated in this first part is the description of a small nation of five hundred families who live a utopian ideal in total isolation from the rest of the world.

Part Two concentrates on the upbringing of Prince Tifan, the savior of Scheschian, who is raised far from the court among simple people. There he learns to value and respect every productive individual. Unaware that he is the legal heir to the throne, the people choose Tifan as the person best qualified to serve as their ruler. Only after his selection do they learn that Tifan is, in fact, the crown prince. The high point of Part Two is reached with the laudation of constitutional monarchy which, with its enlightened monarch and just laws, is the most propitious form of government for safeguarding every citizen's inalienable rights. The novel concludes with a description of youth education programs in the empire, because an enlightened people is more useful and more easily governed.[37]

The narration of these events does not progress smoothly, for Danischmend is frequently interrupted by Shah Gebal with questions concerning the narrative. The ensuing discussions between monarch and court philosopher highlight both the interrelationship of fantasy and reality and the nature of constitutional government. Wieland's contemporaries did not properly understand the function of the framework with its conversations between Danischmend and Shah Gebal; they complained about the disruptions. However, the central artistic and interpretive role of these discourses has subsequently been recognized. Just as in *Agathon* Hippias was not totally rejected and even served as Wieland's mouthpiece, so too Shah Gebal is the spokesman for the author's practical side. The exchanges are, as Sengle notes, "a dialogue between the theoretical and the practical politician"; however, it is not "a dialogue without a conclusion." Rather, Wieland does draw a conclusion, one in keeping with his character. He was less concerned with depicting "that which *should be,* than with showing that which *is* as it should *not* be."[38] The portrayal of the two utopias—the Eldoradolike nation in

Part One and the enlightened reign of Tifan in Part Two—speaks
directly to this problem. Wieland is fully aware of how imaginary his
bucolic people is and consciously shows its origin to be the result of
pure chance and its continued existence to be contingent upon
complete isolation. Just as Candide and Cacambo have little more
than the idea of Eldorado to present upon their return to the real
world, so this paradise is nothing but a mirage outside its valley. The
second utopian state, Scheschian under Tifan's wise rule, is an attempt to meet the objection of impracticality leveled at the Arabian
valley nation by Shah Gebal. Tifan's reign is thus not the result of
chance, and his people do not live in an "unnatural" state. Rather,
the peace and tranquillity he brings evolve as a direct consequence
of his upbringing, which taught him to respect and value every
human being. The constitution he introduces assures the equality of
all citizens and safeguards their rights. Wieland believed that *egalité*
was determined by laws, not by nature; he also held to the feudal
views of the monarch as divinely ordained, but as an enlightener, he
held as well that reason is divine. Consequently, judicious laws
were divine. The constitutional form of monarchy thus represented
an ideal union which could best ensure the general welfare.[40]

When one contrasts the two utopias depicted in the novel, the
point the author is making seems clear: it is more likely that a ruler
can be made sagacious and laws wise than that a nation could evolve
and persevere in a providential state of nature. Even when everything comes together, as in the case of Tifan's reign, there is no
guarantee that the perfect state will be perpetuated. In fact, indications are given that due to internal moral corruption, even Tifan's
empire will fall victim to neighboring princes. Thus the demise
does not first follow in the second version (1794) of the novel.[41] The
novel in part challenges its readers to personally work for the es-
tablishment of a (near) perfect state—one marked by Diogenes'
Weltbürgertum and *Menschlichkeit* rather than narrow nation-
alism—since chance will not do it for us. Wieland is aware of man's
frailty and therefore urges vigilance so that man will not forget his
resolve even as Shah Gebal did.

Der goldene Spiegel is not an *Irrweg*, and its import is not ambivalent. The views presented here in sociopolitical terms are rooted
in the author's concept of man as a hybrid of seraph and sybarite
which dominated his early works. Wieland remained true to this
bifocal view of man throughout his life. The French Revolution did

not essentially alter it.[42] The optimism and confidence which he had brought to his professorship in Erfurt had dissipated in the light of continued opposition. But he did not despair. Like Diogenes and Danischmend, Wieland did not cease to adhere to his ideals.

At the right time, a new opportunity presented itself for Wieland: he received an offer from Anna Amalia, Grandduchess of Saxe-Weimar, to act as court tutor to the crown princes, Karl August and Konstantin. It was not without a sense of relief that he packed his belongings and family into the coach sent for him. His attempt to reform the university had failed, and he was under heavy attack by the rival faction. In addition, his wife had borne him three more girls, his mother had come under his care, and Sophie LaRoche's son, Fritz, had come to live with him as well. The move to Weimar solved his immediate professional problems, and his new job even provided him with a secure financial base. His salary was to be one-thousand Thaler (equivalent to twelve-thousand and five-hundred dollars) for the duration of his tutorship and he was to receive an annual pension of six-hundred Thaler upon retirement. Danischmend had learned much from Shah Gebal.

CHAPTER 6

In Weimar (1772–1813)

I Danischmend at Court

A. New Duties

THE forty year old poet did not know what far-reaching consequences his move to Weimar was to have for the ducal town of
ten-thousand inhabitants and for German culture as a whole. He
also did not expect to spend the rest of his long life there. Except for
seven years in neighboring Ossmannstedt and rare trips to Leipzig
and Zurich (1796), Wieland was firmly rooted in Weimar.

To be sure, the anticipated financial benefits were no minor factor
in the decision to move, yet the prospect of playing Danischmend,
or wise counselor, to a future ruler was equally enticing. The prospect of realizing his poetic dream of an enlightened ruler (Tifan in
Der goldene Spiegel) was exciting. He arrived in Weimar conscious
of his Danischmend role and filled with the desire to work as much
good for his fellow man as possible. Of course, there were the
dangers of sycophantic court life, especially in light of the friendship
which sprang up between teacher and pupil. But the Republican
Swabian loved his independence and privacy too much to become a
courtier. Just as his loyalties had remained with the city of Biberach
despite his acceptance at the Warthausen court, so too did the
author remain aloof from self-aggrandizing court intrigues in
Weimar. This aloofness angered those who hoped to use "Danischmend's" influence over the prince to their advantage and made
life difficult for the poet, even poisoning the duchess' view of the
court tutor for a time. Although Wieland was ultimately cleared of
all accusations and his personal relationship with the Duchess Anna
Amalia eventually developed into a close friendship, the poet found
himself again alone and without many friends.

The result was that he naturally withdrew into his "Schnec-kenhaus." However, this withdrawal was no "resigned flight from unmastered reality into the 'snail house' of private life." Rather it was, as in all instances, a return to his natural habitat. As early as 1752 Wieland had spoken of his aversion to large gatherings, and in the Archytas section of *Agathon* we have an expression of the author's societal ideal. He will present it to us again in the circle of friends surrounding Apollonius (*Agathodämon*), the Johannite family in *Peregrinus* and in Aristipp's relationships (*Aristipp und einige seiner Zeitgenossen* [*Aristipp and Several of his Contemporaries*]) In the privacy of his home, in the midst of his family, he was happiest. His literary life was dependent upon the security of his tranquil homelife.[1] Even the "celebrity" which he had sought since the mid-1760s, and had now attained, had its disadvantages. Besides, Wieland was rather unrefined and ignorant of the customs of high society, as we can see from some previously unpublished anecdotes from K. A. Böttiger's literary legacy in Dresden.[2]

Wieland did not appear to be completely successful as a tutor, or perhaps it was the result of slanders leveled at him; in any event, the author was relieved of any obligations toward the education of Prince Constantin, the younger brother, who was assigned his own mentor, Karl Ludwig von Knebel (1744–1834). After three years, Karl August was declared of legal age (at eighteen), and Wieland found himself without any official duties. Due to the intervention of his former student, the poet was even awarded his full salary of one-thousand Thaler per annum (instead of the contractural six-hundred Thaler) for the rest of his life. Such generosity enabled Wieland to devote himself entirely to his muse. Well, almost entirely. Almost from the very first, the court tutor fulfilled his pedagogical duties only half-heartedly. The reason for this indifference was the founding of a periodical, *Der Teutsche Merkur*. The preparations for the publication of this journal required much attention and were surely a cause of the dissatisfaction with his teaching. Yet, like his tutorship, the editorship of the *Teutscher Merkur*, as we shall see later, resulted from the author's desire to benefit man as well as enrich his pocketbook. Thus in 1775, freed from official court duties but maintaining close contacts, "Danischmend" devoted full time to shaping the opinions of a new pupil: the general public. But first we must look at the poet's muse in the service of the Weimar *Musenhof*.

B. *Dramatic Works*

Sengle argues that the years 1772–1773 represent a creative crisis for Wieland, who supposedly felt that he had reached the end of his artistic productivity. Thus, the preparations for the *Teutscher Merkur* and the writing of the operetta *Alceste* (1773) were "expressions of a creative vacuum."[3] However, this assertion doesn't seem to hold up in light of the literary significance of both the journal and the *Singspiel*. *Alceste* was written during the first months in Weimar and was produced with Anton Schweitzer's music for the first time on May 29, 1773. The premiere was such a resounding success that the poet thought somewhat exaggeratedly that Weimar might now be considered imperial Vienna's cultural equal. *Alceste* was not the first of Wieland's dramatic works to be staged in Weimar: *Clementina von Porretta* and the panegyric operetta *Aurora* were presented in 1772. Others followed *Alceste* as well; most notably *Die Wahl des Hercules* (*Hercules' Choice*, 1773) and *Rosemunde* (1779). Of these, only *Rosemunde*, which found Mozart's approval (he participated in the rehearsals), would seem to approach the quality of *Alceste*.

After such innovative works as *Agathon, Idris und Zenide,* and *Dialoge des Diogenes,* people had come to expect the poet to always produce somthing new. *Alceste* did not disappoint them. Operettas were, to be sure, not new—we need only think of Christian Felix Weisse's productions in Leipzig—yet *Alceste* was, unlike most Leipzig and Paris productions, through-composed. More importantly, the simplicity and sublime tone of the action were striking. Critics have rightfully pointed out that *Alceste* anticipates in style and tone Goethe's *Iphigenie*, since it, too, is "verteufelt human" (terribly human). The titular heroine freely sacrifices her life in fulfillment of an oracle in order to save the life of her husband, King Admet, who is mortally ill. As soon as the promise of a substitute sacrifice is made, Admet recovers. He does not realize until too late to whom he owes his life and is inconsolable over the loss of his selfless spouse. Hercules learns of his friend's sorrow, descends into Hades to retrieve Alceste, and reunites the pair. Nothing is included in the plot which would detract from the singleness of purpose.

To consider the work purely "classicistic," as Sengle does, is to overlook the deep personal experience which underlies the drama. Wieland tells us himself that his beloved wife was seriously ill at that time and that he was truly afraid of losing her. His situation reminded him of the basic idea underlying Euripides' play. True, the external inducement for the writing of the work was Anna Amalia's wish to have a dramatic piece, but the internal motive must not be underrated. *Alceste* is not just a passive product of Danischmend, the court poet.[4] Such a view underestimates the author's own sense of independence as repeatedly expressed in his correspondence.

A detailed analysis of the work's style, structure, and idea would confirm the presence of the "spirit of Weimar classicism" best known from Goethe's *Iphigenie*.[5] Unfortunately, we must content ourselves with merely drawing attention to Wieland's contribution to the classical drama in Germany. The definitive study of Wieland's significance as a playwright has yet to be written. And when it is written, it must resist the temptation to see *Alceste* (and "Die Briefe über die *Alceste*," 1773) through the eyes of the brash young *Sturm und Drang* poets. Goethe, for example, treated Wieland and his *Alceste* unmercifully—and not quite fairly—in his witty farce, *Götter, Helden und Wieland* (*Gods, Heroes and Wieland*, 1774). With its stress on manly vigor and raucous spontaneity, the younger generation was not a fair judge of quiet restraint and sublime sentiment, as Goethe himself came to realize.

C. *The German Parnassus*

With Wieland's move to Weimar, the German Parnassus attained a geographical focus. This proved to be even more the case when Goethe (in November 1775) and Johann Gottfried Herder (in February 1776) also took up permanent residence in the ducal town. They were later joined by Friedrich Schiller (in July 1787). All of them, at one point or another, were part of Anna Amalia's *Musenhof*, of which Wieland was a cornerstone, and which was initiated in 1775 to discuss regularly literary and intellectual questions. From 1775 to the early nineteenth century, Weimar was the focal point of literary endeavors and attracted many visitors. One of the first persons to be sought out was Wieland, whose fame peaked during the 1770s and 1780s. Evidence of his preeminence is provided in the correspondence of a Frenchman traveling through Germany, where we read in a letter dated 1780 that "Wieland is without doubt the best of Germany's authors" and that he "is one of the few German writers, who will be considered classical by future generations, after the writings of most of the others will have been used as dung for the fields."[6]

However, Wieland did not enjoy such acclaim continuously. In fact, he was harshly criticized by such contemporaries as Klopstock, the members of the Göttinger Hain, and Heinrich Wilhelm von Gerstenberg, who branded him as a Francophile and immoralist. The image of Wieland's lack of originality comes from Gerstenberg's reviews in the *Hamburgische Neue Zeitung* (1768, 1770); while the infamous image of Wieland as a slavish imitator of the French comes from Klopstock's *Gelehrtenrepublik (Republic of Scholars,* 1774). The Göttinger Hain even ceremoniously burned his works in protest against this insidious and "un-German" author. Goethe was the most ingenious in his criticism, especially with the image of Wieland as half a man, and consumptive to boot, who dares compare himself to "real men." Wieland's reaction to the criticisms was astounding, but fully in keeping with his character, which demanded honesty of others but even more so of himself: he was tolerant. Certainly, it hurt to be harshly criticized, but he was "big" enough to recognize valid criticism and insightful enough to understand the psychological motivation behind exaggerated criticism. His relationship to Goethe is exemplary in this respect. Despite the damage done to his image with the younger generation by *Götter, Helden und Wieland (Gods, Heroes, and Wieland)*, Wieland published a glowing review of Goethe's piece and highly recommended it. The farce proved to him that Goethe could be a second Aristophanes if he wanted to, even as *Götz von Berlichingen* proved that he could be a second Shakespeare.[7] Goethe was impressed by this maganimity and even a little ashamed of himself.

When the two authors met later in Weimar, they were immediately taken with one another, and a lasting friendship ensued.[8] During his initially difficult years in Weimar, Goethe found in Wieland a substitute father and in his home a haven. When Schiller arrived twelve years later, he too found a haven in his countryman's overcrowded household. Initially, the relationship between the two Swabians was warm; there was even an indication that a lasting union between Schiller and Wieland's second oldest daughter, Karoline, was in the making. But this was not to be. Despite their common cultural backgrounds, Schiller's and Wieland's characters were quite different, and their relationship cooled off, especially after 1794, when Schiller and Goethe became close friends. Schiller apparently did not want to share Goethe's friendship. Despite the venom directed at Wieland in some of the *Xenien (Satirical Epigrams)*—probably composed by Schiller rather than Goethe—Wieland did leave his mark on Schiller.[9]

Wieland's relationship with Herder was initially cool, but warmed up considerably after 1794 (although Herder did not read many of the Swabian's works.) In fact, Wieland's personal warmth and openness were qualities which invariably won him respect, if not friends. Whoever met Wieland personally left with a more favorable impression of the man than he had before entering his home. The attacks directed at him during the early 1770s and again during the late 1790s were, in a way, a tribute to the stature he enjoyed in the public's mind. Like the "Stürmer and Dränger," the young Romanticists denounced Wieland in an effort to establish with great fanfare their own literary platform.[10] The widespread fame which Wieland enjoyed with all classes of the reading public in the later eighteenth century was due, in no small measure, to the circulation of the *Teutscher Merkur*, which Wieland founded in 1773.

II   *Wieland as Popularizer*

A. *Journalist and Essayist*

Wieland had long nurtured the idea of establishing a literary journal. In the early 1750s in Zurich, he had regularly contributed to Bodmer's critical journal *(Crito)*, and in the late 1750s, he had enthusiastically greeted Zimmermann's proposal to initiate a weekly, which bears much resemblance to the subsequently founded *Teutscher Merkur*.[11] However, for various reasons the early plan did not materialize. Only in the 1770s, encouraged by the success of Riedel's *Erfurtische Gelehrte Zeitungen*, to which our author contributed regularly, did the idea of his own journal become dominant again. In September of 1772, scarcely settled in Weimar, Wieland wrote to Riedel concerning his intention to establish an imitation of the successful *Mercure de France*. The title, *Teutscher Merkur*, was suggested by Friedrich Heinrich Jacobi.[12] By spring 1773, the first issue appeared.

The publication of the journal is significant for a number of reasons, the least of which was that it proved—at least initially—to be lucrative. Wieland was clever enough to realize that a carbon copy of the *Mercure de France* in Germany would not succeed.

Thus, he adapted the format and program to Germany's own social and cultural situation, shifting the emphasis from theater to broadly held opinions which he wished, in part, to revise. In addition, he promised to publish all his own literary works in the journal, as well as the poetic works of others. In doing this, Wieland created the prototype of the general literary journal which "took the decisive step from pedantic instruction to literature, from scholarship to entertainment and culture."[13] His journalistic enterprise is thus to be seen in conjunction with his striving for a *Weltbürgertum* based on the ideal of *humanitas*. More than just a moneymaker, the *Teutscher Merkur* was also an expression of the editor's sense of the intellectual's social responsibility.[14] Danischmend shifted his focus here from the court to the reading public, with such success that Goethe could remark in 1825 that "all the upper classes owe their style and taste to Wieland."[15] There is an indication that Wieland's influence was not restricted to the aesthetic tastes of the upper classes. Recent studies have dealt with the influence which the journal tried to exert in sociopolitical matters as well. Finally, the *Teutscher Merkur* is significant because it endeavors to reach a general reading public, one not restricted by geographical location, educational background, or class.

This was the case under Wieland's editorship until 1796, but most especially in the 1770s and 1780s, when the editor was confident of his ability to teach even the lower classes to be "right thinking" men. In a letter to Fr. H. Jacobi written in 1775, Wieland clearly indicates that his journal was not aimed only at the intellectual elite: "Do you think that an honest man, who publishes a *Merkur* is not concerned with average people, with the intellectually deprived, with the intellectually immature and infantile?" Bruford has noted that the *Teutscher Merkur* "made some appeal to the rapidly expanding public of ordinary tradesmen and their wives, as well as to the highly educated, and it had the field almost to itself in southern Germany."[16] Yet, to my knowledge, no study has dealt with this question of a lower class audience for Wieland's works, although we are told, for example, that Seiler Geissler, a leader of the peasant revolt in Saxony in 1790, took many of his ideas from the *Teutscher Merkur*.[17] We also know that the journal was subscribed to by many reading circles throughout Germany whose members came from all walks of life, that servants in many households had access to the families' reading matter, and that even analphabets were exposed to certain writings via village pastors and teachers who would read to them from published material.[18]

The statement to Jacobi cited above was in response to Jacobi's objection that there was no need for Wieland to be as explicit in his self-defense against the accusation of moral turpitude as he had been in the essay "Unterredungen zwischen W.*** und dem Pfarrer zu*** (1775). Clever readers were able to understand allusions and nuances. However, as is evident, Wieland was not writing here primarily for skilled readers, but also for less practiced ones. Wieland's letter to Jacobi seems to validate what has been asserted by a contemporary observer: "No German author knows his public as well as Wieland."[19] For almost a quarter of a century, he was able to attract more than a thousand subscribers (which meant many more thousands of readers) through his ability to capture the reading public's attention. One enticement for the reader was the very personal relationship he enjoyed with the editor. Very frequently, Wieland addressed his reader directly through announcements or through commentaries to the works of other authors. The relationship tends, of course, to parallel the communication established between narrator' and fictive reader in his belletristic writings. Thus, it is not surprising that the essayistic writings reveal rhetorical qualities similar to those of the poetic productions. Even the makeup of the journal contributed to its enduring success and broad appeal: side by side we find philosophical essays and travelogues, incisive book reviews and popularized scientific notes, anecdotes, and reports on foreign affairs. This editorial practice and the editor's unique talent for mixing the humorous with the serious prefigured the feuilleton style of Heinrich Heine.

As Goethe noted in his funeral oration of 1813, the *Teutscher Merkur* mirrors Germany's literary and intellectual life from 1773 to at least 1796. All of Wieland's verse and prose writings of the 1770s and 1780s first appeared in its pages. In addition, other leading authors such as the Jacobis, Goethe, Schiller, and Novalis were represented. During the initial years, emphasis was placed on literary criticism as well, the result no doubt of the influence of Johann Heinrich Merck, who was one of Wieland's best contributors.

The journal was founded the same year in which Goethe composed his *Götz von Berlichingen*. That is significant, for the rush of patriotic sentiment typical of the *Sturm und Drang* was not lost on the journalistic enterprise. After the first issue, the title, *Deutscher*

Merkur, was changed to the *Teutscher Merkur* in recognition of the patriotic flavor of the older "teutsch" with its etymological root of "pertaining to the people." The *Volksmässigkeit* of the journal's tone is evident in biographical essays on Sebastian Brant, Hans Sachs, and Martin Luther. The rampaging Shakespeare adulation found its way into its pages too, in the essay "Der Geist Shakespeares" ("Shakespeare's Genius," 1773) and in the review of *Götz* (1774).

Of interest is the amount of space that Wieland devoted to the lot of the professional writer, with his rights, responsibilities, and problems. For example, the already mentioned "Unterredungen zwischen W*** und dem Pfarrer zu***" was published in 1775. In 1780, a "Schreiben eines Nachdruckers" ("Letter from a Piratical Publisher")—written in a style faintly reminiscent of the sixteenth century *epistolae obscurorum virorum (Letters of Obscure Men)*— appeared. It stressed the financial injustice done to an author by unauthorized reprintings. That work was followed by the important "Briefe an einen jungen Dichter" ("Letters to a Young Poet, 1782–1784) and "Über die Rechte und Pflichten der Schriftsteller in Absicht ihrer Nachrichten, Bemerkungen, und Urtheile . . ." ("On the Rights and Obligations of Writers Concerning their Reports, Comments, and Judgements," 1785). The two essays address themselves, on the one hand, to the financial and legal problems that an author just starting out can expect to encounter. The first is a sober appraisal of the state of German literature and includes an indictment of both Franco-and Anglophobia. The "Briefe" further outline the qualities of a good writer and indicate the difficulties of artistic creation.[20] "Über die Rechte und Pflichten" highlights the need for freedom of expression and of the press. In these and other pieces, a writer's social obligation to always speak the truth impartially is stressed. The state must respect this obligation "um der guten Sache selbst willen" (i.e., the education of the people). The two pieces are especially important for Wieland's concept of the "freier Schriftsteller" and for the role of the free press in the eighteenth century. Finally, an essay from the year 1791 demonstrates the editor's continuing concern for the lack of copywright laws: "Grundsätze, woraus das Mercantilische Verhältniss zwischen Schriftsteller und Verleger bestimmt wird" ("Principles from which the Mercantile Relationship between Author and Publisher Emerges").[21]

In the 1780s, the literary vogue gave way to popular scientific questions—for example, the art of flying in France, the use of coal in hearths in order to save scarce wood, a report of Georg Forster's travels. Also of general interest were essays dealing with super-natural phenomena such as Swedenborg's divination, Mesmer's and Lavater's magnetism, or Cagliostro's magic. Alongside these popular pieces, we find essays treating the life and culture of ancient Rome and Greece.

The late 1780s and early 1790s saw a decided turn to the contemporary political situation in France and its significance for Germany. Unlike many contemporaries, Wieland greeted the revolution (which he had foreseen in *Diogenes*) with tempered enthusiasm. He lauded the efforts to establish a constitutional monarchy. Yet he had been too often disappointed by reality to allow himself to become overconfident that all would end well. He had learned that ideals, although necessary to man, cannot normally be translated into reality. Thus, when anarchy and the Reign of Terror began to dominate French political life, Wieland was not as sorely disappointed as many other political observers. As is evident in his earlier writings, the poet had always been skeptical of democratic rule. His observations of man convinced him that all men did not possess the same talents, nor to the same degree. The slogan "fraternité, egalité, liberté" held only one-third of its appeal for the Swabian. The cornerstone of all of Wieland's thought—religious, ethical, social, political, and the like—was *humanitas;* thus, fraternity was the only ideal he accepted unconditionally. More important than equality and freedom were law and order. Wieland rejected the ideology of equality and freedom because it was inconsistent with reality. As Würzner concluded in his study of Wieland's political stance: "Democracy can never guarantee [law and order], only monarchy can do that; however, not an absolute monarchy but only one bound by constitutional laws and subject to a two-house system which gives no hegemony to any one estate while excluding none. Yet that is, for the time being, only a 'daydream.' "[22] The latter reference is to Wieland's essay. "Gespräche unter vier Augen X: Träume mit offen-en Augen" ("Private Dialogues Nr.X: Day Dreams," 1798), in which the author considers soberly the manner in which a utopian state would have to be implemented. The catchwords are not "Freiheit und Gleichheit" (Freedom and equality) but rather "Sicherheit und Ordnung" (law and order). Because of these views, the political commentator foresaw in 1798 that a strong new leader would rise out of the chaos to restore law and order, which should be the chief function of any state. The only person qualified was Napoleon Bonaparte. This prophecy caused quite a stir, which found its first expression in an article in the *St. James Chronicle* in early 1800.

The "Gespräche unter vier Augen" was Wieland's final comment on the implications of the French Revolution. All of the *Merkur* articles leading up to them revolve around his conviction "that rule by the stronger is an historical fact and, regardless of how much one might complain about it, it is one of the inadequacies of this world."[23] Of concern in this regard is the author's view of "das Volk." Although he felt that the so-called proletariat was too busy to improve itself intellectually, he did not want us to conclude that the common people are incorrigible and uneducable, for he repeatedly emphasized (as for example in the Agathon-Hippias dialogues or in *Agathodämon*) that man must try to better himself if he is not to regress to a complete state of animality. His disparaging comments on the rabble *(Pöbel)* therefore are not to be seen as a rejection of the people *(das Volk)*[24] The rabble acts like animals, but is not ipso facto incapable of improvement. If Wieland had not been convinced that all men have at least the capacity for *Aufklärung*, his entire oeuvre would amount to self-parody.

B. *Translator*

Wieland used his journey to Zurich in 1796–1797 to withdraw from the editorship of the *Teutscher Merkur* (which had been renamed the *Neuer Teutscher Merkur* in 1790). In that same year, he founded the *Attisches Museum*, a journal dedicated to the study of antiquity. This periodical appeared from 1796–1803 and contained many of his own translations.

We have seen from his Shakespeare translations that he had early been interested in presenting world authors to a wider audience. His work on Horace, Lucian, Aristophanes, and Cicero was motivated, at least in part, by the same desire. Wieland translated these authors primarily because he saw something of himself in them and was attracted to them. This was especially true of Horace and Lucian, to whom he dedicated almost a decade of his life. *Horazens Briefe* appeared in 1782 and *Horazens Satyren* in 1786, while *Lucians von Samosata Sämtliche Werke* appeared from 1788 to 1789. Portions of these works had previously been published in the

Teutscher Merkur. These translations were made during a pause in his own belletristic production, but they are far from being fillers and "are not a typical product of an aging poet."[25] In fact, the original Latin and Greek texts have been so masterfully translated that they are still considered "classical" today. The translations are not literal; rather, it was Wieland's intent to "recreate" the spirit of the originals, so that Horace and Lucian would have the same effect on an eighteenth century German reader as they had had on their contemporaries. In order to achieve that end, three things were necessary: the translator had to have a thorough knowledge of late antiquity, he himself had to be a poet, and he had to see in Horace and Lucian an alter ego.

Wieland's identification with Horace and Lucian began early, in Horace's case developing to the point where Wieland felt the Roman poet's spirit residing in himself. *Horazens Briefe* are, in fact, more than a translation; together with Wieland's interpolated essays and notes, they represent a monument to Horace and to himself, for as Wieland himself remarked, the *Epistles* with commentary are an excellent source for acquainting oneself with his own taste and manner of thinking.[26] The greatest parallel between the two poets is their celebrated urbanity and moderation in all things. Similarly, the translation of Lucian's satires is simultaneously an encompassing interpretation of the Greek poet. Like the Greek author, Wieland too mixed humor and earnestness in his battle against hypocrisy and deception. In their endeavors to improve their audiences, both made use of a graceful, congenial style. Here too, the identification between author and translator was so intimate that Sengle speaks of a "symbiosis with Lucian."[27] The translations of Horace's and Lucian's satires earned Wieland the epithet "the German Voltaire" (a designation he did not appreciate, although he saw in the Frenchman a *Lucianus redivivus*).

Later translations of several of Aristophanes' plays (e.g., *The Clouds*, 1798; *The Birds*, 1805), Xenophon's dialogues (1799, 1801), and Cicero's epistles (volumes I–V, 1806–1812; vol. VI was completed by F. D. Gräter in 1818) were also undertaken. However, these did not match the quality of the Horace and Lucian undertakings. Nevertheless Goethe was correct in stating in his funeral oration that "perhaps no one has felt so intimately as [Wieland] did what an intricate business a translation is."[28]

CHAPTER 7

Poet Laureate (1772–1783)

I Literary Program

THE years 1772–1783 represent the second pinnacle of Wieland's poetic muse. Despite his early court obligations and the self-imposed task of producing a highly successful journal, the poet created a number of major and minor classics. We must of necessity be selective and brief in our discussions of the prose and verse creations of these years, which is unfortunate because the verse tales such as—*Das Wintermärchen* (*A Winter's Tale*, 1776), *Geron der Adelich* (1776), *Schach Lolo* (1778), *Pervonte* (1778, 1796)—are true gems. They detail the further development of Wieland's subtle style and present a chronology of the emerging Romantic spirit. However, we will have to concentrate on the two major works worthy of world recognition: *Die Geschichte der Abderiten* (*The Republic of Fools*, 1773–1780) and *Oberon* (1780).

These works, like their companions of the 1770s and 1780s, can be seen as the fulfillment of a "literary plan" particularized in the *Merkur* essay "Gedanken über die Ideale der Alten" ("Reflections on the Ideals of the Ancients," 1777) and sketched again in "Briefe an einen jungen Dichter" (1782, 1784). In the first article, the poet reacts to the ideology of stark realism advocated by the *Sturm und Drang*, as well as to Lavater's apotheosis of the Greeks in the section of his *Physiognomische Fragmente* ("Physiognomic Fragments") entitled: "Über die Ideale der Alten, schöne Natur, Nachahmung" ("Concerning the Ideals of Antiquity . . .") Whereas Lavater had argued that the Greeks enjoyed a more perfect nature than we know and imitated that real perfection in their works, Wieland contends that physical and human nature were no more perfect then than now. Rather, the Greeks created their works according to *Urbilder*, (innate ideas) which they saw with their mind's eye. It was the typical which they saw in the particular and idealized.[1] Sengle rightly points out that Wieland draws here upon Plato's and Herder's concept of "deus in nobis" to clarify his own literary ideas.[2] He sees the work of art as a mediator between the divine forces (of which the poetic imagination partakes) and the sensations of the empirical world (in which the perceiver is rooted). What Sengle overlooks is that this idealistic turn is not a radical change; it is in line with the Swabian's artistic development since *Araspes und Panthea* (1759). We have seen that the idealism in Wieland's literary productions was more or less constant and have heard him officially declare in 1767 that he was departing from Sterne's capricious style and was going to return to his Platonic/neo-Platonic idealism. The significance of the *Merkur* piece lies in its conviction that a classical period in German literature itself was entirely possible. Wieland himself created some of the first classical German works, although he does not say so in his review of the state of German literature in "Briefe an einen jungen Dichter."

This literary program can also be seen in conjunction with Wieland's awareness that true (classical) literature transcends the bounds of narrowly chauvinistic interests which marked much of the literary climate of the 1770s. In 1773, a critical report on the contemporary state of the German parnassus was published in the *Teutscher Merkur*, to which Wieland appended a critical commentary. These remarks foreshadow his own literary program and even anticipate Goethe's and the Schlegels' concepts of *Weltliteratur*. Wieland speaks there of the "common character of poetic virtuosos" despite their cultural and linguistic differences. He further warns of the dangers posed by undue stress on atavistic patriotic tendencies and urges one not to ignore the transnational cultural heritage common to all Europeans since antiquity. The progress of mankind toward harmonious interaction can only be achieved through the dismantling of nationalistic cultural barriers. These views sharply contrasted with the tenor of the times; but they reveal the author as more "progressive" than many another. *Die Abderiten* and *Oberon* represent the fulfillment of Wieland's striving for a "world literature."

II Die Geschichte der Abderiten *(1781)*

Of Wieland's many excellent works, *Die Abderiten* is perhaps most deserving of wide recognition. Just as the novel was read in every part of German-speaking eighteenth century Europe, it surely would be popular with today's English-speaking audiences schooled on *Gulliver's Travels* or *Catch 22*. Along with *Don Silvio*, this novel would serve most propitiously as a first introduction to Wieland's genius. Sengle sees it as signaling a "humorous classicism" and rates it even higher than *Oberon*. Its humorous treatment of human folly anticipates Jean Paul's accomplishments, its aesthetic synthesis of "nature and spirit" prefigures the classical permeation of the object with the idea, and its parody of the German philistines adumbrates the Romantic rejection of the pseudoeducated.[3] In doing this, the novel also demonstrates how the Enlightenment's aesthetic combinatory principle of wit prepared the way for the harmonious union of form and content in the classical period proper.[4]

The work can appropriately be seen as a juncture of the past and the future in a number of other ways. For example, it renews the tradition of fool's literature so popular from the fifteenth to the seventeenth centuries; most specifically, it renews the motif of wrong-headedness which dominates the chapbook, *Das Lalebuch* (*The Book of Lale*, 1597). In contrast to the people of Lale, however, the inhabitants of Abdera never intentionally act foolishly; on the contrary, they pride themselves on being descendants of the wise Athenians. *Die Abderiten* is also the first serialized novel in German literature, appearing in seventeen installments between 1774 and 1780. In 1781, it was published in slightly revised book form (here the "Schlüssel zur *Geschichte der Abderiten*"—the "key"—was added). The serialized novel became, of course, immensely popular in the nineteenth century. Finally "the novel is not only the first comprehensive socially critical novel in eighteenth century German literature . . . it is also the first aesthetically formed, literary documentation of a bourgeois self-criticism."[5] Critics concur that *Die Abderiten* is both a masterpiece of social satire and of ironic literary style. They also agree that the novel represents "a kind of *summa*" for Wieland in the 1770s,[6] and it is in this light that we will consider the novel.

Die Abderiten is clearly divided into two parts comprising five books. The first three books (comprising Part I) treat personal conditions in the town, where everything is the complete reversal of what is considered normal. For example, the supreme court judge was elected because he had a good singing voice; the temples look like baths, the public baths like temples; the libraries are full of useless books; the arsenals have no weapons, the fountains no water; and the people cry at comedies and laugh at tragedies. This wrong-headedness is viewed in Book I by the natural philsopher Democritus, who at first tries to reason with his fellow Abderites, but eventually gives up. Ultimately, he is considered insane by his countrymen, because for them to do otherwise would be to admit their folly. Book II introduces Hippocrates, the famous doctor, who recognizes the people's adsurdity and recommends a strong dose of snuff. Book III concerns itself with the question of aesthetics, especially that of the drama, occasioned by a production of Euripides' *Andromeda.* It is here that Wieland's criticism of contemporary, philistine aesthetic views is most strident.

Books IV and V (Part II) shift the focus to the social and political sphere. Matters of property and justice are raised in Book IV, while Book V centers on the politization of religion and the duping of the people. The legal question in Book IV ("Der Prozess um des Esels Schatten" ["The Lawsuit Concerning the Ass's Shadow"] which must be resolved is whether a man who hires a donkey automatically hires his shadow as well. A dentist hires a donkey on which to make his rounds; however, the sun is so hot that he must sit in the ass's shadow to keep cool. The hinny driver, a shrewd businessman, demands extra payment for the use of the shadow, which was not hired out with the animal. An altercation ensues, and the matter goes to court. However, the townspeople, senate, religious leaders, and judges become so polarized into adherents of the ass and adherents of the shadow that no judgment can be reached. As so frequently happens in Wieland's fiction, chance resolves the conflict. The ass is spontaneously attacked in the market place by the irate Abderites and is torn to pieces, and eaten. Thus the innocent donkey becomes a kind of scapegoat, which brings about a parodistic reconciliation of the two factions.[7] Yet the ultimate question of property—namely, whether the shadow is part of the donkey, is left unresolved. Book IV of *Die Abderiten* is by far the best known, for it was subsequently published separately (like the Biribinker episode in *Don Sylvio*) and has been dramatized by such writers as August von Kotzebue, Ludwig Fulda, and Friedrich Dürrenmatt.

Book V, which narrates the cause for the demise of the Republic of Abdera, is in fact an indictment of the corruption of religion, not of religion itself. There are two rival temples in Abdera, the Temple of Latona and the Temple of Jason. The followers of Latona are guided by the high priest Agathyrsus and revere frogs as sacred beings, whereas the disciples of Jason follow the high priest Stilpon and revere the Golden Fleece. Because the sacred frogs multiply unrestrictedly, they soon begin to overpopulate the city. However, the Jasonites do not stand idly about, for the frogs get them hopping mad. Agathyrsus and Stilpon begin to manoeuver for power within the republic, each using his organized religion to play upon the ignorance of the people, gain more followers, and thus strengthen his position. The result is again a drawn out dispute, which ends when the city is abandoned to the frogs.

From this brief overview of the satire, it would appear that we are dealing with a fantastic tale such as that of Biribinker or Idris. In fact, the author informs us in "Der Schlüssel zur Abderitenge-schichte" ("Key to the History of the Abderites") that "he conceived the idea in a rush of capriccio . . . of letting his imagination run wild."[8] But the scenes from Abdera are not portrayed for their entertainment value alone. In the preface we are informed that the author looks upon his narration as a "contribution to the history of human understanding."[9] Throughout we perceive that Wieland is very concerned with establishing the principle of probability, so that his continuing efforts to understand man in his psychological and sociological context are apparent. The principal thrust of this novel, as opposed to the others we have discussed, lies in the degree of folly depicted. The book version of 1781 closes with the shrewd formulation: "sapientia prima est stultitia caruisse" ("freedom from folly is the first [step to] wisdom") (H, II, 455). When we consider that the citation is only part of a longer quotation from Horace, the dual purpose of this and of all of Wieland's works is poignantly clear. The first part reads: "virtus est vitium fugere" ("to flee vice is [itself] virtue") (H, II, 823) and could easily stand at the masthead of other works such as *Kombabus* or *Die Wasserkufe* (*The Water Trough* 1795). We don't have to make a case for the dual intent of this novel, since critics are in general agreement on that issue.

The success of the novel was tremendous. Not only was it widely read and translated, but university lectures were delivered on it as well.[10] Nevertheless, complaints were heard from various quarters that the work was satirizing specific individuals and places, so that Wieland felt it necessary to add the "Schlüssel" in order to coun-termand these suspicions. Although we can accept his statement that he had no specific models for his characters, but rather took types, because the Abderites "are an indestructible and immortal people . . . who can be found everywhere" (H, II, 452), we know that certain personal experiences did give rise to some situations and characters in the novel. For example, Book III is largely indebted to the author's experiences in Mannheim, where he had traveled for the premiere of his *Rosemunde* in 1777, whereas Book IV reflects experiences in Biberach, and Book V mirrors circumstances in Erfurt.[11] Less important than determining these circumstances, however, is the need for showing that Wieland successfully harmonized experience and idea, reality and poetry, that, in other words, he produced a work of art, not a documentary.

Some of the ideas which went into the making of the novel strike us as radical even in the twentieth century; for example the suggestion in Book I, Chapter 10, that the only hope for the Abderites would be for them all except for several dozen children (who would presumably be taught wisdom by "paternal" Democritus) to fall victim to a plague. Such a suggestion is due no doubt to the misanthropic mood which gave birth to the undertaking, for Wieland reportedly acknowledged: "The Abderites were conceived in an hour of ill humor, when I was looking down from my garret window on the whole world filled with dung and filth and decided to take revenge on it."[12]

Die Abderiten can be seen in line with Wieland's previous works. For example, Democritus, Wieland's spokesman in *Die Abderiten*, resembles Diogenes; neither of them is a fantast like Agathon. In the earlier novels, we can see the author's evaluation of society change, and the individual's role is reassessed. Whereas society in the early novels is the end-all (the goal for which the sometimes foolish individual strives), society in *Die Abderiten* becomes a parody of what it once was. With Democritus, therefore, the aberrant dreamer type à la Don Sylvio, who lives in his own fantasy world, takes on a positive cast, so that the roles of aberrant individual and normative society in *Die Abderiten* are reversed: society is now aberrant, while the "outsider" represents the ideal norm.

With the passing years, Wieland became increasingly skeptical in social and political matters; but he did not become cynical, as the tone of the satire might suggest. If we compare the novel with the *Merkur* article "Stilpon," which appeared the same year as the first installments of the novel (1774), we note a relatively more optimistic tone in *Die Abderiten*. The dialogue "Stilpon" presents the reader with a purely negative view of abderitism. We hear again in the interlocutors, Eukrates and Kleon, the advocates of the head and the heart, as we had once heard them in Hippias and Agathon. The head is, of course, restricted to the world of appearances, while the heart looks behind appearances to what should be. Although Stilpon is consulted as to which view is correct,[13] his advice goes unheeded, and the worst possible leader is chosen, who then bans Stilpon from the republic. The philosopher's cynical laughter at the conclusion of the dialogue offers no hope of improvement.

Laughter is a major motif in *Die Abderiten*, and although "the laughing philosopher" Democritus also leaves his hometown, his perspective is not identical with Stilpon's. By way of explanation, we can cite a statement from another work of the same period, thereby stressing one of the ways in which *Die Abderiten* is a *summum* of Wieland's oeuvre through 1781. In the verse tale *Schach Lolo* (1778), an ironic justification of rule by divine right, we read: "The true seer is he who selects the right perspective."[14] What that "right perspective" is exemplified in Democritus' stance. He is tolerant because he realizes that he himself is neither omniscient nor perfect; he is patient with the foolish and bad behavior of others because they have to tolerate his. In a word, he knows that the Abderites "were all in all men like other men despite their abderitism; in a certain sense they were the more human the more abderitic they were." Thus, Democritus says, in effect, to himself: "But for the grace of God, there go I." Democritus is an Abderite like his fellow townspeople; yet because of his "superior" perspective (because he is widely traveled), he can recognize the blindness of their judgments. They are like children who do not know better, who are foolish not by intent, only through ignorance. And where there is ignorance and not evil purpose, there is the prospect that the void can someday be filled with insight. This is the basis of Democritus' "right perspective" and explains the nature of his laughter. The narrator suggests in Book II, Chapter one, that the philosopher laughed because he saw in mankind's actions "empty trifles and children's games." Thus, it is "more amiable to smile at human life than to sneer at it. And one can say that he who smiles at it does mankind a greater service than he who laments it, because the first gives us a modicum of hope." Democritus' basic attitude is described here, and we notice that it ends on a positive note. Yet the philosopher did not necessarily remain a passive observer. In a footnote the narrator explains further: "A wise and good man laughs or smiles . . . bemoans or bewails, excuses or exculpates according to the people and concerns, time and place, involved."[15] In *Die Abderiten*, Wieland, in the *persona* of Democritus, found it fitting to smile and try to improve by example alone. In other contributions to the *Teutscher Merkur*, he found it appropriate to assume a more active role, as, for example, in the essays on the French Revolution.

The laughter in this novel about folly is humanitarian, for it derives from a feeling of *Sympathie* with all members of the human race. It is related to the instinctual bond which unites *Weltbürger* with one another, such as Democritus with Hippocrates and Euripides. Cosmopolites operate on a second level as well, that of reason; and theirs is a "secret" society based on the principles of reason. It is the lack of this commonality with the Abderites which prevents their direct influence on society such as the "Turm-gesellschaft" was later to exert in *Wilhelm Meister*.

To be sure, the novel is, as Martini asserts, to a great extent a parody of "the Enlightenment's pedagogical optimism" and, as Sengle says, an expression of "the impotence of reason."[16] Nonetheless, Democritus (Wieland) hopes that Abderites all over the world can be cured of their wrong-headedness. He places his trust not in reason—for reason is not the only determinant of human action, as we have already seen in both *Don Sylvio* and *Agathon*— but in the goodness of the human heart. With Danischmend, Democritus holds that "philosophy is situated in the heart, not the head."[17] Because he does not rely solely on reason to dispel wrong-headedness, Democritus can still be optimistic. Although cognizant that the majority of people will not attain the use of salubrious reason, he senses intuitively that its attainment must still be ultimately possible. For the present, the sage can only observe and comment from a distance, waiting for the foolish "children" to come to their senses.

Wherever familial feelings dominate in Wieland's writings, a tolerable social community evolves. Although there is no explicit solution proferred in *Die Abderiten*, we might conjecture as follows without departing from Wieland's manner of thinking. As suggested, a natural catastrophe could eliminate all adults from a society, thus freeing the children from the cycle of foolhardiness and opening them up to true education by wise men. Wieland, as

Danischmend, of course, saw himself as a qualified teacher. Yet radical as the idea would seem, he did not advocate taking children from their parents by force. Chance (or providence) would have to come to man's rescue. That Wieland's idea is not without some validity can be seen from the Chinese communalization of all aspects of private life. For the Chinese as well as for Wieland, private life is merely the prelude to social life. The familial situations we encounter in Wieland's works are due no doubt to this "enlightened" insight.

  Die Geschichte der Abderiten is not only a thematic *summum,* but also a stylistic one. As a stylist, Wieland reached "the zenith of his mastery" in this novel,[18] where he used all the techniques he had learned to enlist the active participation of his reader. By means of unexpected twists, dialogue, shifting perspective, *Sympathie* and irony, Wieland endeavors to raise his reader to his own lofty vantage point. In the process, the reader must learn to recognize folly and prejudice not only in others but also in himself. When enough people reach this "right perspective," a "perfect" society will evolve. No arrogance is implied by the narrator's position because he does not consider himself inherently better than others. It is all a matter of perspective. These concepts echo Wieland's early concerns; the style mirrors his early approaches.

  The work would appear to have almost more in common with comic than with epic technique (as do *Musarion* and *Der neue Amadis*). For example, the five books might be seen as a five act comedy, for each is a self-contained unit, with its own scenic dimensions artfully executed. This is particularly true of Book IV, "Der Prozess um des Esels Schatten," which readily lends itself to stage production. The elements of comedy include typecasting of characters, interlacing of humorous motifs, pithy formulations, and unexpected reversals or developments. The latter extend to the novel's very syntax and are reflected in Wieland's preference for the periodic sentence. It has been noted that Wieland's interest in the theater was more than a passing fancy. What apparently appealed to him was the immediacy of the stage, with its stress on eliciting audience reaction through the play's effect.[19] These elements, and the entire third book, would seem to verify this assertion. Comedy, of course, requires the audience to maintain a distance from which it can view the totality of the action and the relationships depicted without losing the capacity to respond to what is perceived. It is the appropriate attitude for the reader who is about to be enlisted as an equal partner in the author's ironic interplay with the characters and the work.

Irony is one of the most characteristic traits of Wieland's urbane style, and as Blackall asserts: "The full flower of this irony is to be seen in *Die Abderiten.*"[20] A proper understanding of the poet's irony is prerequisite to a judicious appraisal of his work. Rarely boisterous or caustic, his brand of irony is, rather, engaging and playful. In 1769, he wrote very revealingly to Sophie LaRoche: "Irony, for which I like to think I have some talent, is admittedly my favorite device. It is, to be sure, a dangerous talent. Fortunately, nature has equipped me with a good and honest heart. My cynicism is only feigned; I love mankind by nature. If I mock the failings of the one or the inadequacies of the other, I do it usually amiably and with the intention of speaking beneficial truths in a joking manner, truths which one, at [other] times, would not dare utter."[21] Wieland's ironic style derives from the dialectic methods of the Enlightenment and is marked by a multiplicity of perspectives, the basic pattern of which is dialogic. In fact, dialogue comprises the real "action" of this work, for it appears variously as conversation between intimates, as discourse between teacher and students, as easy social chatter, as essayistic digression, and as polemical diatribe. Furthermore, a dialogue arises between the narrator and his work, as well as between narrator and fictive reader. This dialogic approach causes almost constant shifts in the point of view, so that the reader must learn to distinguish the changing perspectives in order to appreciate the author's harmonization of source material, personal experience, and idea. *Die Abderiten* is especially rich in points of view.

The fiction of the manuscript upon which the "history" is based is treated lightly. Already in the preface, we are informed that the ensuing work is based on ancient documents, but that this historicity is not the ultimate criterion for veracity. "Discerning readers" will note that the author had followed nature in his endeavor to reconstruct the history of Abdera. Nature, we are assured, is a better guarantor of truth, so much so that it would behoove historians to observe her operations more closely (H, II, 125). Nature is here equated with human nature seen in a psychological and sociological light. The narrator's benign duplicity evolves from this bipolar basis as he mixes and reverses fantasy and reality. Throughout the narrative there are references, even footnotes, detailing the documentation for this history. The reader is called upon to accept the absurd and grotesque actions of the Abderites as historical. Yet is is not the historical documentation which makes the story—despite its absurdity—true, but the understanding which evolves between narrator and reader. The attentive reader realizes that the historicity is a parody of itself. Furthermore, it is ironic that the illogical antics of this philistine people are essentially logical, when we consider that salubrious reason has been totally replaced by "unreason." We find here a parallel to the logic of the fantastic, fairy tale atmosphere of the Biribinker episode in *Don Sylvio*. Each world is consistent in itself.

Not all of Wieland's readers were astute enough to understand this relationship between the empirically real and the fictionally real. The author did, however, attempt to raise his readers to this level of insight. The tone of this educative process is sounded in the first chapter of Book I. Within the framework of the entire novel, the chapter is structurally designed to introduce the reader to the character of the Abderites. The rest of the novel then provides specific illustrations, a rather straightforward, didactic method which even marks the sentence structure of Wieland's ornate, but clear, style. However, more important for Wieland's major contribution to the evolution of an elastic, rhythmic German prose style is the narrator's treatment of the reader. The narrator unexpectedly interrupts himself with the exclamation: "To what end (our readers cry) this insignificant determination of the origin and fate of the town of Abdera in Thrace?" (H, II, 127). The parenthetical remark forces the individual empirical reader to identify with the fictive readers addressed and to repeat the question: "Yes, to what end?" Thus he feels himself directly addressed when the narrator next urges: "Be patient, well-disposed readers! Be patient! We must agree upon the terms before I continue the narration" (H, II, 127).

The narrator then puts himself in the empirical reader's position. He realizes that none of them *has* to read this story and begins to cite the various obligations which this, that, and the other reader probably has (e.g., visit the sick, write a report, just bought some oxen, just took a wife). The author's purpose in mixing examples from current bourgeois activities and from the biblical parable of the marriage feast to which the invited guests would not come is not lost upon the attentive reader. The author shows here his awareness that all persons who should read *Die Abderiten* will not have sense enough to do so. They are not interested in anything that might be beneficial. Thus, the narrator exclaims:

In God's name, go study, visit, refer, review, translate, buy, and celebrate! Pre-occupied readers are seldom good readers. Now they like everything, now nothing; now they only half-understand us, now not at all, now (and that is the worst of all) wrongly. Whoever will read with enjoyment, with profit, must have nothing else to do or even think. And if this happens to be your case, why shouldn't you take two or three minutes to learn something which took a Salmasius, a Barnes, a Bayle—and to be honest—myself (because I did not think to check the article on Abdera in Bayle) many hours to find out? (H, II, 127).

Wieland does not want a distracted or lethargic reader. He seeks one who is active and willing to learn to play the game according to the "terms agreed upon." These terms require the reader to be flexible.

The empirical reader is attracted by the author's candor (he was too stupid to check Bayle's *Dictionnaire* before "wasting" hours on unnecessary research). The author shows himself to be further at fault (like his reader) when he admits, in Chapter Six of Book I, that he cannot answer all the reader's questions about the Ethiopian beauty Gulleru because he has not given her much thought! She is only incidental to his story. The bond between narrator and reader is further cemented by the numerous parenthetical comments inserted by the narrator and by such phrases as "our man." They establish the norm by which the reader is to judge the events.

After having interrupted his initial report to draw the reader into the work, the narrator attempts to return to his depiction of Abdera: "The Abderites were (according to what we have already—" However, he is not allowed to finish his sentence, for a reader interrupts him: "Without interrupting, who were the three calenders about whom you were just speaking?" The narrator replies politely: "Excuse me, madame, we were not speaking about calenders but about the Abderites (H, II, 128). (The reference was to the three dervishes in *Der goldene Spiegel*.) The narrator then refers the woman to sources for similar stories, explains that there is a difference between "Geschichte der Kalender" and "Kalendergeschichten" (namely, trivial stories in almanacs) and tries to return to the Abderites once more. This time he manages to complete the sentence begun previously before being interrupted a second time: "The Abderites (according to what was already reported) were said to be as fine, active, witty, and clever a people as ever lived under the sun.—And why that?" The question is interjected by a fictive reader. A note of irritation might be detected in the narrator's initial reaction to the repeated distraction, but his response is friendly enough: "This question is presumably not put to us by the scholars among our readers. But then who would want to write books if all readers were as knowledgeable as the author? The question 'why' is always a very sensible question (H, II, 128). The questioner is not reproved for interrupting; he is even praised. Obviously, the "terms" of the narrative include an obliging, understanding attitude on the narrator's part.

One of the means by which the reader is taught to react with just as much understanding and tolerance toward the Abderites is the narrator-reader relationship outlined in the first chapter. The explanation for this accommodation lies in the awareness that author and reader are human too and thus imperfect. There is no sense of superiority over the befuddled townspeople.

The introduction of Democritus refines the reader's perception of the irony involved and strengthens the narrator–astute reader perspective. Democritus lives among his compatriots as a wise man among fools, and through his eyes, the reader experiences the Abderites from the vantage point of a naturalist and world traveler. The juxtaposition of his cosmopolitan humanitarianism and the Abderites' shallow myopia gives frequent rise to ironic contrasts, which are not drawn by Democritus directly, but rather inferred by the reader. This positive contrastive point of view is expanded by other characters in the novel as well. For example, Hippocrates (in Book II) is also a cosmopolite (here, an advocate of salubrious reason in all things) and, in addition, represents the healing power of medicine. A third representative of Wieland's own position is the dramatist Euripides (Book III), whose special function within the structure of the novel is to demonstrate the beneficial influence of art. Under the spell of his aesthetic competency, the citizens of Abdera are temporarily restored to psychic health, their wrong-headedness set aright. This deliverance ("Rettung," as Martini calls it),[22] is attained at the end of Book III.

In dramatic terms, Book III coincides with the climax of the third act and tends to highlight Wieland's conviction that all men can be brought to their senses. In terms of the novel's division into two parts, the effect of Euripides' play marks the end of Part I with its ostensible spokesmen for right-mindedness. Although Part II (i.e., Books IV, V) lacks a clearly positive contrast to abderitism, we should not assume that Wieland had become so cynical during the final years of the novel's composition as to believe that there was no hope for Abderites anywhere. Otherwise "who would write books, if all readers were as knowledgeable as the author?" The Abderites have learned from the fiasco with the ass's shadow to laugh at their own folly. That is at least a beginning toward *stultitia caruisse*. Book V concludes with a vision of an indefinite time in the future when abderitism will have been overcome. The author is not willing to estimate when that time will come, even though he makes reference, albeit ironic, to the reform efforts of his contemporaries. He is less confident that the reform will be achieved quickly; yet he is not without hope that *Weltbürgertum* will someday hold sway. The all-too-human quality of the *Geschichte der Abderiten* encompasses more than the total perversion of reason; it includes the hope against all hope of improvement.

The significance of *Die Abderiten* can be summarized as follows: It offers another corrective to Winckelmann's idealization of ancient Greece, it initiates the modern trend of bourgeois self-criticism in literary form, and it perfects the supple, rhythmic qualities of classical German prose begun with such works as the *Sympathien* (1755). Furthermore, it teaches its wise audience, more than any other work of its age, how to read satiric literature. On the basis of this satire alone, Goethe was fully justified in calling Wieland the "deutscher Lukian" in his funeral oration of 1813.

III   Oberon *(1780)*

In 1744, Alexander Pope's *The Rape of the Lock* (1712) was translated into German; in the same year, Friedrich Wilhelm Zachariä published his mock heroic poem *Der Renommist (The Braggart)*, which was admittedly modeled after Pope's work. In their wake followed a rash of comic verse tales. Between 1744 and 1783 approximately forty comic epics, mock heroic poems, or burlesque tales were written, twenty-one of them by Wieland. We have already discussed some of these tales conceived during the 1760s. Now it is time to turn our attention to the versifications of the poet's second major creative period. All of his verse productions with one exception were first published between 1773 and 1783 in the *Teutscher Merkur*. The list is long (twelve) and demonstrates the Swabian's astounding ability to shape the German language into subtle rhythms marked by musical modulations. The twelve verse works, composed mostly in four to six iambic lines, fall into three major categories based on Diderot's theory of narrative: (1) comic verse narrative, (2) verse fairy tales, and (3) verse narratives and parodies with chivalric atmosphere.[23]

The verse narrative achieved perfection in Wieland's capable hands at a time when Weimar and many parts of Germany were being shocked by the explosive, irregular prose of the Storm and Stress writers. That Wieland went his own way is significant for German literary history because his mastery of language and tight form not only in *Alceste* but also in these verse narratives points forward to the classical ideals later adopted by the better writers among the young Titans.

Nevertheless, the *Sturm und Drang* movement left its mark even on these refined works. For example, the young generation's titanism is mocked outright in the burlesque tale *Titanomachie, oder das neue Heldenbuch* (*War of the Titans, or The New Book of Heroes*, 1775) and is mirrored in the medieval atmosphere of such works as *Das Sommermärchen* (*The Summer's Tale*, 1777) or *Geron der Adeliche* (1777) with the many public and private adventures of their heroes. The latter tale even acknowledges the *Sturm und Drang*'s bourgeois criticism of their largely feudal society in that the sobriquet "der Adeliche" refers rather to Geron's nobility of character than to his nobility of blood. His noble birth is justified only by his noble deeds. (We can't help but think here of Werther's frustrating experiences with "high" society.) Merck called *Schach Lolo oder Das göttliche Recht der Gewalthaber* (1778) a "classical fairy tale."[24] It treats ironically the question of rule by divine right. Finally, the *Sturm und Drang* interest in the naive, childlike *Volk* found its way into *Pervonte* (1778–1779), intended as a children's fairy tale. Its titular hero, a very simple fellow, rises by virtue of the fairies' aid to understanding, wealth, and power. His wife, a princess, gives herself over to the excesses of court opulence, whereas Pervonte longs only to live for her and for his children in rural solitude. When his wife runs off with a lover, he decides he has had enough of "society life" and uses his last wish to restore everything to its original state. The fairies do his bidding, but see fit to leave him his understanding. The didactic intent of this and the other tales is summed up by Pervonte as he returns to his mother's simple abode:

> "Ich bring euch aus dem Feenland
> Gesunden derben Menschenverstand."[25]

In Pervonte's simple requirements, we have a similar rejection of the ruling class's excesses. Obvious in *Pervonte*, as well as in the tale *Hahn und Gulpenheh* (1778), is the combination of a folksy atmosphere with that of the oriental fairytale world, a mixture which later marks the Burgtheater productions of Ferdinand Raimund and Franz Grillparzer in Vienna.[26]

Goethe's comment to Johannes David Falk on January 25, 1813, concerning *Pervonte* is sufficient to persuade us that the verse tales preceding *Oberon* (1780) are more than just preliminary steps toward mastery in the celebrated epic. Goethe said: "The plasticity, the mischievousness of this poem are singular, exemplary, indeed, completely priceless. In this and similar products it is his true nature . . . which gives us pleasure . . . . It is an incomparable propensity which is dominant in him: everything is in flux, everything is genius, everything is in good taste." And Falk adds: *"Pervonte* is [Wieland's] most ingenious product; there he became himself surprisingly creative."[27]

Yet we choose to discuss *Oberon* in some detail because it was singled out by Goethe and by Wieland himself in a special way. On July 3, 1780, Goethe wrote to Lavater: "As long as poetry remains poetry, gold remains gold, and crystal remains crystal, *Oberon* will be loved and admired as a masterpiece of poetic art." In the same rush of enthusiasm, he sent Wieland a poet's laurel, recognizing in him a prince of poets for his astounding accomplishment. As a young student in Leipzig, Goethe had wondered at the "Rosenfarb und Silber" (rose color and silver) of *Musarion*. To those qualities are now added gold *(humanitas)* and crystal (classical lucidity). Years later, Wieland admitted that he was so astonished at his *Oberon* that he himself could not grasp how he was able to compose such light-flowing verses.[28] It was not easy.

Wieland revised the poem seven times before sending it to the presses for the *Teutscher Merkur* in 1778; in 1796, he subjected it to a final thorough revision for the definitive edition of his works. This polishing was designed to remove the last vestiges of the Sternesque narrative style so characteristic of his earlier works. Thus the change in narrative mode from *Der neue Amadis*, where the act of narration itself was the main topic of the tale, to the objective style of *Oberon* is striking. The highly visible narrator of *Idris* or *Der neue Amadis* represented a marked stylistic advance over the previously limited possibilities of the genre and stressed the difference between Wieland's open modernity and Pope's or Zachariä's rugged narrowness. The basic regularity and objectivity of *Oberon* now signals a move toward classical proportions. The shift was not sudden. Already in the other verse tales of the later 1770s there were signs that the poet's "Geist Capriccio" was being "reigned in." The narratives became simpler, more direct, more popular *volkstümlich*).[29] Wieland's poem does for the epic what *Iphigenie* did for the drama.

Wieland has been called "der undeutsche Klassiker"(the un-German classicist).[30] It is a designation which expresses his literary impressionableness. An openness to foreign—as opposed to narrowly German—literary stimulation is more characteristic of Wieland than of his cohabitants on the German parnassus. Goethe has his *Faust, Hermann und Dorothea*, and *Wilhelm Meister*; Schiller has his *Wallenstein, Wilhelm Tell*, and *Die Glocke (The Bell)*. Only Wieland has *Die Abderiten* and *Oberon*. The celebrated verse epic, which made its author famous as "the German Ariosto," is paradigmatic for his "un-German classical" art.

In the foreword to the poem Wieland explicitly names his sources: the chivalric romance *Histoire de Huon de Bordeaux*, Chaucer's *Merchant's Tale* and Shakespeare's *A Midsummer Night's Dream*.[31] Furthermore, *A Thousand-and-One Nights* evidently provided the model for the heroine, Rezia. Wieland also explains that his Oberon is not related to the roguish hybrid of man and elf in the French romance. He is rather like the good-natured king of the fairies in the *Merchant's Tale* or *A Midsummer Night's Dream*. None of the above works strikes us as being typically German. What the poet did with these impulses (and others, for we are speaking only of the major stimuli) is awe inspiring. Since any "clod" could come up with an "original" idea, whereas "true ingenuity lies in the adaptation of the subject matter,"[32] Wieland considered the weaving together of motifs to be the heart of artistic creation. The medieval romances, the fabulous tales of gods and men in ancient Greece and the

Orient, were for Wieland "a gold mine of poetic topics" (as he says in the foreword to *Oberon*, H, V, 162) because almost every idea has been thought before. The truth of this view is seen not only in *Musarion*, but also in *Oberon*.

Again in the foreword to his epic, Wieland asserts: "The manner in which the story of [Oberon's] quarrel with his wife Titania is combined with the story of Hüon and Rezia strikes me . . . as being the special beauty of the plan and the composition of this poem" (H, V, 162). Indeed, it would seem to be so. To be exact, *Oberon* consists of three principal plots: Hüon's knightly adventures, his and Rezia's love story, and the reconciliation of Oberon with Titania. Yet these story lines do not exist independently of one another, since all three are so tightly bound together that none could exist without the other two, and the happy conclusion is totally dependent upon the others. For example, Hüon would never have been able to fulfill Charlemagne's absurd demands without Oberon's aid. Furthermore, without Hüon's perfect love for Rezia and hers for him, Oberon would not have taken an interest in Hüon's adventures, because only such a love as theirs could bring about his reconciliation with Titania. Thus, Wieland concludes, "a kind of unity arises" out of these mutual needs which for him has "the merit of novelty." Based on a quasi-philosophical concept, this aesthetic unity enhances the work's novelty and is best expressed in Hüon's love for Rezia. Their love is independent of their actions, and even of Oberon's influence.

These motifs are laid out in twelve cantos (fourteen in the first version of 1778), a format reflecting the influence of Vergil's *Aeneas*.[33] Also in common with *Aeneas* is the relative directness of the action, despite the levels of interaction and non-chronological order of narration. Like *Agathon*, it begins in medias res, and the reader is brought up to date by means of flashbacks. When the story opens, Hüon is already on his way to Baghdad to carry out the emperor's command. In Lebanon he meets a hermit, Scherasmin, his father's former squire, and naturally both recount their experiences. Hüon and his father, one of the twelve peers of France, had fallen out of favor at court. Having slain a miscreant son of Charlemagne in a joust, Hüon is banned, his return contingent on the fulfillment of seemingly impossible tasks: Hüon is to travel to Baghdad and—without further ado—behead the courtier sitting to the left of the calif, claim the princess as his bride, and demand from the calif four molars and a handful of hair from his gray beard.

Scherasmin decides to accompany his former master's son on his journey. During a storm they seek shelter in a cloister, where they encounter a group of nuns and monks on a pilgrimage to the Holy Land. However, the group is anything but devout, and as punishment for their hypocrisy, they are overcome by an irresistible urge to dance wildly at the sound of a horn. Suddenly, with the horn, Oberon appears. Out of compassion for the wildly gyrating nuns and monks, who are obviously not enjoying themselves, Hüon implores Oberon to cease playing the horn. Touched by the hero's *Menschlichkeit*, Oberon gives him the horn as a present. When it is played softly, all adversaries will be forced to dance; when blown loudly, Oberon himself will appear and aid the endangered Hüon. The fairy tale motif continues, for Hüon also receives a magic cup which always holds refreshment for an honorable man (*Biedermann*) but nothing for the rogue. In the third canto, Hüon also acquires a magic ring, but not from Oberon. He takes the ring from an evil giant whom he had to slay in order to save the distressed damsel, Angela. The ring, like the horn, is a token of Hüon's noble compassion for his fellow man.

Armed with these magical prerequisites and his own youthful confidence, Hüon fulfills his impossible task and departs with Rezia, his newly won bride, for the western Mediterranean. The two lovers brought together by fate never want to part again, so inflamed are they by their passion. However, Oberon commands them to remain chaste until their betrothal. During their lonely journey across the sea, and due to the frailty of human nature, the lovers find the command impossible to keep. Immediately after they give in to their passion, a storm arises and Hüon must be sacrificed to the waves in order to save the ship. He recognizes his transgression and willingly accepts his fate with the august words: "the universal fate of mankind—to be weak—is my only crime. I now atone for it in dreadful fashion, but without complaint because I do not regret this sweet crime. If to love is wrong, then may heaven forgive me!" (VII, 25–26). Rezia, no less capable of the ultimate sacrifice, throws herself into the waves with him. Although Oberon has taken back his horn and cup, Rezia still wears the magic ring which Hüon had given her as a sign of his undying love. Through its power, they remain afloat until they reach a deserted island, where they begin their own idyllic "Robinsonade." Nine months after that fateful night on the ship, a son is born to them. The only other companion during the ensuing years is the old hermit, Alfonso, who becomes like a father to them. The sage has withdrawn from the world ("Fortunens Spielraum") in search of true contentment in the *unio mystica*. Yet like Trevrizent in *Parzival* and the hermit in *Simplizissimus*, Alfonso imparts to the pair the wisdom he has gained from life. Hüon tells him his story and is encouraged by Alfonso to live chastely with Rezia to atone for his transgression. Surely the king of the fairies will be appeased by renewed effort. Hüon follows the advice and in fact does live chastely for more than one hundred weeks. As the narrator tells us: "It was the best victory Hüon ever reaped" (VIII, 39). The growing family learns to be content with simple needs and finds its greatest joy in being closely knit with "a feeling heart and clear disposition" (VIII, 80).

The paradise could not last forever. In a quick sequence of events, Alfonso dies, the island retreat disappears, Rezia is abducted by pirates, Hüon is left to die, and the child vanishes through Titania's intervention. Titania's presence on the island is not coincidental; she had withdrawn to its seclusion after her quarrel with Oberon. Thus, the interaction between the fairy world and the human sphere is unforced. (Titania had also assisted at the child's birth.) Through a series of flashbacks, we are also informed of what has happened to Fatme, Rezia's nurse, and Scherasmin, whose adventures have brought them to the sultan's palace in Tunis as slaves. The pirate ship on which Rezia is held prisoner is destroyed miraculously by a bolt out of the blue off the shores of Tunis, and Rezia, as the sole survivor, is taken to the king's court. Oberon meanwhile takes pity on Hüon and magically conveys him to Tunis, where he meets Fatme and Scherasmin again. Posing as a palace gardener, Hüon unwittingly attracts Rezia's amorous attention, although neither recognizes the other. (In this case of loving without recognizing, there is a definite echo of the main theme in the comic tale *Cephalus und Aurora*.) Also irresistibly attracted to him is Queen Almansaris, while Rezia attracts King Almansor. When Hüon learns that Rezia is at court, he makes plans to free her and flee. However, Almansaris thwarts his plans through her repeated attempts at seducing him. Her advances spurned, she denounces him to Almansor, who condemns him to death by immolation. Fatme is able to reach Rezia and inform her that Hassan is really Hüon. Horrified, Rezia reveals to Almansor who she and Hüon (Hassan) are and pleads for his life. The sultan declares himself ready to pardon Hüon, if she will become his queen. Rezia's response is quick and inalterable: "Barbarian, I too know how to die" (XII, 51). The term "barbarian" stresses the sultan's baseness of spirit, not birth, and prefigures the nuances of the term in the classical period, when "barbarian" designated the lack of *Menschlichkeit*.

In the last moment, Oberon, appeased by their perfect fidelity, saves them from the flames, and is himself reunited with Titania. Hüon and Rezia are transported to France after Hüonet, their child, has been restored to them (Titania had watched over him). Arriving in time to enter the lists in a contest to determine to whom his lands should fall, for it was thought that he would never return, Hüon remarks: "Let now be mine out of virtue what was mine by birth. If I don't earn it, let the emperor give it to him who is worthy of it!" (XII, 82). Naturally, the hero is victorious, and the poem ends with general reconciliation.

Despite the three principal levels of action, and despite the flashbacks and stories within a story, the poem's action is unambiguous, because these various perspectives have been successfully woven into a flawless fabric and are all related to the same *leitmotif*: the love theme. We have seen that ever since the poet's odes to Doris and his *Natur der Dinge* of the early 1750s love has played a central role in his works. Despite his so-called metamorphosis, his thoughts on love have apparently not changed significantly. Love is the unifying theme not only in *Oberon*, but is a focus in most of the other verse narratives as well. An explanation for this obsession is contained in the opening lines of the prologue to *Gandalin oder Liebe um Liebe* (1776): "What? Love again? Always love! Yes indeed! What on earth is more worthy of our attention than love? What is it other than love and love again which everywhere, on earth and in heaven, imparts life and causes action, forming and animating all things?"[34] Citing various kinds of love, the poet grants that pure love is frequently sullied by human weakness; but nevertheless love is still the best thing in life. *Oberon* is animated by pure love even as *Iphigenie* is infused with noble simplicity or *Maria Stuart* with sublime control over herself.

Love is central to the unity of the epic, as can be seen in the arrangement of the narrative events, which are designed to bring the two lovers together and test their fidelity. Chronologically, the discord between Oberon and Titania arises before Hüon sets out on his adventures. Structurally, however, the nature of the quarrel isn't clarified until the latter half of Canto Six. The occasion for the discord is narrated by Scherasmin in the form of a fairy tale intended to warn Hüon and Rezia of the impending peril. Gangolf, who is old and blind, has taken a pretty, vivacious girl (Rosette) as his wife and is so jealous of her that she is virtually a prisoner in his dreary home. Thus it is understandable that she one day yields to the amorous advances of a young man and deceives her husband. Oberon, who chances to observe this scene, is appalled at the wife's betrayal. While Oberon argues that a wife must always be faithful, Titania defends Rosette's behavior as understandable. Her curt reply reveals the affinity of her attitude to that of the current women's equal rights movement: "Is Gangolf guiltless? Is freedom your lot and ours only patience?" (VI, 89). The dispute escalates until Oberon takes an oath to live separated from Titania "until a faithful pair, chosen by fate itself, becomes one by virtue of their chaste love and, steadfast in tribulation as well as joy—hearts undivided even when physically apart—atones for the guilt of the faithless through their own fidelity." He can only be joined again with Titania when this pair has suffered everything for their love and "true to their first love, is determined rather to choose death at the fiery stake, than to be unfaithful . . ." (VI, 101–102). Significantly, this momentous oath is sworn at the very midpoint of the epic, coalescing all preceding events and all subsequent developments.

The phrase "chaste love" *(keusche Liebe)* is carefully chosen. Chaste *(keusch)* means pure, without sully. Chaste love is therefore true love; true love, however, involves a union of minds and bodies.[35] These are precisely the qualities which mark Hüon's and Rezia's love, the physical consummation being only an apparent misstep. The final proof of the purity of their love is brought when both prefer to die a fiery death to becoming unfaithful. The deepening of this pure ardor is reflected in the classical structure of the medieval epic: the hero quickly advances to the possession of his bride, then loses her so that a second heightened possession can follow. The first success normally results from some kind of divine intervention; the second victory is more truly earned by the hero—his virtue is proof of his love. Such is the case in *Oberon*. From the first, Providence has destined Hüon for Rezia. We recognize this fact when Hüon, long before he even sees her, is able to resist lovely Angela, whom he rescues because "an unknown something which draws him like a magnet to Baghdad, seems to dull his

senses so that all her charms are lost on him" (III, 43).[36] The culmination of the first ascent is the physical union of the lovers, whereas
the second ascent peaks with the total harmony of physical and
spiritual love, after both (but most especially Hüon) have been
tested. Hüon is, in fact, tested three times, a symbolic figure sig-
nifying completeness.

Twice the couple is separated—once on the island when they
resolve to abstain from sensual love and once when Rezia is abducted by pirates. The two separations tend to underscore the duality of all human existence, and the final reunion can be seen as a true
recementing of the two halves of man. When the two lovers utilize
their total natures in the act of love, Oberon's ethical dictum is
realized. True love thus partakes of the corporeal and the spiritual.
In this connection we should not overlook the fact that a child is
produced by the initial union and that this child makes their reunion
complete (number "three") at the conclusion of the epic. Not only
are they one again, but so too are Oberon and Titania. The ring
which Hüon had taken from the giant and given to Rezia proves to
be the pledge of Oberon's love for Titania. After Rezia loses it when
she is overpowered by the pirates, Titania finds it again and now
returns it to her spouse to complete the circle. The ring thus stands
as a symbol of unity for each pair and each domain (heaven and
earth).

The *Sympathie* motif observed in Wieland's earlier works plays a
significant role here, too, as it tends to emphasize the spiritual bond
between the lovers and is cited as the cause of love at first sight even
before first sight. Furthermore, Hüon and Rezia see each other for
the first time in a prophetic dream and realize that they are destined
for one another. The dream motif is thus meaningful as a heighten-
ing of reality. For example, Hüon exclaims: "If such a dream can be
false, then everything is illusion! Then truth itself can deceive!" (IV,
8). The general significance of the dream motif has far-reaching
repercussions for Wieland's aesthetic and philosophic concepts.[37]

Also of significance for the love theme is the heroine's name
change from Rezia to Amanda, for it illuminates the shift in her
function for our eighteenth century Parsifal. From mere attraction
(her heathen name "Rezia" recalls "Reiz"), she goes to total in-
volvement. Her Christian name derives from Latin *amare* (feminine
gerundive, *amanda*) and calls to mind the state of being loved. All of
Hüon's actions from Canto Seven to the end of the poem are various
expressions of his love for her.

Finally, the many references to *menschlich* and *Menschlichkeit* in the epic place Hüon's individual love of Rezia in a broader human context. Hüon is a "good" man; that is, he is respectful, noble-minded, compassionate, and helpful. He is sensitive to the needs of others without being mindless of his own worth. Charlemagne's order to slay another knight without provocation or warning, and to demand four of the Sultan's molars and part of his beard, is below Hüon's dignity. It is also unchivalric to claim a woman as his bride without courting her by word and deed. The emperor's command, therefore, confronts the young hero with an apparent dilemma. How can he obey his commander without compromising his knightly honor or without denying his innate sensitivity to his fellow man (regardless of race or creed)? The narrator, working behind the scenes, deftly solves the problem, for the courtier sitting to the left of the sultan turns out to be a coward, ingrate, and braggart who lacks all sense of dignity and honor. On the previous day, Hüon had saved his life, but the only thanks he receives from the haughty knight is to have his Christian God blasphemed and his horse stolen. In addition, when the Arab is offered refreshment from Hüon's magic cup, it goes dry, burning his hands—a sure sign of the knight's inner guile. Obviously he is unworthy of Rezia, yet she is about to be betrothed to him against her will. Thus Hüon's slaying of the man is not an outrageous murder but an act of revenge for breaking the code of *Menschlichkeit* and for blasphemy. His claiming of Rezia is not an unfeeling imposition, but fulfillment of a destiny foreshadowed in the dream each had. Both exclaim spontaneously: "Sie ist's, Er ist's!" ("It's him! It's her!") Finally, Hüon himself does not take the sultan's teeth and hair; they are later delivered to him by Oberon in a small chest. Thus at no time is the hero forced to stray from the path of true humanity.

The reciprocal fusion of the sensual and the spiritual noted in the love theme is also evident in the style itself. After having read *Oberon*, Johann Anton Leisewitz entered the following notation into his diary on April 25, 1780: "I believe no one has mastered the secret of the curving line [*Wellenlinie*] as well as Wieland; even Lessing's style is angular by contrast."[38] This *Wellenlinie* is analogous to Schiller's *Schlangenlinie* (a line typically made by a snake), a symbol of his artistic ideal of the inherent unity of the many in the one.[39] Despite the rhythmic changes—the basic meter being Alexandrine— the whole progresses toward the same goal. More important than the intermittent movements themselves is the aesthetic effect of the gentle transitions on the perceiver, for they appear entirely natural and free despite the poet's tight control of his medium. Schiller, of course, referred to this impression of beauty in poetic depiction as "the free movement of nature in the fetters of language."[40] Preisendanz demonstrates how Wieland's "Poesie des Stils" anticipates Schiller's *Schlangenlinie* theory by at least a decade. In so doing, he refines the terminology of the poet's artistic accomplishments by introducing such subcategories as "Kunst der Darstellung" (art of depiction), "Kunst der Periode" (art of sentence structuring), and "Kunst des Übergangs" (art of transition). The latter two deal more directly with Wieland's proximity to Schiller's ideal of the *Schlangenlinie*. In *Oberon,* Wieland is interested in conveying a sense of dynamism which determines how he structures his ideas. He tries to pack into each sentence as many temporal moments as possible and to display them in their synchronic relativity. Chronological order or detailed sequence is unimportant. Decisive is the ordering force of the respective perceiver, be it the narrator himself or (more frequently) one of the characters. In this organizing principle, the author's perceptual and epistemological concerns are clearly evident. Indispensable to this "continuum of narration" is Wieland's "art of transition," which is the supple shift from one temporal perspective to another.

We must limit ourselves to citing examples only of the poet's "art of depiction," for in it is expressed most saliently the fusing of matter and spirit. Besides, the other two categories are subordinate. The nexus of material and immaterial qualities is achieved in a threefold manner. First, the bifocal depiction is accomplished via the infusion of erotic overtones, which are always ambivalent with Wieland, appealing, as they do, to both the intellect and the senses. Second, the portrayal endeavors to express inner psychological reality in terms of gesture and movement; thus, reflection appears as action. Third, objective situations are related in terms of their effect on the perceiver; that is, the person responds to the stimulus by crying out or by asking a rhetorical question. Of course, when the character reacts thus, so does the reader. In this way, the narrative manner is characterized by a constant interaction between internal and external impulses. It is a true "Geschichte der Wirkungen" ("history of interaction").

As an example of Wieland's talent for using erotic motifs ambivalently, we can turn to Canto XI, stanza 61, where Almansaris tries to

win Hüon's affections through her musical performance. It is remarkable how the poet delineates her appeal not only through the
music but also through her own sensuous movements.

> Wie rasch durchläuft in lieblichem Gewühl
> Der Rosenfinger Flug die seelenvollen Saiten!
> Wie reizend ist dabei aus ihrem offnen, weiten
> Rückfallenden Gewand der schönen Arme Spiel!
> Und da aus einer Brust, die Weise zu betören
> Vermögend war, das mächtige Gefühl
> Sich in Gesang ergiesst, wie kann er sich erwehren,
> Auf seinen Knien die Göttin zu verehren?[41]

The words "Gewühl" ("bustle") and "der Finger Flug" ("flight of
fingers") designate kinetic sense perceptions. But joined with "lieb-
lich" ("charming") "Rosen" ("rosy") and "seelenvoll" ("tender"), the
concrete action takes on emotional overtones. "Gewühl" refers not
only to the fingers crowded on the lute but equally to the feelings
crowded in her heart and seeking expression in the "tender" strings,
which reflect, therefore, both the player's internal sensation and the
listener's impression of softly melodious notes. The strings themselves are surely not tender. In the next two lines, the narrator uses
the natural baring of Almansaris' arms while playing the lute to
reveal the effect of sense objects on Hüon's emotional state. That is
the purpose of the adjectives "reizend" and "schön." These first four
lines are divided into two two-verse declarations; the first pair centers on the player, the second on the listener.

The last half of the stanza comprises one four-line statement which
tends to unite player and listener in that his impression begins to
harmonize with her expression. Her aural and optical messages are
understood as they are meant. The "Brust" (bosom) of line five is
physical, not metaphorical, but it quickly assumes a metaphorical
meaning as well when "das mächtige Gefühl" is encountered in the
next line. And since this powerful feeling spills over into audible
song, the aesthetic appeal of the music is seemingly lost in its sensual attraction. This final sentence climaxes in a rhetorical question:
How can Hüon not fall on his knees at the goddess' feet? In this
gesture, be it real or metaphoric, both impassioned and reverent
adulation resound. Throughout this stanza, then, which must stand
for many others, the sensual and immaterial appear entwined in
erotic interplay.

Another stanza may serve to show how completely the psychological reality of impatience and expectation assumes concrete shape:

> Unmutig kehrt sie um und mit sich selbst im Zwist,
> Beisst sich die Lippen, seufzt, spricht etwas und vergisst
> Beim dritten Wort schon, was sie sagen wollte.
> Zürnt, dass Nadine nicht die rechte Antwort gibt
> Und nicht errät, was sie erraten sollte;
> Die schöne Dame ist mit einem Wort—verliebt!
> Sogar der Blumenstrauss erfährts—wird ohn' ihr Wissen
> Zerknickt und Blatt für Blatt verzettelt and zerrissen. [42]

These verses are an excellent example of Wieland's "Kunst der Darstellung." Nothing is static, nothing abstract. An immaterial state (being in love) is expressed in a series of realistic images. For one idea there are many translations into phenomenal reality. No Baroque metaphors here, and no sterile accumulation of exempla. Almansaris paces up and down, bites her lips, sighs, speaks disjointedly, is irritated with Nadine, and plucks all the petals from a flower without realizing it. There is no doubt that these signs say much more than the mere phrase "in love."

Finally, Wieland also imbues factual occurrences with metaphorical meaning. For example, Almansaris ultimately realizes that all her seductive powers are useless against Hüon. Disappointed and ashamed, she flees his sight: "Sie eilt, sich zu verhüllen,/Verhasst ist ihr das Licht, der weite Saal zu eng."[43] The bright light and the spacious hall are not perceived objectively, because their significance is purely subjective; they are designed to lead the reader from externals into Almansaris' soul. Similarly, the narrator informs us that Hüon prefers to be falsely accused rather than himself impune the honor of a lady: "Er schmiegt den edlen Arm in unverdiente Bande/ Und Hüllet schweigend sich in sein Bewusstsein ein."[44] Refering to Hüon's proud refusal to defend himself, the second verse is clearly metaphorical. The first line, however, is simultaneously metaphorical and literal. On the first level it signifies his willing submission to another's power, whereas on the second it means that his arms really were put in bonds.

These few examples will suffice to convey a sense of Wieland's mastery of form and narrative technique. Everything is ambivalent, has at least two meanings and seems to be in constant flux. "Sein" is apparently unimportant for the poet; as for Goethe, so for Wieland, true reality can be perceived only in progression. The Swabian's dynamic style of narrative progression of *Schlangenlinie*, prefigures, after a fashion, Goethe's concept of *Werden*. Wieland's artistic playfulness, the infusing of his material with a spirit of lightness and freedom, anticipates Schiller's aesthetic ideal of "the free movement of nature in the fetters of language." Because these linguistic fetters are not visible in a masterpiece like *Oberon*, Wieland was often mistaken for a facile writer. The ease of his style belies the agony of the effort; he often wracked his brains for hours to find just the right word, just the right turn of phrase to achieve the intended response. On the basis of Wieland's response-oriented aesthetics, Müller-Solger argues that we should rather speak of the poet's "Kunst der Wirkung," according to which the reader's consciousness of an art work is lost in his response to it. In this light, Wieland points beyond Classical Aesthetics to Romantic concepts.[45] Wieland saw in the epic a synthesis of logic and emotion, of the cult of reason with the cult of feeling. In a letter of December 28, 1779, he wrote that *Oberon* was the best product which his head and his heart had jointly given birth to.[46]

The immediate reception of his epic was relatively disappointing for the poet. He complained repeatedly in his correspondence with Merck about the paltry acclaim the work had apparently been given by the general public. Critics were also strangely quiet in these initial years. Perhaps, as Sengle argues, Wieland's image had been so badly tarnished in the public's mind by the many diatribes that his newest accomplishment could not be fittingly judged.[47] Goethe's spontaneous praise is even more striking in its isolation. Yet by the late 1780s, this disappointing picture had altered radically. In Jena, Karl Reinhold, professor and popularizer of Kantian philosophy, held public lectures on *Oberon*. There was standing room only, and the crowds spilled over into the streets. In 1785, Reinhold had married Wieland's oldest daughter Sophie and for a time had breathed new life into the *Merkur* with his essays on Kantian philosophy, until he was made professor in Jena. Sengle would see in Reinhold's lectures merely a maneuver to reestablish Wieland's supposedly waning reputation. But more recent scholarship has shown that Wieland's popularity was still strong and even increasing.[48] I do not think, therefore, that we have to ascribe the large attendance at Reinhold's lectures solely to the lecturer's personal appeal. At first sight it might be perplexing that a professor of philosophy would speak on a work noted for its charm and grace, its original design or—to speak with Madame de Staël—for "uniting fantastic fiction with true sentiment." Yet a deeper attraction was noticed by an early fan of *Oberon*, William Taylor of Norwich, who remarked that the poem was "the masterpiece of Wieland—the child of his genius in moments of its purest converse with all the beauteous forms of ideal excellence; . . . an epic poem, popular beyond example, yet as dear to the philosopher as to the multitude."[49] We can only conjecture as to Taylor's exact meaning regarding the poem's attraction for the philosopher, but we have seen the influence of perceptual theories and ethical concepts on the making of *Oberon*. John Qunicy Adams was so enthralled with the poem that he translated it into English. Had William Sotheby not translated *Oberon* in 1798, Adams' translation, which was completed in May 1800, might have introduced the English-speaking world to the classic. Sotheby's translation is still considered the best in English. The poem was also rendered into several other languages, including Portuguese and Swedish, although Wieland contended that *Oberon* (*and Musarion*) were untranslatable. He surely meant that the finely balanced "Kunst der Darstellung" could not be duplicated.

After the inimitable *Oberon*, Wieland produced only two more works in verse: *Clelia und Sinnibald* (1783), an epyllion, and *Die Wasserkufe* (1795), a shorter verse narrative. The 1780s were, as we have seen, filled with essayistic and translation work. It is as if Wieland had been aware of having reached a pinnacle in his mastery of prosody. The appearance of *Oberon* and *Die Abderiten* marks the end of a second fertile period.

CHAPTER 8

"Vater" Wieland (1781–1813)

I *The Quiet Life*

SENGLE tends to overstate the negative influence of the literary attacks, during the 1770s and 1790s, on the poet's retiring way of life, for already in Zurich Wieland had preferred the quiet company of a close circle of friends. Just as many of his works use the bucolic arbor or aromatic garden as the ideal environment, Wieland himself chose to spend much of his time in a leafy retreat. In the early 1780s, he purchased a home in Weimar with a garden; and in 1797, he finally attained what Horace, Cicero, and Pope had secured before him, a country estate. It was situated ten kilometers from Weimar near the village of Ossmannstedt, and there he had a small cottage built, his "museum," where he could spend quiet hours working and writing. Unlike Horace's *Sabinum* or Cicero's *Tarentum,* however, Ossmannstedt was not the gift of a mighty patron. In keeping with the rise of the professional writer in eighteenth century Europe, a new kind of patron made the Swabian's *Osmantinum* possible: the reading public. Wieland earned his miniature Arcadia through his belletristic and journalistic undertakings. Ossmannstedt represents the culmination of a long-nurtured desire, for on his estate he could grow his own food, raise his own cattle, breed his own sheep, and receive visitors in manorial style. Although the idyll lasted only seven years (1797–1803), because the estate proved to be more expensive to operate than anticipated, these years were contented ones for the aging author in the midst of his family and close friends. Anna Amalia, Goethe, Herder, Böttiger, Jean Paul, and others frequently made the short trip from Weimar to visit him. In 1799, he was able to receive Sophie LaRoche in the splendor of his manor; it was the first time that he had seen her in over twenty years. She brought with her her granddaughter Sophie Brentano, the sister of Clemens and Bettina Brentano. Sophie returned alone the following year to spend—as it turned out—the final months of her life in spiritual intercourse with the aging poet. Charmed by her beauty and melancholy manner, Wieland transformed her youth and freshness into the tragic figure of Lais in the novel *Aristipp*. When she died suddenly, he laid her to rest in the same plot which was to receive his wife's and his own earthly remains. Scarcely a year later, his wife followed Sophie in death (November 1801). Her passing was a great loss for Wieland; he later complained that since her death he had lost interest in life. His financial situation also worsened, so that he had to give up the estate.

In 1803 he moved back to Weimar, not far from the Grand Duchess' palace, where he had the use of her gardens. Her "Musenhof" was still functioning, and Wieland was a frequent guest at the small gatherings. This fairly secluded way of life (interrupted only once by an extended journey to Zurich) found poetic expression as well. For example, Democritus in *Die Abderiten*, Alfonso in *Oberon*, Archytas in the 1794 version of *Agathon*, Agathodämon and Aristipp from the later novels of the same names all appear more or less as father figures, and all reveal close similarity to Wieland's personal way of life.

The importance of fatherhood in the poet's view is poignantly underscored in an anecdote told by Bertuch, who had first met Wieland in Erfurt when the poet was a professor there. Bertuch had visited the poet just after the birth of his second daughter, Caroline. The renowned author placed the child in Bertuch's arms and said: "Look, here is something which is worth more than all my doggerels and of which I am prouder than of all the products of my mind."[1] Ten years later, we are informed by the *Briefe eines reisenden Franzosen (Letters of a Traveling Frenchman)* that "Wieland is a good 'Hausvater' (family man), who lives more for his family than for the public." In that he was very unusual. Wieland himself checked the lives of poets to verify that none had as many children as he did.[2] Evidently he saw himself first as a father, then as a writer. From the late 1760s onward, the family replaced the close circle of friends as the primary focus of his social life. During the mid-1780s, the poet's family increased through the marriages of three daughters and the arrival of the first grandchildren. With that, just about everyone in Weimar began to refer to him as "Vater

Wieland." It was a happy, harmonious family in which each member fulfilled certain obligations willingly for the benefit of the whole. The patriarch was an understanding, wise leader of the clan. Little wonder that Wieland's essays on the momentous political events in France echo the principles of his own private life. Mankind was for him but an extension of his own family. The manner in which he tried to treat his relatives and in-laws is expanded into the ideal of the enlightened monarch and that of the *Weltbürger*, and the ultimate goal of mankind is a *Weltbürgertum*.

With his fiftieth birthday, Wieland reached a turning point in his literary production. He himself sensed that a culmination had been reached, and he began to fret over his loss of poetic inspiration. He turned first to his old friends Horace and Lucian, spending hours reproducing their works in classic translations, thereby advancing his ideal of a transnational literature and culture. Later he turned to Aristophanes, Euripides, Xenophon, and Cicero. In order to advance his countrymen's salubrious use of reason and to train their judgment, he contributed essays on religious and philosophical themes to the *Teutscher Merkur*. His political commentaries in the *Merkur*, astute and prophetic as they were, reflect his ideal of the commonality of all men. If man would only use common sense, he would avoid excess and achieve lasting happiness; but man seemed prone to excess, be it political or religious. Thus Wieland began to direct more attention to the cause of these extravagances, which he sought in religious concerns. These ideas reemerge in dominant constellation.

The Enlightenment's disparagement of superstition of all kinds was still much in evidence. Realizing, however, that man had an innate proclivity to irrationality and recognizing its potential benefit, Wieland was a more cautious critic than most. If reason could not bring mankind to a proper perspective of life's priorities, he thought, perhaps a proper use of belief could. In his essay "Enthusiasmus und Schwärmerei" (1776), Wieland had distinguished between true and false enthusiasm, the former being beneficial for man and corresponding to truth. Therefore, true enthusiasm should not be disparaged. False enthusiasm, however, brings havoc into man's ideas and life. He watched the evolving Romantic movement with skepticism because he was not sure whether the new generation would distinguish between true and false inspiration. These irrational concerns move into the forefront of Wieland's late works because he felt that man must try to get a different perspective on things. If man could only learn to judge himself and his actions from a different point of view, he might be better able to avoid past mistakes. Reason alone no longer seemed sufficient to resolve man's private and public problems because all too often it did not guide man's actions. Man must learn why he so frequently acts irrationally. To attain "the right perspective" for this undertaking, Wieland began to focus on worldly events from a point outside of time. We might want to see in this move a parallel to the remoteness of his own "snail house". Thus many of these works, even the *Merkur* essays such as *Göttergespräche* (1791) or *Gespräche im Elysium* (*Elysian Dialogues*, 1796), view human events from beyond the grave. In selecting this point of view, the author participates in a European literary tradition which had been popular since the late seventeenth century: the *Totengespräch* ("dialogue of the dead"). Its chief purpose was to illuminate topical problems, revise false conceptions, or satirize contemporary political situations.[3] Greater distance was achieved by fixing the action in the period of late antiquity which had many intellectual and political parallels to eighteenth century Europe and could thus serve as a prototype of human existence.[4]

The majority of Wieland's works after about 1780 reflect these standpoints and concerns. At the same time, they are, in great part, a fulfillment of earlier plans.[5] That was the case, for example, with the translations and with the last major novel, *Aristipp und einige seiner Zeitgenossen* (1800–1801). Others, such as *Geheime Geschichte des Philosophen Peregrinus Proteus* (1789), evolved from the author's study of Lucian. A focal consideration is the phenomenon of *Schwärmerei*, because it poignantly expresses the contrast between the dreamy idealism of the enthused individual and the disappointing sobriety of his earthly environment. *Schwärmerei* is a major symptom of man's predilection for irrationality and is thus a logical focal point for the author's consideration of the human condition. *Schwärmerei* connotes more than just religious fanaticism; it includes any undue interest in the wondrous.

A link between the fairy tale atmosphere of certain works of Wieland's first and second phases (e.g., *Don Sylvio*, *Oberon*) and the third one is represented in the collection *Dschinnistan oder auserlesene Feen- und Geistermärchen* (*Dschinnistan, Selected Fairy Tales and Ghost Stories*, 3 vols., 1786–1789). Only two of the twelve tales are original creations: "Der Stein der Weisen" ("The Philosopher's Stone") and "Die Salamandrin und die Bildsäule" ("The Female Salamander and the Statue"). Fairy tales were extremely popular at the time (as evinced by Karl Musäus' collection of folk tales [1782–1787] and the translations of the *Arabian Nights*), which is surprising because it was the heyday of the Enlightenment. Wieland addresses himself to this phenomenon in the introduction in *Dschinnistan*, where he remarks: "It seems strange that two so contrary inclinations as the proclivity to the wondrous and the love of truth should be equally natural and fundamental to man."[6] The explanation is, of course, that certain truths are sometimes better said in the guise of a fairy tale than directly. Wieland's original contributions to the collection demonstrate that the seemingly wondrous has a natural explanation if man gets to know himself well enough.

II *Probing the Limits: The Final Period*

In his final creative phase, Wieland wrote almost exclusively prose, and predominantly novels. Between 1789 and 1805 he composed three major novels, two shorter ones, and a collection of three fairy tales and three novellas—all this in addition to revising his earlier works for the definitive edition of his oeuvre, to his translation projects, and to his voluminous journalistic efforts in the *Merkur* and *Attisches Museum*. Despite his increasing age and general estrangement from younger writers, therefore, Wieland did not slow down. Compared to the products of his youth and prime, the literary works of Wieland the sage have received relatively little critical attention. One reason for the neglect can be seen in the difference of tone. For the most part, these later works lack the freshness of expression and the (relative) vivacity of movement characteristic of the earlier works. The style is not raucously ironic, the content not electrifying, with the result that the reader must frequently make an effort to "get into" the mood of the work. Once the reader has done that, however, he is rewarded by the flowing language, the charm of subtle ironies, the dazzle of erudition, and the profundity of content. Yet *Peregrinus, Agathodämon,* or *Aristipp* would not propitiously serve as a first introduction to Wieland's art. Even an astute reader like Ludwig Tieck—prejudiced against Wieland—commented: "[the] later prose works are too long, e.g. *Agathon*. Reading them is a task." However, Tieck did single out one of the works from the final phase as being good: *Peregrinus Proteus*. For his part, Friedrich Schlegel praised the "rather high level of vividness of individual characters."[7]

Peregrinus is the first of the late novels, and its titular hero has much in common with Don Sylvio and Agathon, all three of whom are *Schwärmer* types.[8] The novel is considered Wieland's vindication of the sincere fantast, that is, enthusiast, not *Schwärmer*. The apparent model for the hero was Johann Kaspar Lavater, the author of the famous *Physiognomische Fragmente* (*Physiognomic Fragments*, 1775–1778) and advocate of magnetism. A case has also been made for seeing the novel as an apology for the young Rousseau.[9] Peregrin's life is recounted in dialogic form designed to clarify the reasons for his self-immolation in A.D. 165. In his account of the events, Lucian had depicted the fantast as a charlatan, but Wieland suspects that Lucian, in his skepticism, had presented a biased picture of the fanatic's true intentions. Thus, the author brings the two men together sixteen hundred years later in Elysium. The time and vantage point allow Peregrinus to explain his motivation and to clarify the "wondrous" aspects of his life. Furthermore, their presence in Elysium guarantees the veracity of the narration, for prejudice is not possible in the hereafter.[10]

Since little is known about the historical Peregrinus (as was also the case with Agathon), Wieland resorts to his psychological sensitivity and tried technique of perspective to portray the seemingly bizarre fantast in anthropological terms. The "facts" of Lucian's historical account concerning the hero's immolation are included as part of the novel; however, in the course of the narration they are revealed by means of the writer's poetic fancy to be primarily fiction. Thus, Wieland's fictive account of Peregrin's life is truer than that of the eyewitness because the author has looked deeper into the enthusiast's soul for an answer to his apparently irrational behavior. These psychological insights are provided in narrative passages which complement the colloquy between protagonist and antagonist, a hybrid technique which strikes Sengle as being "the appropriate form for the cautious, all-encompassing narrative style of [Wieland's] old age."[11] Because the cool skeptic Lucian judged the warm fantast only on the surface, and only according to reason, he rejected Peregrin as an impostor. Like Hippias, Lucian is guided only by his head and thus misjudges the power of the heart.

Lucian comes only gradually to an appreciation of Peregrinus'

sincerity. His shift from complete skepticism toward the protagonist to congenial acceptance of his uniqueness at the novel's end
is doubly significant. Not only does it evince the power of
psychological perspective, it also mirrors structurally the reader's
growing understanding of the causes of *Schwärmerei*. Lucian assumes here the role which the fictive reader played in earlier works
(e.g., in *Die Abderiten*), so that the empirical reader tends to view
Peregrinus through the skeptic's eyes. In this regard, the nature and
use of irony are indicative of the change Wieland wants his readers
to undergo. Only initially is Lucian caustic in the expression of his
disbelief. At the end, irony disappears entirely, because he accepts
the enthusiast as an equal. As the interlocutors warm up to each
other, Peregrin begins to speak ironically of his own "theophanic"
experiences. From his view from beyond the grave, he can recognize how duped he had been by others—not by his own feeling. His
feeling was true, its object false. The hero's use of irony against
himself, combined with Lucian's waning use of it, tends to shift the
reader's sympathies to the enthusiast.

When Peregrinus speaks of his disillusionments, he uses motifs
and language parodying the fairy tale; yet this parody is not directed
at Peregrinus' sense of the divine in man or at his striving for an *unio
mystica*, but at the misapplication of his fervor, at the mistaken
belief that union with the gods is possible on earth. The function of
the wondrous fairy tale elements is actually twofold. On the one
hand, they underscore the illusion and delusion by parodying them;
on the other, the idealism of the fairy tale atmosphere prefigures a
future state of perfection which sharply contrasts with present reality. This type of fairy tale is like dreaming with your eyes wide open.
Future perfection and present inadequacy enter the perceiver's
consciousness simultaneously.[12]

Just as the fiction reader disappears in this novel (and in the suc-
ceeding ones as well), so does the personal narrator vanish from the
page. In these developments we can observe a parallel to the transition from Wieland's subjective, personal narrative style in the early verse narratives to a more sober, classical distance in *Oberon*.[13] The
absence of a personal guide through the maze of perspectives and
opinions means that the work lacks an obvious social norm, as previously expressed, for example, by Archytas or Democritus. The
reader himself must decide which of the subjective perceptions presented should serve as the norm. By contrasting *Peregrinus* to *Don*

Sylvio and *Agathon,* we can verify our suspicion that there is no longer a common social norm for Wieland. Don Sylvio was integrated into an aristocratic society from which he had deviated; Agathon found his appropriate place in Archytas' utopian community at Tarentum after having failed to integrate himself into the imperfect societies at Athens and Syracuse; and Peregrinus—well, he doesn't fit anywhere. As his name indicates, he is destined for other times, other societies. Lucian and Peregrinus accept one another as equals when they realize that each is different—the one rational, the other intuitive—yet both justified. Each has a right—an obligation:—to evolve according to his individual inward form.

The justification for Peregrinus' asocial actions lies in the concept of the daemonic, which is defined as the power of divination[14] and which is the result of God's presence in us *(deus in nobis)*. However, not all men are aware of this force, for the sensual side of human nature often proves too distracting. Peregrinus' ascetic way of life (despite his occasional relapse into carnality) is seen as a means of liberating this spirituality. Since the hero is following the divine inner voice, "this incorruptible judge in our bosom,"[15] his *Schwärmerei* is not false. His fiery renunciation of the world with its corporeality is analogous to Alfonso's rejection of the world in *Oberon.*

On January 10, 1788, Wieland wrote to the classical philologist Christoph Gottlob Heyne that he wished "to place Peregrinus in the proper light."[16] The "proper light" is the right perspective from which to judge the defamed enthusiast. Three years later, in the eighth "Göttergespräch," of the *Neue Göttergesparäche* (1791) an unknown god ("ein Unbekannter"—i.e., Christ, who was unknown in Greek mythology) converses with Jupiter about the events which are taking place on earth (i.e., the French Revolution). The political upheaval is seen as an attempt to bring about general happiness, but the events seem to be taking a wrong turn (i.e., the Reign of Terror). The unknown god argues that the path to the general welfare is the same as the avenue to personal happiness: man must learn to be content with little. The idea is an echo of Alfonso's statement in *Oberon:* "Nature requires much less than we think. He who is not satisfied with little will not be satisfied with much" (VIII, 31).

The connection between the private sphere and the political is made explicit by the unknown god:

My plan, as grandiose as it is, is basically the simplest in the world. The manner in which I would surely bring about universal happiness is the same in which I lead every individual man to happiness. What guarantees my certitude is *that there is no other possibility.* By the way, I conclude the way I began: it is impossible not to be deceived as long as one perceives things piecemeal as they appear individually. They are not *real* except in their *total context.* The *perfection* which *arises from the combined whole*—toward which everything strives and in which everything will rest—is the *only* point of view from which all things are correctly seen."[17]

The antiquarian novels of this final period all strive to lead the reader to this proper perspective of the whole.

Agathodämon (1796) can be seen as a pendant to *Agathon* and *Peregrinus Proteus;* in it the author intended to give his final views on the reform of mankind and plans for universal happiness.[18] The protagonist, Apollonius von Tyana, is, in a sense, the result of an intensified study of enthusiasm. "Study" is not an inappropriate word for the major novels of this period—including the third version of *Agathon*—since they all deal with philosophers and with the meaning of life. *Agathodämon* (i.e., "good spirit") occupies a special place in the poet's oeuvre. It is an epistolary-dialogic work in which Apollonius discusses his life from the vantage point of old age, beyond the rush of life. Whereas in *Peregrinus* he appeared as a charlatan and deceiver (Kerinthus), Apollonius is here transformed into a repentent, sincere enthusiast. The mystery and secrecy he practiced were intended to lead men to happiness. He realizes only much later that the only path to true contentment was through the highest personal sincerity, which prepared man for the ultimate union with totality. The seventh and last book of the novel deals with Christ, who is depicted as the full realization of that which Apollonius only appeared to be. Again we face the question of perception, again the distinction between true and false enthusiasm.

Wieland himself thought very highly of this seventh book, which cost him great effort. Of *Agathodämon* as a whole he said that "it was the most important and best of his works in more than one respect" and that the novel conveyed his "present religious convictions."[19] To his daughter Sophie Reinhold he had written, in November 1796, that Appollonius of Tyana, rather than Archytas, was the true expression of his own *Hausphilosophie.*[20] An explanation for the latter assertion might be sought in the marked shift toward the recognition of truth through intuition and religious belief rather than through rational processes. Martini aptly observes that Wieland's highest humanistic ideals, his visions of the contented individual and of the harmonious state "lead beyond the limits of rationalism" and "repeatedly brush up against the province of religion."[21] This assertion is completely justified by the passage quoted from the eighth "Göttergespräch" and by the novel *Agathodämon*.[22]

Yet the religious questions were not the sole motivation for this and many of the other works, whose antiquarian tone is intended to convey a more accurate picture of antiquity. What bothered the aging poet intensely was Friedrich Schlegel's inaccurate grasp of Greek culture in his translation of the elegy "Hermesianax." Schlegel's translation has, Wieland contended, "no sense [*Fünkchen*] of the Greek spirit or of Greek taste."[23] Even granting a certain bias against Schlegel resulting from the Romanticist's vicious attack on him, the assertion is bold.

The right perspective from which to judge human events is mystical in nature. The only way to avoid deception by appearances and by one's own sensuality is to partake as little as possible of the world of things. In life this is virtually impossible. Total spirituality can at best be approximated in the hermitage, a vantage point far removed from temptations of the flesh, of power, and of things. Man's material nature prohibits the realization of his true destiny and the attainment of lasting happiness. Apollonius lives in a cave on a plateau high above the surrounding communities and enjoys a panoramic view of the sea. When Hegesias, his interlocutor, visits Apollonius, he must literally climb upwards, leaving the morass of phenomena behind him. The ensuing conversations deal almost entirely with spiritual questions and are accompanied by descriptions of endless vistas which convey a sense of the infinite. The style itself attempts to overcome the inherent finiteness of language through the use of ornate yet clear and rhythmically flowing sentences. In addition to the prose, certain symbols underscore the tendency to reach beyond the known. For example, the novel is divided into seven books, with Christ figuring prominently in the seventh, the crowning book. The fact that Book VII focuses on Christ is doubly symbolic. First, as God-man, he represents the union of the infinite and the finite. Second, the number seven can be interpreted in cabbalistic fashion: consisting of the mystical three (divinity) and the worldly four (four elements, four directions), the number represents the interconnection of the finite and the infinite, the empirical and the ideal. Finally, elevating song and music accompany the discussions and enhance the evocative function of the language, so that we can see in this technique the continuity of Wieland's *Wirkungsästhetik*, which is here designed to induce the reader to "probe the limits."

The goal of the style and content is, therefore, to lead the reader to Apollonius' insight that the world of appearances is not the real world. Ultimate reality is, rather, reflected in the ideal realms created by (moral) philosophers and poets who are more in tune with the daemonic in man, who rise above material existence. Thus, introspection leads man beyond the world of deception to a perception of the infinite, the perfect. Enthusiasm—or the sense of the infinite, the effect of the *deus in nobis*—is the perception of the totality pared of its individual components.[24] Wieland obviously chooses to express these ideas in novelistic form because art treats of the ideal, of the whole, whereas the documentary treats of individual phenomena.

Aristipp (1800–1801) is a compendium of Socratic philosophy in artistic form. It complements the "narrowly" religious view of the preceding novels with a dazzling multiplicity of anthropological, sociological, and especially philosophical views, which are formally underscored by the novel's basic epistolary structure. Several friends correspond with one another and relate not only their own experiences but also what others have said or done. Thus, the point of view is in a constant state of flux. Yet all the perspectives refer back to a common experience of the world and of human nature so that a definite unity evolves. Each of the individuals is searching for the same thing—true happiness. Felicity is more or less equated with the "proper" perception of reality.

It would not be inappropriate to see in this novel an answer to the Romantic search for the expression of the totality in which the true meaning of each separate entity is rooted. Wieland enthusiastically claimed in conversation with a friend, Heinrich Lüttkemüller, that the richness of that period of Greek life and culture which he intended to recreate in *Aristipp* is "like the fountain of youth which our Romantic 'Ritterhelden' [cavaliers] sought but did not find."[25] The early Romantic school was marked by a striving for a mystical union of all things, since it was convinced that there is one dominant view despite the plurality of perspectives. In the same conversation, the poet confided that the richness of his material "shows [him] a perspective which allows [him] more to intuit than to see." Although the report breaks off at that point, it would seem from the author's plan for the work that the perspective referred to is that applied from a superior vantage point, one encompassing all finite perspectives from below. Thus the hetaera Lais, whose passionate love radically contrasts with Aristipp's restrained enjoyment and quiet married life, is indispensible to the whole.[26] By the same token, Plato's "fantastic" visions are complemented by Hippias' materialistic skepticism. In between, the gamut of philosophical opinions is reviewed. Wieland accepts differing philosophic (and religious) paths to truth because each man's personality is regulated by a unique "inward form." The "inward form"—a concept borrowed from Shaftsbury—is likened to the morphological laws of plant life. The commonality of man, despite the different "inward forms," is rooted in the divine presence existent in each person.[27]

With each new work, Wieland hoped to achieve the crowning feat of his long career, and he felt very strongly that *Aristipp* best fulfilled this function. In fact (as he wrote to Göschen on December 14, 1799), he required fifty years of professional experience in order to be capable of writing this one novel.[28] It took him that long to achieve the proper perspective from which to depict the life and times of Aristippus, a symbol of his (and our) own age. The fundamental principle of Aristippus' *philosophy of life* is moderation in all things, because the avoidance of emotional and intellectual extremes is the only way in which man can achieve continuous contentment in life. Peregrinus and Agathodämon were impractical as models for life because their attention was turned away from this finite world to the infinite yonder. Aristippus' middle way is a model for the here and now. Yet Aristippus is fully aware of man's true calling and knows that the path he treads is the safest way to avoid grave disappointment and deception. He tells Lais:

There is no other highest *bonum* . . . for man than 'to be and become that which he should be and can become according to nature's design.' But this is just the point which he will never reach, although man will eternally draw closer to it. Where there is a higher level above each step, there is no highest state—except by deception. It is like the man who wants to climb a mountain the summit of which appears to be the highest until he has reached the pinnacle and sees that other pinnacles tower above him, disappearing into the clouds.

Everything in man's earthly existence which appears to be the absolute is absolute only in a relative sense because of the limited perspective. Aristipp thus concludes: "for immortal man there is no highest good other than eternity."[29] *Aristipp* is a comprehensive statement of its author's major concerns since *Die Natur der Dinge*. In the figure of Aristippus, it offers a model for dealing with everyday life while not losing sight of the ultimate goal. Lais' sensuality is just as much a part of this plan as is Plato's seraphic spirituality. The head and the heart both fulfill vital functions in guiding man through life, each correcting the deviations of the other. The ideal social environment is described in terms of Aristippus' family life.

Justice cannot be done to the thematic richness and stylistic eminence of this neglected work. Sengle's judgment that it represents merely "several hours of somewhat flimsy chit-chat with the aged poet"[30] would seem to miss the significance of the novel's content within the context of his oeuvre. The content represents a kind of *summum* of all his works since *Die Abderiten*. The language—which Wieland endlessly reworked and refined—reaches a classical roundness and precision comparable to that of his friends Jean Paul and Goethe. Of course, we must judge the *Altersstil* (late style) by somewhat different standards; otherwise we would conclude with Schiller that the novel is not to be considered as an "aesthetic composition."[31] The mixture of literary, scientific, and essayistic styles points forward to Thomas Mann and Robert Musil rather than back to Sterne or Fielding.[32] As Goethe's *Wanderjahre (Wilhelm Meister's Travels)* Thomas Mann's *Joseph und seine Brüder (Joseph and his Brothers)* or Musil's *Mann ohne Eigenschaften (Man Without Qualities)* are not to every reader's taste, neither is *Aristipp*.

After *Aristipp*, Wieland composed two more short novels and a collection of fairy tales and novellas. In each, a principle of comparison and contrast can be observed. In *Das Hexameron von Rosenhain* (1805), Wieland combined three prose fairy tales with three novellas. Whereas the atmosphere of the first group is wondrous and "unnatural," the latter group is placed in a contemporary, prosaic setting; the former tends to be idealistic, the latter realistic. In this double approach, the dipolar basis of Wieland's world view is reflected. The three novellas are especially important for literary history, for they pay tribute to the then newly rediscovered artistic requirement of thematic originality; furthermore, they influenced the development of the emerging *Novelle* form in Germany. One of these novellas, "Freundschaft und Liebe auf der Probe" ("Friendship and Love Tested"), even provided the stimulus for Goethe's novel *Die Wahlverwandtschaften (Elective Affinities)*. In Wieland's treatment of the theme there is, typically, no trace of tragic development. I say typically because Wieland was, as we have seen, a man of the middle who, in accordance with his *Weltanschauung*, urged avoidance of extremes and excesses.

The two novels, *Menander und Glycerion* (1804) and *Krates und Hipparchia* (1805), are complementary. Both treat in comic fashion the theme of love and marriage. In the first novel, Glycerion realizes that Menander's passionate but unsteady love is not the basis for a marriage and weds another. Menander weds a fiery dancer, who all too soon leaves him for someone else. The moral is clear: passionate love is transitory and cannot lead to true happiness. In the second work, the beautiful Hipparchia does everything she can to marry the penniless and ugly Krates. The lesson here is that marriage must be founded on more solid ground than wealth, beauty, or momentary passion. Both novels can be seen as continuing the ideal as depicted in Aristipp's marriage with Kleone, which is rooted, in turn, in Wieland's own personal experiences. These final works reiterate, therefore, the poet's solution to the practical problem of attaining happiness in life.

After 1805, "Vater Wieland" wrote no more fictional works. His own epoch passed him by and, in the process, he became a living "classic," a role underscored by events of the early nineteenth century.[33] For example, in 1803 Herder died; Schiller followed in 1805. Two old friends, Sophie LaRoche and Duchess Anna Amalia, departed in 1807. In addition, the poet came to be revered by political masterminds, such as Frederick II of Prussia, who commended the master poet for having spread Germany's fame abroad. In 1808, Wieland was singled out by Napoleon for two audiences and was praised for his many accomplishments. Father Wieland shocked many onlookers at the first interview when he broke all rules of protocol by appearing in a velvet cap and in cloth boots and by requesting, after a short while, that the audience conclude. "I am an old man," Wieland said, "who is not accustomed to standing so long, and it is late for me." In this manner, the Swabian demonstrated to the end his independence.

Not only had the poet gained the esteem of political leaders in Prussia and France, but in Russia as well. In 1804, Karl August's son was betrothed to Maria Pavlovna, sister to the Russian czar. Between her and the aging poet a very cordial relationship developed, and when her brother the czar visited Weimar in 1805, Wieland discovered in him an admirer of his works, especially of *Idris und Zenide*. Particularly satisfying to the author was the acclaim given him by Madame de Staël during her two trips to Weimar (1804, 1809). She recognized him as Germany's best known writer, according him a prominent position in her book *De l'Allemagne* (1810) and defending him against his fiercest opponent, August Wilhelm Schlegel. Most flattering was perhaps Goethe's clever idea of replacing the busts of Vergil and Ariosto with those of Schiller andWieland on the occasion of the premiere of *Tasso* in Weimar in 1807. When Wieland died, on January 20, 1813, Germany lost the "dean of [its] parnassus"[34] and one of its most renowned cultural envoys. His physical remains were placed beside his wife, Dorothea, and beside his Indian Summer maiden, Sophie Brentano; but his spirit still lives on.

CHAPTER 9

Wieland's Legacy

A remarkable writer in several ways, Wieland occupies a prominent position in German letters. For one thing, he made remarkable contributions to the evolution of the German language as a vehicle of poetic expression, anticipating in his writing the lucidity of form and sublimity of sentiment which distinguish the Classical period. His prefiguring of the Romanticists' pantheistic appraisal of life is also remarkable. As a versatile writer, Wieland is again noteworthy, for he wrote everything from erotic Rococo verse poems to instructive essays, hilarious satires, and antiquarian novels. The range of this versatility is also expressed in his roles as teacher, translator, and journalist. As a teacher, he interpreted the humanistic idealism of past ages to younger generations (e.g., the concepts of *die schöne Seele,* virtuoso) and waged a battle against all kinds of prejudice and superstition. As a translator of Shakespeare, he ushered in a wave of poetic fervor among his countrymen; as a translator of Horace and Lucian, he provided German-speaking peoples with classical renditions of classical authors. Finally, as a journalist, he educated whole generations of Germans to aesthetic taste and to an appreciation of opposing points of view. His *Teutscher Merkur* was one of the longest-running and most influential periodicals of the eighteenth century. All in all, Wieland was one of the few men of genius who truly deserve to be known as a *praeceptor Germaniae* (educator of Germany).

Furthermore, Wieland was a receptive and innovative writer. Perhaps no other German writer except Heinrich von Kleist was so consciously responsive to epistemological debates in the eighteenth century or allowed them to shape both the content and the form of his works so extensively. Of the classical German authors, Wieland was the most politically and socially engaged, taking his lead from such French thinkers as Bonnet, Helvetius, Montesquieu, and

156

Rousseau. Not only did he have rare insights into the mechanisms of society, but he also anticipated the results of later research in the areas of anthropology and depth psychology—disciplines which did not exist in his day—and all this because he took the maxim "know thyself" seriously.

That he was an innovative writer would seem to be astounding when we consider that he imitated such writers as Ariosto, Boccaccio, Cervantes, Euripides, Fielding, Lucian, Ovid, Shakespeare, Sterne, Tasso, Xenophon, and others. Yet precisely because of his openness to other cultures and styles, the Swabian learned early to experiment with form and meter, to adapt the best of other cultures to his own. As a result, he helped usher in the modern novel with its personal narrator and reader, producing in *Don Sylvio* the best German imitation of *Don Quixote* and in *Agathon* the first *Bildungsroman* in the eighteenth century. In *Der Neue Amadis*, Wieland unconsciously recreated the epyllion (short epic) and introduced the Italian *ottava rima* into German. With *Die Abderiten*, he introduced the first comprehensive social critique of bourgeois society. The ironic interplay between author and reader in these works required the reader to become an active participant in the narrative process and to gain independence from both self and fiction. As for his essays in the *Merkur* and elsewhere, they point forward to the classical nineteenth century type. Last, Wieland's thoughts on the dangers of a strictly nationalistic literature, as opposed to the intellectual and social advantages of a world literature, look forward to Goethe's celebrated idea of a *Weltliteratur*.

Obviously, Christoph Martin Wieland's many-faceted significance for German literary history cannot be summed up in a word. Yet Fritz Martini came close when he wrote: "Wieland's importance does not lie so much in the individual poetic find or even in the particular momentous thought, but rather in the totality of the impulses which he imparted right up into his old age to German culture, to the broad reading public as well as occasionally to intellectual giants such as Goethe, Schiller, even Novalis and Kleist."[1] Wieland recognized very early the talent of younger authors and encouraged them to excel, to surpass even his own achievements. We have seen how unselfish he was in his praise of Goethe's genius, even before their friendship. Friedrich von Hardenberg and Heinrich von Kleist also gained his respect. For example, when the other giants of the German parnassus spurned Kleist as eccentric, Wieland opened his arms to the tortured youth as to a son and gave him encouragement, seeing in him a great dramatic talent capable of unifying the genius of Aeschylus, Sophocles, and Shakespeare.[2]

Yet despite the author's contributions and stimuli—or perhaps because of them—few writers were as harshly treated by his countrymen as he. In the nineteenth century he was overshadowed by Goethe and Schiller—a paradox, since Wieland had had a substantial hand in preparing the *Bildungsmasse* (broad public) for an appreciation of the two. When Wieland was remembered, it was mostly for his supposed licentiousness, plagiarism, and desultoriness. With foreign critics during the nineteenth century Wieland fared better, for to them he appeared as an instigator of "both the Hellenic and the Romantic revival"[3] and as "one of the most fertile and most profound of modern thinkers."[4] Not until our own century has the public image of Wieland undergone radical change in Germany. In the process, Goethe's judicious appraisal of the Swabian's significance for German letters, especially as expressed in the funeral oration, "Zum brüderlichen Andenken Wielands" ("In Fraternal Memory of Wieland," 1813), has been re-examined. A milestone in this reevaluation is Sengle's biography, which appeared in 1949 and which is to be soon reissued. Furthermore, an updated, comprehensive biography is currently in preparation by Professor Hansjörg Schelle of the University of Michigan. These undertakings attest to the continuing interest in the poet's germaneness to our own age.

Wieland lived in an age of extremes, of hope, and of uncertainty. Reason had liberated man from the bonds of orthodox belief, science had opened up new frontiers, and philosophy had interpreted the world in increasingly anthropologic terms. It was an exciting—and unnerving—age which culminated in a paradox: politically it led eventually to the new adventure of democracy; philosophically it peaked in Romantic solipsism. The former resulted from an optimistic rationalism which felt that reason could solve all of man's problems; the latter issued from a growing disillusionment with the powers of reason to answer all of man's questions and from the realization that life cannot be equated with logic. The paradox was unavoidable, since man himself is a composite of paradoxes: spirit and flesh, head and heart, capable of the best logic and the worst fanaticism.

Our own computer age is marked by the same "convergent" and "divergent" problems. Whereas "convergent" problems are germane to the fields of logic such as physics, chemistry, astronomy, and mathematics, "divergent" ones are related to higher forces such as the moral good of intuition and resist logical solution. Wieland confronted this dilemma of human nature by suggesting self-knowledge as the basis for improving mankind's lot. Because he realized that life is bigger than logic, he approached the Cartesian thinking of his epoch skeptically. Because his study of himself revealed the fraternity of mankind in its relationship to a higher order, he cajoled his reader through compassionate irony to recognize the folly of pursuing transitory goods to the neglect of the only permanent good. Because of the insights into his own nature, he could better understand others. This perception made him tolerant and made him a great educator. In a recent essay on similar concerns in the twentieth century, E.F. Schumacher remarks: "If we asked a great teacher to solve our dilemma, he or she would no doubt reply irritably: 'All this is far too clever for me. The point is: you must love the little horrors.' Love, empathy, understanding—these are faculties of a higher order than those required to carry out any policy of discipline or of freedom. To mobilize these higher faculties, to apply them constantly and permanently, requires a high level of self-awareness, and that is what makes a great educator."[5] The intent of the present study was to depict Wieland as such as educator, not just as one of the eighteenth century's most astute critics and urbane poets.

Notes and References

Preface

1. Letter to Ludwig Gleim cited by Johann Gottfried Gruber, *Wielands Leben mit Einschluss vieler noch ungedruckter Briefe Wielands* (Leipzig: Göschen, 1828), III, 151. Gruber's biography appears as volumes 50–53 of *Wielands sämmtliche Werke*, ed. J.G. Gruber (Leipzig: Göschen, 1818–1828). Hereafter this edition is cited as Gruber with the volume indicated by Roman, and the page by Arabic, numerals.

2. Letter to Friedrich Justus Riedel (December 15, 1768). Renate Petermann and Hans Werner Seiffert, eds., *Wielands Briefwechsel. Briefe der Biberacher Amtsjahre (6.Juni 1760–20.Mai 1769)* (Berlin: Akademie-Verlag, 1975), III, 559 (this volume hereafter cited as Petermann/Seiffert).

3. Laurence Sterne, *The Life and Opinions of Tristram Shandy, Gentleman* (New York: New American Library, 1962), p. 161.

4. *Christoph Martin Wieland. Werke*, ed. Fritz Martini and Hans Werner Seiffert (Munich: Hanser, 1965), III, 300. Hereafter this edition will be referred to as H.

Chapter One

1. Two of the most informative sources for the author's early life are a letter written to the Swiss literary critic Johann Jakob Bodmer (1698–1783) on March 6, 1752, and one of December 28, 1787, to Leonhard Meister, professor in Zurich. The first is found in *Wielands Briefwechsel. Briefe der Bildungsjahre (1.Juni 1750 – 2.Juni 1760)* (Berlin: Akademie-Verlag, 1963), ed. Hans Werner Seiffert, I, 49–52 (hereafter cited as Seiffert). The second letter is in *Ausgewählte Briefe von C.M. Wieland* (Zurich, 1815), III, 379–93 (hereafter cited as AB). Also of note is Wieland's letter of August 10, 1768, to Riedel, professor in Erfurt. See Petermann/Seiffert, III, 531–38. Gruber's biography is also highly informative.

2. Cited by Gruber, L, 25.

3. Petermann/Seiffert, III, 532.

4. Letter to Meister (December 28, 1787), AB, III, 382–83. See also letter to Bodmer (March 6, 1752), Seiffert, I, 50–51, and Gruber, L, 29.

5. Petermann/Seiffert, III, 532.

6. H, IV, 11: "O how your friend loves you! O how happy he is when you greet him with your honey-sweet kisses and when your softly quivering lips begin to distend like a budding rose!"
7. Cf. Ann B. Shteir, "Albrecht von Haller's Botany and *Die Alpen*," *Eighteenth-Century Studies*, 10 (Winter 1976–1977), 170–71.
8. Seiffert, I, 63.
9. Ibid., p. 78.
10. C.M. *Wielands Briefe an Sophie von LaRoche*, ed. Franz Horn (Berlin, 1820), p. 332 (hereafter cited as Horn).
11. Bernhard Seuffert, "Mitteilungen aus Wielands Jünglingsalter," *Euphorion. Ergänzungsheft*, 3 (1897), 63–101, discusses the reasons for Wieland's move.
12. See Gotthold Ephraim Lessing, *Werke* (Munich: Hanser, 1973), V, 42 (hereafter cited as Lessing, *H*).
13. *Wielands gesammelte Schriften*, ed. Deutsche Kommission der Kgl. Preuss. (Berlin: Deutsche Akademie der Wissenschaften, Weidmann, 1909), Ser. 1, I, 54,70 (hereafter cited as AA). See also Wieland's letter to Schinz (Seiffert, I, 78), where he states: "In my system there are no purely spiritual beings, and the angels embrace one another even as we do."
14. Ibid., pp. 54, 118: "No Platonic thinker, regardless of what ideas he thought up, ever separated spirit from substance. . . ." "God is the source of joy because all delight comes from perfections and permeates all spiritualities. The source of both is God." Emil Ermatinger, *Die Weltanschauung des jungen Wieland* (Frauenfeld: Huber, 1907), and Karl Hoppe, *Der junge Wieland. Wesensbestimmung seines Geistes* (Leipzig: J.J. Weber, 1930), subject the poem to close analysis, judging it as a philosophical and literary work. Thomas P. Saine, "Was ist Aufklärung?", *Aufklärung, Absolutismus und Bürgertum in Deutschland*, ed. F. Kopitzsch (Munich: Nymphenburger Verlagsbuchhandlung, 1976), esp. pp. 324–32, renews the discussion of the general religious and philosophical atmosphere out of which *Die Natur der Dinge* grew.
15. See Cornelius Sommer, *C.M. Wieland* (Stuttgart: Metzler, 1971), p. 15.
16. Petermann/Seiffert, III, 532–33. Despite the catalytic role love played in the making of this poem, its general tone is so dignified and restrained that Georg Friedrich Meyer, a professor in Halle, thought that the author must be a sixty year old nobleman! See Seiffert, I, 62.

Chapter Two

1. E.g., in a letter to Zimmerman (March 27, 1759), Wieland urges his friend to put aside a few bottles of good wine for his visit (Seiffert, I, 415). See also the letter to Bodmer (February 4, 1752) which stresses his "preference" for water (Seiffert, I, 39).
2. Ibid., pp. 87–89.

3. Wolfgang Paulsen, *C.M. Wieland* (Berne and Munich: Francke, 1975), pp. 47–51. For detailed study of Wieland's personal and literary relationship with Bodmer see Fritz Budde, *Wieland und Bodmer* (Berlin: Mayer und Müller, 1910).

4. Seiffert, I, 570.

5. Hans Werner Seiffert, "Wielands Beiträge zur Zürcher Monatsschrift *Crito*," *Festgabe für Eduard Berend zum 75. Geburtstag* (Weimar: Böhlau, 1959), pp. 324–35, examines Wieland's contributions to Bodmer's critical journal.

6. Cf. letter to Zimmermann (April 26, 1759): Seiffert, I, 430.

7. Paulsen, however argues (pp.60–63), that Wieland had never taken his engagement to Sophie that seriously.

8. Cf. Letter to Sophie (March 20, 1754): Seiffert, I, 196–98. It is a restrained letter that reflects Wieland's desire to relieve Sophie of any sense of guilt because he apparently loved her dearly and wanted her to be as happy as possible. In a letter written almost three years later to his confidant Zimmermann, his sense of loss is scarcely concealed, as he speaks several times of his incomparable Sophie in sentimental fashion. His conclusion ("But enough of this silly talk!") is anything but ironic when we consider that he had just opened his heart to his best friend (See Seiffert, I, 294–96).

9. Seuffert, "Mitteilungen," p. 100, speaks of Wieland's awareness of the need to experiment with various verse and prose styles. See p. 93 for a list of Bodmer's influences on Wieland.

10. See Seiffert, II, 174–75. Wieland's rapprochement with the group began about the same time that Sophie broke with him, so that the move can be seen as a conscious distancing from his goal-oriented existence in Bodmer's house.

11. Wieland's letter of January 11, 1757, to Zimmermann clearly reveals the author's attitude toward women and insinuates that Sophie's break with him was the catalyst (see Seiffert, I, 294–96). For a detailed analysis of Wieland's attitude toward women as revealed in his works see Matthew G. Bach, *Wieland's Attitude toward Woman and her Cultural and Social Relations* (New York: Columbia University Press, 1922).

12. Julius Steinberger, *Wieland in Mainz* (Heidelberg: Weissbach, 1925), pp. 41–42. See also Wieland's letter of November 8, 1758, to Katharina Zimmermann, his friend's wife (Seiffert, I, 383–84).

13. Gruber, L, 207–208.

14. Seiffert, I, 265.

15. See "Sympathien," H, III, 124–27.

16. Once while saying good night he took her hand and, looking languishingly into her eyes, wished he were twenty years older so that there would be no barrier between them. She, for her part, lamented that she was not twenty years younger! See Gruber, L. 212.

17. Ibid., pp. 213, 228; Seiffert, I, 366.

18. Seiffert, I, 390.

19. Ibid., p. 288.

20. Cf. Bernhard Seuffert, *Prolegomena zu einer Wieland-Ausgabe* (Berlin: Akademie der Wissenschaften, 1904), pt. II, p. 33 (hereafter cited as *Proleg*).

21. AA, ser. 1, vol. 2, 201–202.

22. Gruber, L, 227–28, reports that in 1758 Wieland was planning to write a treatise on the role of love which surely would have reflected Diotima's view of the types of love ascending from the physical to the mystical.

23. Fritz Martini, "C.M. Wieland und das 18. Jahrhundert," *Festschrift für Paul Kluckhohn und Hermann Schneider* (Tübingen, 1948), p. 263. Manfred Dick, "Wandlungen des Menschenbildes beim jungen Wieland: *Araspes und Panthea* und Shaftesburys *Soliloquy*," *Jahrbuch der Deutschen Schillergesellschaft*, 16 (1972), 145–75, subjects the narrative to a detailed analysis while delineating Shaftesbury's influence on it. However, Dick interprets the influence as a refutation of Wieland's two souls theory rather than as a complementation of his then predominant spirituality. Dick has failed to note that Wieland saw physical and Platonic love as inherently related to love of absolute beauty (p. 171).

24. AA, ser. 1, vol. 3, 87. Luise Bröcker, "Das Zweiseelen problem bei Goethe und Wieland" (Diss, Münster, 1947), scrutinizes this aspect.

25. AA, ser. 1, vol. 3, 84.

26. Paulsen, pp. 133–34 and fn. 81, argues that Wieland had Sophie in mind, and not Frau Grebel-Lochmann, as Gruber (L, 211) had suggested.

27. Seiffert, I, 313.

28. Paulsen, p. 134.

29. AA, ser. 1, vol. 2, 202.

30. Cf. *Proleg.*, pt. I, p. 52. Friedrich Sengle, *C.M. Wieland* (Stuttgart: Metzler, 1949), p. 99, reports that Bodmer had urged Wieland to compose a Cyrus epic for Frederick the Great, but that Wieland had not shown any interest. Victor Michel, *C.M. Wieland: La formation et l'évolution de son esprit jusqu'à 1772* (Paris: Boivin, 1937), p. 174, suspects that the idea was even older.

31. See Seiffert, I, 319, 324.

32. Hermann Müller-Solger, *Der Dichtertraum* (Göttingen: Kümmerle, 1970), p. 87.

33. Seiffert, I, 371.

34. Karl Wilhelm Böttiger ed., *Literarische Zustände und Zeitgenossen. In Schilderungen aus Karl August Böttigers handschriftlichem Nachlasse* (1838; rpt. Frankfurt: Athenäum, 1972), I, 154.

35. A free translation of "Vive les femmes idiotes!" (Seiffert, I, 483).

36. Ibid., p. 496.

37. Cf. Gruber, L, 325–26.
38. Seiffert, I, 501, 505, 518.
39. Ibid., p. 527.
40. August 11, 1756, cited by Gruber, L, 268.

Chapter Three

1. Paulsen, pp. 91–94, believes that Wieland unconsciously wanted to avenge the pain that Sophie had caused him ten years earlier. This argument is implicitly based on several assumptions: (1) that despite the lapse of time, his love for Sophie in 1763 was just as intense as in 1753, (2) that the influence of the Swiss women was negligible, and (3) that Bibi was scarcely more than an *ersatz* Sophie. The first two points are possible but improbable; the third seems to overlook Paulsen's own view (p. 242 et passim) that Wieland had wanted only a Platonic relationship with Sophie. Bibi was no intellectual match for Sophie; therefore, she represented no threat from that angle. The poet's love for Bibi was quite physical. How, then, could he want (even subconsciously) to hurt Sophie, whom he supposedly loved only intellectually? Only if Wieland had been frustrated in his physical attraction to Sophie would Paulsen's argument seem to be valid. Gruber (L, 316–25) argues, on the other hand, that Wieland's feelings toward Sophie had altered extensively—i.e., that he had "gotten over" his love for her by 1763, treating his former emotions as a topos.

2. For a brief discussion of Count Stadion and his relationship to Wieland, see Gabriele Koenig-Warthausen, "Friedrich Graf von Stadion," *Schwäbische Lebensbilder*, 8 (1975), 113–36.

3. Cf. Petermann/Seiffert, III, 252.

4. Koenig-Warthausen, p. 128, stresses the count's aversion to excesses.

5. See Friedrich Gundolf, *Shakespeare und der deutsche Geist* (Munich and Düsseldorf: Küpper, 1959), pp. 145–62 and, especially, 165–72.

6. *Proleg.*, III, 5–6. Sengle, p. 163, believes that the success of the *Sturm* performance in Biberach's amateur theater under Wieland's direction gave the poet the idea of translating the other plays as well.

7. Jeffrey Gardiner and Albert R. Schmitt, "C.M. Wieland: 'Theorie und Geschichte der Red-Kunst und Dicht-Kunst. Anno 1757.' An Early Defense of Shakespeare," *Lessing Yearbook*, 5 (1973), 219–41.

8. Lessing, *Hamburgische Dramaturgie*, 15. Stück (June 19, 1767), Hanser, IV, 300–301; Johannes Falk, *Goethe aus näherm persönlichen Umgange dargestellt* (Leipzig, 1832), III, 57; letter to Gessner and Co. (May 8, 1766) in Petermann/Seiffert, III, 375.

9. Cf. Johann Georg Jacobi's views on the matter published in Wieland's journal *Der Teutsche Merkur*, October 1773, fourth quarter (Weimar, 1773), p. 10.

10. See the reference in the first stanza to her singing voice, which compares favorably with Philomela's (H, IV, 70).
11. Petermann/Seiffert, III, 297.
12. Gruber, LI, 416–18. Hans Sittenberger, "Untersuchungen über Wielands *Komische Erzählungen*," *Vierteljahresschrift für deutsche Literaturgeschichte*, 4 (1891), 281–317, 406–39; and 5 (1892), 201–23, investigates in detail the relationship between form and content for each of the tales.
13. Cf. John A. McCarthy, "Wielands Metamorphose?", *DVLG*, 49 (Sonderheft, 1975), 149–67.
14. Cited by Gruber, LI, 408–409. Charles Antoine Coypel (1694–1752) was a successful artist of the French Rococo.
15. Petermann/Seiffert, III, 425. He contends further that these tales are as moral in their fashion as the *Briefe von Verstorbenen* in theirs. In 1775, he finally wrote his own defense in "Unterredungen zwischen W** und dem Pastor zu***." See H, III, 295–327.
16. See Sengle, p. 176; Lieselotte E. Kurth-Voigt, *Perspectives and Points of View* (Baltimore and London: The Johns Hopkins University Press, 1974), pp. 136–37; Gruber, LI, 418.
17. Petermann/Seiffert, III, 298.
18. Ibid., pp. 431–32.
19. H, IV, 109.
20. Ibid., p. 180.
21. Ibid., p. 142.
22. See Kurth-Voigt, pp. 136–66, for an admirable analysis of the mythical narrative.
23. In addition to Kurth-Voigt, studies which deal with the significance of point of view for Wieland include: John McCarthy, *Fantasy and Reality: An Epistemological Approach to Wieland* (Berne and Frankfurt: Lang, 1974); Steven R. Miller, *Die Figur des Erzählers in Wielands Romanen* (Göppingen: Kümmerle, 1970); and Jan-Dirk Muller, *Wielands späte Romane* (Munich: Fink, 1971).
24. Otto Guldenberg, "Wielands *Komische Erzählungen* im Spiegel des literarischen Rokoko" (diss, Halle, 1925), p. 104.
25. H, IV, 140–41: "Yet they heard (gods have acute hearing), I don't know what, which caused them to conclude that the lady was not alone in the bath."
26. Petermann/Seiffert, III, 471. Cf. also AB, II 322–23.
27. Seiffert, I, 321.
28. Sengle, p. 212.
29. Gruber, LI, 424–27.
30. Cf. Wieland's letter to Riedel published as an introduction to *Idris und Zenide* and the preface to the same (H, IV, 183–91). See also the letters to Gessner and Riedel in Petermann/Seiffert, III, 408, 499–500, and the one to Zimmermann (1767) cited by Gruber, LI, 379.

31. Friedrich Beissner, "Poesie des Stils. Eine Hinführung zu Wieland," *Wieland: Vier Biberacher Vorträge* (Wiesbaden: Insel, 1954), pp. 5–34. See also Otto Brückl, " 'Poesie des Stils' bei Wieland," *Festschrift für Herbert Seidler* (Salzburg and Munich: Pustet, 1966), pp. 27–48. Almost fifteen years later, Wieland wrote in "Briefe an einen jungen Dichter" *(Teutscher Merkur*, August 1782): "When a poetic work . . . is that which Horace calls 'completely polished and rounded,' when it has acquired by means of elegant refining a sense of complete ease, when the language has been purified and the diction made appropriate, when the rhythm seems like music and the rhyme occurs naturally . . . ; in short, when everything is a harmonious whole . . . so that nowhere a sign of effort can be found, then you can rest assured that the poet—regardless of how great his talent might be—has worked with enormous care for details" (H, III, 441–42).

32. Letter of July 21, 1766, in Petermann/Seiffert, III, 396. Antoine d'Hamilton (1645–1719) was a French writer of fairy tales in the manner of *1001 Nights.*

33. Ibid., p. 408; Sengle, p. 205. Herbert Rowland's recent study, *'Musarion' and Wieland's Concept of Genre* (Göppingen: Kümmerle, 1975), investigates Wieland's innovative approach to form and style, which draws upon the forms of the didactic poem, the comedy and verse narrative.

34. Johann Wolfgang von Goethe, *Werke* (Munich: dtv, 1962), XXIII, 55 (=*Dichtung und Wahrheit*, 2. Teil, 7. Buch).

35. Cited by Emil Staiger, "Wieland: *Musarion*," *Die Kunst der Interpretation* (Munich: dtv, 1972), p. 92.

36. Elizabeth Boa, "Wieland's *Musarion* and the Rococo Verse Narrative," *Periods in German Literature*, ed. James M. Ritchie (London: Wolff, 1968), II, 25. B. A. Sørensen, "Das deutsche Rokoko und die Verserzählung im 18. Jahrhundert." *Euphorion*, 48 (1954), 148, calls *Musarion* "the epitome of historic-intellectual aspiration of the German Rococo."

37. Staiger, p. 89.

38. H, IV, 325.

39. Joachim Müller, "Wielands Versepen," *Jahrbuch des Wiener Goethe-Vereins*, 69 (1965), 14.

40. H, IV, 361–62.

41. Ibid., p. 364.

42. Seiffert, I, 217.

43. Gruber, XII, 145. Book 5 of *Die Grazien* is especially instructive concerning Wieland's understanding of these qualities. See Gruber, XII, 133–45.

44. Cited by Gruber, LI, 455.

45. C. W. Böttiger, "Christoph M. Wieland nach seiner Freunde und seinen eigenen Äusserungen," *Historisches Taschenbuch*, ed. Friedrich von Raumer, 10 (Leipzig: Brockhaus, 1839), 381.

46. Petermann/Seiffert, III, 492.

47. Ibid.; pp. 289–90. Lessing had written in 1759 in "Briefe die neueste

Literatur betreffend": "Rejoice with me for Mr. Wieland has descended from the ethereal realms and again walks the earth!" (Lessing, H, II, 185).
48. See Paulsen, pp. 229–39; Gruber, LI, 418–23. In *Musarion* itself reference is made to both kinds of love: "And Amor, not the little rogue whom Coypel portrays, another one, a cupid of ideas" (H, IV, 349).
49. See Gruber, LI, 383.

Chapter Four

1. J. G. Robertson, "The Beginnings of the German Novel," *Westminister Review*, 142 (1849), 190 and Wolfgang Kayser, "Entstehung und Krise des modernen Romans," Sonderdruck from *DVLG*, 28 (1954), 13 et passim argue that *Don Sylvio* marks the beginning of the modern novel in Germany. However, Lieselotte E. Kurth, "W.E.N.—Der teutsche Don Quichotte, oder die Begebenheiten des Marggraf von Bellamonte. Ein Beitrag zur Geschichte des deutschen Romans im 18. Jahrhundert," in *Jahrbuch der deutschen Schillergesellschaft*, 9 (1965), 106–30, convincingly shows that the techniques of the modern novel existed in Germany before the publication of *Don Sylvio*.
2. Lessing, H, IV, 555.
3. Fritz Martini, "Nachwort," in H, I, 934, considers *Don Sylvio* to be the "best example of German Rococo style in novel form." See also Sengle, p. 180.
4. Petermann/Seiffert, III, 169–70.
5. Cf. *Proleg.*, I, 56; Sengle, p. 113.
6. Petermann/Seiffert, III, 206–207.
7. Cf. Klaus Oettinger, *Phantasie und Erfahrung* (Munich: Fink, 1970), esp. pp. 53–57, 141–45.
8. See McCarthy, *Fantasy*, pp. 43–70, for a discussion of the influence of epistemological concerns on the structure and style of *Don Sylvio*. Kurth-Voigt, *Perspectives*, p. 133, uses the term "the perspective portrayal of man."
9. H, I, 135.
10. Wolfgang Preisendanz, "Die Auseinandersetzung mit dem Nachahmungsprinzip in Deutschland und die besondere Rolle der Romane Wielands *(Don Sylvio, Agathon)*," in *Nachahmung und Illusion*, ed. Hans R. Jauss (Munich: Eidos, 1964), p. 84.
11. Some readers consider the Jacinte episode to be parodistic rather than imitative. See Guy Stern, "Saint or Hypocrite? A Study of Wieland's 'Jacinte Episode,' " *Germanic Review*, 29 (1954), 96–101.
12. H, I, 338.
13. Ibid., pp. 342–47. Miller, directs much of his attention to the question of how reliable historical truth is.
14. *Die Abenteuer des Don Sylvio von Rosalva*, ed. Wolfgang Jahn (Munich: Goldmann, n.d.), "Nachwort," p. 337. Peter J. Brenner,

"Kritische Form." Zur Dialektik der Aufklärung in Wielands Roman 'Don Sylvio von Rosalva,' " *JDSG*, 20 (1976), 162–83, dresses up his discussion with fashionable terminology à la Adorno, Horkheimer, and Lukács, but does not provide new insights.

15. H, I, 137–38. Emil Ermatinger, "Das Romantische bei Wieland," *Neue Jahrbücher für das klassische Altertum, Geschichte und deutsche Literatur*, 21 (1908), 223–27, examines Wieland's use of the concept of "Sympathie" in some detail.

16. H, I, 17.

17. Kayser, pp. 13–15, cites the personal narrator as a major mark of the modern novel and notes the need to recognize the various roles the narrator (and the fictive reader) assumes (p. 15). Kurth-Voigt, *Perspectives*, pp. 121–27, applies the distinctions of *ingenú* and *vir bonus* to *Don Sylvio*, granting that hers is only a preliminary attempt. See most recently Ralph Farrell and Keith Leopold, "Wieland's *Don Sylvio von Rosalva:* The first Modern German Novel?", in *Festschrift für Ralph Farrell*, ed. Anthony Stephens et al. (Berne: Lang, 1977), who concentrate on the role of the narrator. The role that the fictive reader plays is also deserving of closer study.

18. A free translation: "To be sure, the Muses have to entertain us; yet they use this 'obligation' to instruct us most effectively" (H, IV, 193).

19. See Alfred Martens, *Untersuchungen über Wielands 'Don Sylvio' und die übrigen Dichtungen der Biberacher Zeit*, Diss. Halle-Wittenberg 1901 (Halle: Karras, 1901), p. 61.

20. Martini, "Nachwort," H, I, 922.

21. Ibid., p. 353.

22. See Gruber, LI, 332. Paulsen, p. 177, speaks of the archetypal moment in Wieland's encounter with Ion.

23. Petermann/Seiffert, III, 61.

24. Martini, "Nachwort," H, I, 950–52.

25. Ibid., p. 865.

26. Cf. "Über das Historische im Agathon," Gruber, IX, 3–5. Oettinger, pp. 85–91 et passim, stresses the "Modellcharakter" of the experiences depicted in this "history." In so doing, he laudably demonstrates that chance is a "fundamental principle for structuring the events" (p. 85), which, in turn, necessitates the utopian conclusion that the novel ultimately receives. Oettinger's summation makes clear the conflicting empirical and speculative forces at work here: "The History of Agathon is concerned with depicting a world which draws equally upon Lockean and Leibnizian concepts and which is thus simultaneously empirical and utopian" (p. 99).

27. H, I, 375. Gerd Matthecka, "Die Romantheorie Wielands und seiner Vorläufer" dissertation, Tübingen, 1957), p. 163, asserts: "The central idea of the novel is the law of psychological probability." Heinrich Funck, "Gespräche mit C. M. Wieland in Zürich," *Archiv für Literaturgeschichte*, 13

(1885), provides the following evidence for the continuity of Wieland's psychological concerns: On May 8, 1754, Wieland stated: "The study of psychology should be given greater care. Before we assume certain principles and try to link various systems together, we should first strive for greater understanding of our own souls" (p. 492). The conversations in the following months dealt in great part with psychology and self-knowledge. Then, on March 15, 1755, he made a comment directly applicable to *Agathon:* "Our knowledge of an individual can reach a high degree of accuracy if we observe him in various relationships and study the motives for his actions" (p. 496).

28. Eric Gross, *C. M. Wielands "Geschichte des Agathon." Entstehungsgeschichte* (1930; rpt. Nendeln/Liechtenstein: Krauss, 1967), pp. 66–82 et passim, discusses the impact of physiological and milieu theories on the novel.

29. Alexander Pope, "Essay on Man," Epistle II, verses 1–2.

30. Gruber, IX, v. For consistency's sake, the third edition of the novel will be cited. The Hanser edition (vol. I) reproduces the first edition.

31. Martini, "Nachwort," H, I, 936.

32. Paulsen, (p. 215) sees in the psychological equation of Psyche and Delphi the "Urzelle" of the novel.

33. H, IV, 799–800, fn. 4 to *Neuer Amadis.*

34. Petermann/Seiffert, III, 207.

35. Cited by Martini, "Nachwort," H, I, 964.

36. Lessing, H, IV, 555. Cf. Marianne Spiegel, *Der Roman im frühen 18. Jahrhundert 1700–1767* (Bonn: Bouvier, 1967), p. 101.

37. Cf. Gruber, IX, 298–99n, 301; and H, I, 896, fn. to p. 420.

38. Gruber, IX, 149.

39. Ibid., pp. 81–82. Cf. H, I, 422, where Agathon's reply is more laconic and reminiscent of Bonnet's maxim: "Je sens, donc je suis."

40. Gruber, IX, 89.

41. Ibid., pp. 152, 157 (my emphasis).

42. Jan-Dirk Müller, pp. 89–90.

43. Gruber, XI, 353, 356; 374–76.

44. Gruber, LI, 336.

45. Gruber, XI, xiii–xiv. Also H, I, 379–80.

46. Petermann/Seiffert, III, 140.

47. See Paulsen, pp. 207–27.

48. Gruber, IX, 281–82; and H, I, 543–44. (my emphasis).

49. Böttiger, *Literarische Zustände,* I. 259. Cf. Eric A. Blackall, *The Emergence of German as a Literary Language* (Cambridge: Cambridge University Press, 1959), pp. 420–21.

50. Marga Barthel, *Das "Gespräch" bei Wieland. Untersuchungen Über Wesen und Form seiner Dichtung* (1938; rpt. Hildesheim: Gerstenberg, 1973), examines the significance of dialogic form for Wieland's prose and

verse style, which, for her, is marked by grace (p. 126). Blackall (p. 44), on the other hand, speaks of it as a "combining the culture of wit with the culture of feeling in an overall ideal of grace." More recently, Jürgen Jacobs, *Wielands Romane* (Berne and Munich: Francke, 1969), p. 88, refers to the urbane quality of Wieland's dialogic style.

51. Martini, "Nachwort," H, I, 960. My detailed analysis of Wieland's later essay, "Was ist Wahrheit?" (1776), has revealed the author's indebtedness to rhetorical traditions. Cf. John A. McCarthy, "Wieland as Essayist," *Lessing Yearbook*, 8 (1976), 125–39.

52. Kurt Wölfel, "Daphnes Verwandlungen," *JDSG,* 8 (1964), 41.

Chapter Five

1. Cf. Sengle, p. 166.

2. See Petermann/Seiffert, III, 432–34; and AB, II, 330, where Wieland states that he "is becoming as greedy as Pope and Voltaire." The time when he received only eight Louis d'or for a work such as the *Komische Erzählungen* is over (cf. AB, II, 267). Wolfgang von Ungern-Sternberg, *Chr. M. Wieland und das Verlagswesen seiner Zeit* (Frankfurt a.m.: Buchhändler vereinigung GMBH, 1974), traces Wieland's efforts to establish himself as a free-lance writer.

3. Cf. Sengle's chapter heading, p. 223.

4. Gruber, LI, 498–500; Jacobs, p. 86.

5. Fr. H. Jacobi, *Auserlesener Briefwechsel* (1825–1827; rpt. Berne: Lang, 1970), I, 35–36.

6. Böttiger, "Christoph Martin Wieland nach seiner Freunde," pp. 425–26. Friedrich Schulze-Maizier's *Wieland in Erfurt (1769–1772),* Diss. München, 1919 (Erfurt: Villaret, 1919), represents one of the most thorough studies of this period.

7. Cited by Gruber, LI, 515.

8. Cf. Walter H. Bruford, *Culture and Society in Classical Weimar (1775–1806)* (Cambridge: Cambridge University Press, 1962), pp. 428–31.

9. Gruber, LI, 536–37.

10. Böttiger, "Christoph Martin Wieland nach seiner Freunde," p. 427.

11. Cited by Gruber, LI, 538.

12. Horn, p. 132.

13. Cf. Sengle, pp. 176–78.

14. AB, II, 330; 332–33.

15. See the prefaces to the 1771 and 1794 editions: H, IV, 370, 374. The 1794 edition was thoroughly reworked; the 1771 copy which was used for the revisions is preserved in the Goethe-Schiller Archives in Weimar and provides evidence of the author's "Poesie des Stils." In the 1794 preface Wieland speaks of "Korrektheit des Stils."

16. H, IV, 377: "Of errant knights and traveling beauties, sing, comic muse, in free 'errant' tones! Sing of the hero who has long traversed the

world, up and down mountains, in search of the image of a beauty descended from the realm of ideas to inflame his young heart; [sing of a hero] who, in order to find this counterpart more surely, gave himself up unnoticed to all beauties, having gone from the one to the other until finally the unlikely Olinde succeeded with her quiet merit in capturing the fantast in her arms."

17. Michel, p. 363. Wolfgang Preisendanz, "Wieland und die Verserzählung des 18. Jahrhunderts," *Germanisch-romanische Monatsschrift*, 43 (1962), 17–31, demonstrates how the narrator-reader-subject relationship becomes the "thematic reality" in *Der neue Amadis* and *Idris*.

18. Cited by Gruber, LI, 546.

19. Sengle, pp. 216–18; Michel, pp. 363–73.

20. Sengle, pp. 224–45.

21. Sengle (p. 233) feels the sociopolitical works of these years lead Wieland away from his "Kern."

22. Gruber, LI, 572.

23. Jacobs, pp. 70–73. Seuffert, in *Proleg.*, V, 16, #163, wonders whether the two planned histories of the human spirit (1755 and 1770) might be related. It would seem that they are, since both were apparently designed to amend Rousseau's ideas on the role of experience in the shaping of man's concept of reality.

24. H, II, 19.

25. Klaus Bäppler, *Der philosophische Wieland* (Berne and Munich: Franke, 1974), p. 36.

26. Gruber, LI, 582.

27. Bäppler (pp. 30–61) titles his chapter on *Diogenes* in this manner.

28. H, II, 86. This episode was probably inspired by a similar one in *Tristram Shandy*.

29. Ibid., pp. 69–72. Richard Samuel, "Wieland als Gesellschaftskritiker," *Seminar*, 5 (1969), 45–53, points out Wieland's unexpectedly unorthodox views here and elsewhere.

30. Bäppler, p. 60.

31. H, II, 74.

32. Ibid., p. 36.

33. Böttiger, *Literarische Zustande und Zeitgenossen. In Schilderungen aus Karl August Bättigers handschriftlichem Nachlasse*, I. 205.

34. Sengle (pp. 260 and 267) uses these terms. Hans Würzner, "C. M. Wieland. Versuch einer politischen Deutung," (Diss. Heidelberg, 1959), corrects Sengle's judgment and focuses on the continuity of Wieland's political thought, which he sees based on the author's anthropologic views. Würzner further argues (pp. 30–32) that Montesquieu's influence on Wieland's thought has been underrated. Peter U. Hohendahl, "Zum Erzählproblem des utopischen Romans im 18. Jahrhundert," *Gestaltungsgeschichte und Gesellschaftsgeschichte*," ed. Helmut Kreuzer (Stuttgart:

Metzler, 1969), pp. 102–114, reaffirms the serious political and aesthetic concerns underlying the novel.

35. Hohendahl, pp. 111–12.

36. Gruber, XVI, 16.

37. Bernd Weyergraf, *Der skeptische Bürger* (Stuttgart: Metzler, 1972), p. xiii, bases his study on the premise that Wieland was not concerned with the interests of the fourth estate. That premise misrepresents the scope of Wieland's concern not only in 1772 but also in 1793.

38. Sengle, p. 267.

39. Gruber, LI, 609.

40. Cf. Bäppler, pp. 84–85, 94–95 et passim; Alfred Ratz, *Freiheit des Individuums* (Berne: Lang, 1974), pp. 79–80. Ratz also argues, parodoxically, that man for Wieland was without reason in the state of nature (see pp. 81–83). Saine (pp. 319–343) indicates Wieland's position in eighteenth century political thought.

41. James A. McNeely, "Historical Relativism in Wieland's Concept of the Ideal State," *Modern Language Quarterly*, 22 (1961), p. 280, fn. 15, has corrected the view promulgated by Sengle that the fall is not indicated in the 1772 edition.

42. See Walter Siegers. *Menschheit, Staat und Nation Bei Wieland*, Diss. Munich 1929 (Alfeld a.d. Leine: Stegen, 1930), pp. v, 142.

Chapter Six

1. Fritz Martini, "Wieland-Forschung," *DVLG*, 24 (1950), 275, speaks of a "flight." Hansjörg Schelle, "Unbekannte Briefe C. M. Wielands und Sophie von LaRoches aus des Jahren 1789 bis 1793," *Modern Language Notes*, 86 (1971), 657–60, recognizes the poet's need for quiet.

2. Cf. Bernd Maurach, "Ein Zeitgenosse über Wieland," *Weimarer Beiträge*, 22, no. 7 (1976), 167. Cf. also *Briefe eines reisenden Franzosen über Deutschland an seinen Bruder zu Paris.* tr. Johann Kaspar Riesbeck, II (1784), 54.

3. Sengle, p. 291.

4. Cf. Sengle, p. 287. He does not mention the personal experience. Emilie Marx, *Wieland und das Drama* (Strassburg: Trübner, 1914), pp. 80–104, is more judicious. More recent treatments of this play and the author's other dramatic works include: L. John Parker, *C. M. Wielands dramatische Tätigkeit* (Berne and Munich: Francke, 1961), pp. 89–101; and Otto Schmidt, "Die dramatische Gestaltung bei C. M. Wieland" Dissertation, Munich, 1964), pp. 81–130.

5. Schelle, pp. 86, 660. Seuffert, "Der junge Goethe und Wieland." *Zeitschrift für Deutsches Altertum und Deutsche Literatur*, 26 (1882), 252–87, was the first to compare *Alceste* und *Iphigenie*.

6. *Briefe . . . Franzosen,* II, 51, 52.

7. Cf. Gruber, LII, 105–106.

8. To be sure, the friendship did have its ups and downs, as can be seen from recently published anecdotes about their mutually biting comments. (see Maurach, p. 167). Still, neither was capable of bearing a grudge.

9. Walter Hinderer, "Beiträge Wielands zu Schillers ästhetischer Erziehung," *JDSG,* 18 (1974), 348–87, is a recent contribution to the many parallels between the two authors' ideas. See also Wolfgang Preisendanz, "Die Kunst der Darstellung in Wielands *Oberon,*" *Formenwandel* (Hamburg: Hoffmann and Campe, 1964), 252–53 and fn. 24.

10. For a discussion of Wieland's reaction to his auto-da-fé in the first number of *Athenäum* see Albert R. Schmitt, "Wielands Urteil über die Brüder Schlegel mit ungedruckten Briefen des Dichters an Carl August Böttiger," *Journal of English and Germanic Philology,* 65 (1966), 637–61. Due to space limitations, the major phases of Wieland's reception by his contemporaries could only be sketched very briefly. For a thorough treatment of the topic, see Manfred A. Poitzsch, *Zeitgenössische Persiflagen auf C.M. Wieland und seine Schriften* (Berne: Lang, 1972), and Käthe Kluth, *Wieland im Urteil der vorklassischen Zeit,* Dissertation, Griefswald, 1927 (Grimmen: Grimmen Kreiszeitung, 1927).

11. See Hans Wahl, *Geschichte des Teutschen Merkur* (Berlin: Mayer & Müller, 1914), pp. 6–7.

12. *Auswahl denkwürdiger Briefe von C.M. Wieland.* Ed. Ludwig Wieland (Vienna: gerold, 1815), I, 304. See also Wahl, p. 39.

13. Wahl, p. 42.

14. Cf. Martini, "Wieland-Forschung," p. 277.

15. Conversation with Eckermann of January 18, 1825. There Goethe uses the term *Oberdeutschland,* which could mean either "upper" (i.e., southern) Germany or the educated classes of Germany.

16. Jacobi, I, 220; Bruford, p. 52.

17. Hedwig Weilguny, *Das Wieland-Museum im Wittumspalais zu Weimar* (Weimar and Berlin: Aufbau, 1968), p. 59.

18. See Rolf Engelsing, "Dienstbotenlektüre im 18. und 19. Jahrhundert," *Zur Sozialgeschichte deutscher Mittel- und Unterschichten* (Göttingen: Vandenhoeck & Ruprecht, 1973), pp. 180–224; and R. Engelsing, *Analphabetentum und Lektüre* (Stuttgart: Metzler, 1973).

19. *Briefe . . . Franzosen,* II, 52.

20. H.J. Meessen, "Wieland's 'Briefe an einen jungen Dichter,'" *Monatshefte,* 47 (1955) 193–208, examines the significance of these letters for German literary history.

21. In addition to Ungern-Sternberg's study, see Hansjörg Schelle, "Wielands Beziehung zu seinen Leipziger Verlegern. Neue Dokumente (Teil I)," *LY,* 7 (1975), 151–59, who gives a brief survey of the rise of *freie Schriftstellerei.* Schelle's continuing work ("Teil II," *LY,* 8 [1976], 140–239;

"Teil III," *LY*, 9 [1977] 166–258 provides important material for the study of the *Teutscher Merkur*. It would thus appear evident that the *Merkur* had no "subordinate" function for Wieland, as Sengle (p. 407) claims.
   22. Würzner, p. 168.
   23. Sengle, p. 441.
   24. Weyergraf, pp. 45–51 et passim, discusses the complex nature of Wieland's skeptical attitude toward the common people and his rejection of democracy as a viable political form.
   25. Seiffert, "Nachwort," H, V, 883.
   26. Horn, p. 281 (letter of January 2, 1788).
   27. Sengle, p. 398.
   28. Goethe, *Werke*, 31, 162.

Chapter Seven

   1. "Gedanken über die Ideale der Alten," H, III, 366, 383, 393 et passim. Müller-Solger, pp. 179–228, reinterprets Wieland's essay as an expression of his fundamental idealism, which remained constant.
   2. Sengle, p. 328.
   3. Ibid., p. 331; Martini, "Wieland—*Geschichte der Abderiten*," in *Der deutsche Roman*, ed. Benno von Wiese (Düsseldorf: Bagel, 1963), I, 81.
   4. Martini, "*Abderiten*," I, 68.
   5. Ibid., p. 77. Maria Tronskaja, *Die deutsche Prosasatire der Aufklärung* (Berlin: Rütten and Loening, 1969), pp. 187–213, gives an overview of criticism and delineates the intellectual and social sources of the satire.
   6. Albert Fuchs, *Geistiger Gehalt und Quellenfrage in Wielands 'Abderiten'* (Paris: Société d'edition "Les belles Lettres," 1934), p. 4.
   7. See John Whiton, "Sacrifice and Society in Wieland's *Abderiten*," *LY*, 2 (1970), 213–234.
   8. H, II, 450.
   9. Ibid., p. 125.
   10. *Proleg.*, V, 38.
   11. Gruber, LI, 364, speaks of the Biberach influences; B. Seuffert, *Wielands 'Abderiten'* (Berlin: Weidmann, 1878), and Ernst Hermann, *Wielands 'Abderiten' und die Mannheimer Theaterverhältnisse* (Mannheim: Bensheimer, 1885), discuss the Mannheim input; and Schulze-Maizier, pp. 73–102, exposes some Erfurt connections.
   12. Böttiger, *Literarische Zustände und Zeitgenossen. In Schilderungen aus Karl August Böttigers handschiftlichem Nachlasse*, I, 179.
   13. H, II, 769.
   14. Ibid., V, 92.
   15. The preceding quotations are found respectively in H, V, 180, 296, 205, 206n.
   16. Martini, *Abderiten*, I, 79; Sengle, p. 334.

17. Gruber, XVIII, 180. The quotation is from the sequel to *Der goldene Spiegel, Die Geschichte des Danischmend (History of Danischmend*, 1775), so that we again recognize the thematic interrelationship of *Die Abderiten* with other products of the 1770s.

18. Hans Hafen, *Studien zur Geschichte der deutschen Prosa im 18. Jahrhundert*, Diss. Zurich, 1952 (Olten: Genossenschafts-Druckerei, 1952), p. 76.

19. Cf. Sengle, p. 332; and Martini, *Abderiten*, I, 72. Also Hafen, p. 82.

20. Blackall, p. 423.

21. Cited by Martini, *Abderiten*, I, 65.

22. Ibid., p. 83. Tronskaja, pp. 201–202, appears to misjudge the significance of this breach of style for the novel's didactic intent.

23. Seiffert, "Nachwort," H, V, 860.

24. Cited by Walter Hinderer, "Nachwort,"*Hann und Gulpenheh. Schach Lolo-Verserzählunger* (Stuttgart: Reclam, 1970), p. 51.

25. H, V, 160: "From the land of the fairies, I bring you good common sense."

26. J. Müller, p. 32. Cf. also Eugen Thurnher, "Raimund und Wieland," *Sprachkunst als Weltgestaltung. Festschrift für H. Seidler* (Munich: Pustet, 1966), pp. 317–33.

27. Böttiger, *Literarische Zustände und Zeitgenossen. In Schilderungen aus Karl August Böttigers handschiftlichem Nachlasse*, I, 257. Conversation with Falk, January 25, 1813. In conversation with Eckermann on April 11, 1827, Goethe further claims that the verse narratives of the 1770s were written at his instigation.

28. Böttger, *Literarische Zustände und Zeitgenossen. In Schilderungen aus Karl August Böttigers handschiftlichem Ncchlasse*, I, 233.

29. Ibid., I, 186–87; Preisendanz, "Wieland und die Verserzählung," pp. 25–27.

30. Hinderer, "Nachwort," p. 39.

31. H, V, 162–63. All subsequent references to the *Oberon* poem will be cited in the text. Roman numerals indicate the canto, Arabic numerals indicate the stanza.

32. Böttiger, *Literarische Zustände und Zeitgenossen. In Schilderungen aus Karl August Böttigers handschiftlichem Nachlasse*, I, 255.

33. J. Müller, p. 33.

34. H, IV, 666.

35. J. Müller, p. 40.

36. Cf. Müller-Solger, pp. 281–83.

37. Müller-Solger analyzes the motif for Wieland's aesthetic production through *Oberon*.

38. Cited by Preisendanz, "Die Kunst der Darstellung," p. 252. The following discussion of style is based in large part on Preisendanz' excellent analysis. Müller-Solger's treatment of theme and style in *Oberon* is one of the most exhaustive (See pp. 263–302).

39. Friedrich Schiller, *Werke in drei Bänden* (Munich: Hanser, 1966), II, 374–75.

40. Ibid., II, 381: "Die Schönheit der poetischen Darstellung ist *freie Selbsthandlung der Natur in den Fesseln der Sprache.*"

41. XI, 61: "How quickly the rosy-colored fingers fly over the spirited strings in lovely confusion! How alluring is the play of the delightful arms stealthfully issuing more and more from the gaping sleeves! And since her powerful passion pours forth in song from a breast which was capable of confounding the virtuous, how can he resist falling on his knees before the goddess?"

42. XI, 20: "Annoyed, she turns away and at odds with herself, bites her lip, sighs, says something but forgets already by the third word what she wanted to say. She is angry that Nadine doesn't give the right answer and doesn't guess what she was supposed to guess. The beauteous dame is, in a word, in love! Even the bouquet learns of it: without her realizing it, the flowers are broken, the petals plucked and shredded."

43. XI, 65: "She hastens to hide herself; the light is loathsome to her, the spacious hall too confining."

44. XII, 25: "He places his noble arm in undeserved bonds and wraps himself up in his consciousness, uttering not a word."

45. Müller-Solger, pp. 216–20, 268n. Because Wieland's art is designed to lead the reader to a type of theophany, Müller-Solger prefers to speak of "energetic" structure (i.e., vertical motion) instead of "morphological" structure (i.e., horizontal, symbolic). See pp. 224–28. As a result he cannot agree with the parallels Preisendanz draws between Wieland's and Schiller's "Wellenlinie des Stils" (p. 267n).

46. AB, III, 308.

47. Sengle, p. 373.

48. Cf., for example, Lieselotte E. Kurth-Voigt's excellent study, "The Reception of Wieland in America," in *The German Contribution to the Building of the Americas: Studies in Honor of Karl J.R. Arndt,* eds. G.K. Friesen and W. Schatzberg (Hanover, N.H.: Clark University Press, 1977), pp. 97–133. The author has collected a wealth of material documenting Wieland's popularity not only in North America, but also in Europe and Germany itself.

49. Madame de Staël and William Taylor are cited by Kurth-Voigt, "Wieland in America," pp. 102–04.

Chapter Eight

1. Böttiger, *Literarische Zustände und Zeitgenossen. In Schilderungen aus Karl August Böttigers handschriftlichem Nachlasse,* I, 264.

2. *Briefe . . . Franzosen,* II, 53. The letter in question is dated 1780.

3. J.-D. Müller, p. 17. Müller's study is one of the few detailed considerations of Wieland's post-1781 novels.

4. Ibid., p. 198.

5. See Gruber, LIII, 274.

6. *Dschinnistan oder auserlesene Feen- und Geister-Märchen* (Winterthur: Steiner, 1786), I, v.

7. Cited by Ludwig Hirzel, *Wielands Beziehungen zu den deutschen Romantikern* (1904; rpt. Hildesheim: Gerstenberg, 1974), pp. 65–66, 7.

8. See McCarthy, *Fantasy and Reality*, pp. 110–12, 153–56. Kurth-Voigt, "Wieland in America" pp. 119–221, delineates striking parallels between *Peregrinus* and Charles Brockden Brown's novel *Wieland or the Transformation*.

9. Karl Raab, "Studien zu Wielands Roman *Peregrinus Proteus*," *Jahresbericht des Staatsgymnasiums mit dt. Unterrichtssprache in Prag-Altstadt* (Prague: Rohlitek and Sievers, 1909), pp. 29–32. Raab, pp. 14–15, also addresses himself to the question of Lavater's role as a kind of model for Peregrinus.

10. Cf. Gruber, XXXIII, 42, and also XXXIV, 186.

11. Sengle, p. 480.

12. Cf. J.D. Müller, pp. 95–105, 185. Cf. also the contrasting reactions of the protagonist and his grandfather to the effect of the wondrous in fairy tales. Where the grandfather found amusement, the youth found premonition of a higher state (Gruber, XXXIII, 49–50).

13. Cf. Matthecka, pp. 25ff. Preisendanz, "Wieland und die Verserzählung," demonstrates this stylistic shift for the verse tales.

14. Gruber, XXXIII, 26.

15. Thus Wieland in the essay "Unterredungen zwischen W** und dem Pfarrer zu ***" (H, III, 342).

16. AB, III, 397.

17. Gruber, XXVII, 327. Derek M. van Abbé, *Christeph Martin Wieland* (London: Harrap, 1961), p. 131, inexplicably contends: "Thus Wieland is seen as a novelist who reflects, shrewdly, the malaise of his time but does not offer authoritative analysis or possible cure." Our cited passage, the antiquarian novels themselves, and most especially Wieland's political essays in the *Merkur* belie this contention.

18. Böttiger, *Literarische Zustände und Zeitgenossen. In Schilderungen aus Karl August Böttigers handschriftlichem Nachlasse.* I, 161.

19. Letter to Göschen (February 28, 1799) in Gruber, LIII, 283; Maurach, p. 169.

20. Robert Keil, ed., *Wieland und Reinhold* (Leipzig and Berlin: Friedrich, 1885), p. 226.

21. Martini, "Wieland-Forschung," p. 274. Mark O. Kistler, "Dionysian Elements in Wieland," *GR*, 40 (1960), 88–92, discusses the Orphic elements of Wieland's pantheism.

22. Wieland himself claimed that the eighth *Göttergespräch* was the *Keimzelle* (spore) of the novel. Cf. Margrit Wulff, "Wielands späte Auseinandersetzung mit Aberglauben und Schwärmerei" (Dissertation, University of Texas, Austin, 1966, p. 177.

23. Cf. Gruber, LIII, 284.

24. The original motto of the book was: "est deus in nobis, agitante calescimus illo" ("a god is in us and through his presence we become inflamed"). H.P.H. Teesing, "Wielands Verhältnis zur Aufklärung im *Agathodämon*," *Neophilologus*, 21 (1936), 112, notes that this pantheism, despite its similarity to Spinoza's, is not based on reason.

25. Cited by Gruber, LIII, 278.

26. Ibid., p. 279.

27. Cf. J.D. Müller, pp. 93–96. Herbert Grudzinski, *Shaftesburys Einfluss auf Ch. M. Wieland* (Stuttgart: Metzler, 1913), traces the Briton's impact from 1755 through *Aristipp*.

28. Cited by Gruber, LIII, 293; see also Lütkemüllers report, cited by Gruber, LIII, 277.

29. Ibid., XXXVII, 153.

30. Sengle, p. 507.

31. Fritz Jonas, ed., *Schillers Briefe* (Stuttgart: Deutsche Verlags-Anstalt, 1892–1896), VI, 235.

32. Cf. e.g., the recent study by Otto Fiene, *Das humoristisch-ironische Spiel des Erzählers bei Wieland und Thomas Mann: Studien zur fiktiven Erzähler-Leser-Beziehung* (Aachen: Author, 1974).

33. In the preface to his collected works, which began to appear in 1794, Wieland had angered younger writers by claiming that the dawn of German literature had begun with his first writings and now dusk seemed to be settling with his last (Gruber, I, xvii). However, he subsequently retracted the statement (ibid., p. ix).

34. Goethe as cited by Beissner, p. 12.

Chapter Nine

1. Martini, "Wieland-Forschung," p. 279.

2. See Hermann Behme, *Heinrich von Kleist und C.M. Wieland* (Heidelberg: Winter, 1914), pp. 8–10.

3. Cited by van Abbé, p. 162.

4. Cited by Kurth-Voigt, "Wieland in America," p. 25.

5. E. F. Schumacher, "The Nature of Problems: An Argument Against Final Solutions," 1, no. 4, *Quest/77*, (September-October 1977), 78. Schumacher employs the terms "convergent" and "divergent" problems.

Selected Bibliography

Because a comprehensive bibliography by Hansjörg Schelle is currently in progress, this one will be highly selective. The notes contain some further references.

PRIMARY SOURCES

A. Collected Works

Wielands gesammelte Schriften. Ed. Deutsche Kommission der königl-preussischen Akademie der Wissenschaften. Berlin: Akademie der Wissenschaften, 1909N. When completed, this edition will be the definitive one of the author's entire oeuvre. Approximately one hundred volumes are envisioned, each volume of text eventually accompanied by one of commentary.

C. M. Wielands sämmtliche Werke. Leipzig: Göschen, 1794–1811. This "Ausgabe letzter Hand" (authentic edition) appeared in four different formats.

C. M. Wielands sämmtliche Werke. Ed. Johann Gottfried Gruber. Leipzig: Göschen, 1818–1828 (folio) and 1824–1828 (octavo). 53 vols. Volumes 50–53 contain Gruber's valuable biography of Wieland based on many personal experiences.

C. M. Wielands sämmtliche Werke. Leipzig: Göschen, 1853–1858, 36 vols.

Wielands Werke. Ed. Heinrich Düntzer. Berlin: Hempel, 1879ff. 40 vols. Contains most of the author's verifiable contributions to the *Teutscher Merkur.*

B. Selected Works

Chr. M. Wieland, Ausgewählte Werke in drei Bänden. Ed. Friedrich Beissner. Munich: Winkler, 1964ff. 3 vols. Concise and annotated with helpful afterwords.

Christoph Martin Wieland. Werke. Ed. Fritz Martini and Hans Werner Seiffert. Munich: Hanser, 1964–1968. 5 vols. Most useful, with insightful commentaries.

Christoph Martin Wieland. Ausgewählte Werke. Ed. Wolfgang Jahn. Munich: Goldmann, 1964ff. 6 vols.

Wielands Werke in vier Bänden. Ed. Hans Böhm. Berlin and Weimar: Aufbau, 1967.

C. Correspondence

Auswahl denkwürdiger Briefe von C. M. Wieland. Ed. Ludwig Wieland. Vienna: Gerold, 1815. 2 vols.

Ausgewählte Briefe von C. M. Wieland an verschiedene Freunde in den Jahren 1751–1810 geschreiben und nach der Zeitfolge geordnet. Zurich: H. Gessner, 1815f. 4 vols.

C. M. Wielands Briefe an Sophie von LaRoche. Ed. Franz Horn. Berlin, 1820.

Neue Briefe C. M. Wielands, vornehmlich an Sophie von LaRoche. Ed. Robert Hassencamp. Stuttgart: Cotta, 1894.

Wielands Briefwechsel. Ed. Deutsche Akademie der Wissenschaften. Berlin: Akademie-Verlag, 1963ff. Represents "Abteilung III" of *Wielands gesammelte Schriften.* Three volumes, covering the correspondence from 1750 to 1769, have been published to date under the specific editorship of Hans Werner Seiffert and Renate Petermann.

Wieland und Reinhold. Originale Mittheilungen als Beiträge zur Geschichte des deutschen Geisteslebens. Ed. Robert Keil. Leipzig and Berlin: Friedrich, 1885.

See also entries under Hansjörg Schelle.

D. Translations into English

All of Wielands's major works were translated into English shortly after their initial publication in German. With the exception of the following items, these early translations are no longer easily accessible, so that the need for modern translations of the more important works should be obvious.

The Adventures of Don Sylvio de Rosalva. New York: Dutton, 1904. reprint of the 1773 anonymous translation, with a brief introduction by Ernest A. Baker.

Oberon, A Poetical Romance. Tr. John Quincy Adams. New York: F. S. Crofts, 1940; reprint Hyperion: Conn., 1977.

Oberon, A Poem from the German of Wieland. Tr. William Sotheby. London: Cadell and Davies, 1798.

SECONDARY SOURCES

ABBÉ, DEREK M. VAN. *Christoph Martin Wieland (1733–1813). A Literary Biography.* London: Harrap, 1961. The only other full-length treatment in English. Fairly well written, but frequently inaccurate and too superficial.

BÄPPLER, KLAUS. *Der philosophische Wieland. Stufen und Prägungen seines Denkens.* Dissertation, Amherst, 1972. Berne and Munich:

Francke, 1974. A well-considered inquiry into the nexus of practical philosophy and social criticism in Wieland's several phases.

BARTHEL, MARGO. *Das "Gespräch" bei Wieland. Untersuchungen über Wesen und Form seiner Dichtung.* 1938; rpt. Hildesheim: Gerstenberg, 1973. Useful earlier study of Wieland's style.

BEISSNER, FRIEDRICH. "Poesie des Stils. Eine Hinführung zu Wieland." In *Wieland: Vier Biberacher Vorträge.* Wiesbaden: Insel, 1954. A milestone in the evaluation of Wieland's polished style.

BLACKALL, ERIC A. *The Emergence of German as a Literary Language 1700–1775.* Cambridge: Cambridge University Press, 1959. Focuses on Wieland's balance of the eighteenth century cult of feeling with that of wit.

BOA, ELIZABETH. "Wieland's *Musarion* and the Rococo Verse Narrative." *Periods in German Literature,* ed. James M. Ritchie, II, 23–41. London: O. Wolff, 1968. Excellent evaluation.

BÖTTIGER, KARL WILHELM, ed. *Literarische Zustände und Zeitgenossen. In Schilderungen aus Karl August Böttigers handschriftlichem Nachlasse.* 1838; rpt. Frankfurt: Athenäum, 1972. 2 vols. Contains important excerpts from Wieland's letters and conversations of the final phase.

————. "Christoph Martin Wieland nach seiner Freunde und seiner eigenen Aüsserungen." *Historisches Taschenbuch,* ed. Friedrich von Raumer, 10 (Leipzig: Brockhaus, 1839), 361–464. Informative.

BUDDECKE, WOLFRAM, C. M. *Wielands Entwicklungsbegriff und die "Geschichte des Agathon."* Palaestra 235. Göttingen: Vandenhoeck and Ruprecht, 1966. Significant interpretation of the novel as a *Bildungsroman.*

CRAIG, CHARLOTTE. *Christoph Martin Wieland as Originator of the Modern Travesty in German Literature.* Chapel Hill: University of North Carolina Press, 1970. Focuses on Wieland's parodistic vein.

DICK, MANFRED. "Wandlungen des Menschenbildes beim jungen Wieland: *Araspes und Panthea* und Shaftesburys *Soliloquy.*" *Jahrbuch der Deutschen Schillergesellschaft,* 16 (1972), 145–75. Good comparative analysis, but tends to overemphasize the materialistic elements of Wieland's philosophy.

ELSON, CHARLES. *Wieland and Shaftesbury.* New York: Columbia University Press, 1913. Valuable study of philosophical influences.

ERMATINGER, EMIL. *Die Weltanschauung des jungen Wieland.* Frauenfeld: Huber, 1907. Good study of young Wieland.

————. "Wieland und die Ironie." In *Deutsche Dichter: 1750–1900. Eine Geistesgeschichte in Lebensbildern,* pp. 33–54. Bonn: Athenäum, 1961. Concise and readable.

FINK, GONTHIER/LOUIS. "Wieland und die Französische Revolution." In *Deutsche Literatur und Französisc e Revolution. 7 Studien,* ed.

Richard Brinkmann. pp. 5–38. Göttingen: Vandenhoeck und Ruprecht, 1974.

FUCHS, ALBERT. *Les apports français dans l'oeuvre de Wieland de 1772 à 1789.* Paris: H. Champion, 1934. Comprehensive analysis of French influence on Wieland during one of his most prolific periods.

GOETHE, JOHANN WOLFGANG VON. "Zum brüderlichen Andenken Wielands." In *Werke.* vol. 31, pp. 201–19. Munich: dtv, 1961–1963. Important early evaluation.

GROSS, ERICH. C. M. *Wielands "Geschichte des Agathon." Entstehungsgeschichte.* 1930; rpt. Nendeln/Liechtenstein: Krauss, 1967. Good analysis of philosophical influences, especially those of French materialism.

HECKER, JUTTA. *Wieland. Die Geschichte eines Menschen in der Zeit.* Stuttgart: Mellinger, 1971. Well written, concise, historically accurate. Recommended.

HINDERER, WALTER. "Beiträge Wielands zu Schillers ästhetischer Erziehung." *Jahrbuch der Deutschen Schillergesellschaft,* 18 (1974), 348–87. Descries many parallels between the two authors.

HOHENDAHL, PETER UWE. "Zum Erzählproblem des utopischen Romans im 18. Jahrhundert." In *Gestaltungsgeschichte und Gesellschaftgeschichte.* Ed. Helmut Kreuzer, pp. 79–114. Stuttgart: Metzler, 1969. Especially useful for interpreting *Der goldene Spiegel.*

HOPPE, KARL. *Der junge Wieland. Wesensbestimmung seines Geistes.* Leipzig: J. J. Weber, 1930. Excellent study of the early works; designed to demonstrate the continuity of Wieland's thought.

JACOBS, JÜRGEN. *Wielands Romance.* Berne and Munich: Francke, 1969. Stresses urbanity of style and role of relativity in shaping form and content.

KAUSCH, KARL HEINZ. "Die Kunst der Grazie. Ein Beitrag zum Verständnis Wielands." *Jahrbuch der Deutschen Schillergesellschaft,* 2 (1958), 12–42. Analyzes a major stylistic concept.

KURRELMEYER, WILHELM. "Die Doppeldrucke in ihrer Bedeutung für die Textgeschichte von Wielands Werken." In *Abhandlungen der Preuss. Akademie der Wissenschaften.* Philosophisch-historische Klasse. Berlin, 1913. Central for an appreciation of Wieland's style and popularity.

———. "The Sources of Wieland's *Don Sylvio.*" *Modern Philology,* 16 (1919), 637–48.

KURTH-VOIGT, LIESELOTTE E. *Perspectives and Points of View: The Early Works of Wieland and their Background.* Baltimore and London: The Johns Hopkins University Press, 1974. Highly recommended study of Wieland's early use of a rhetorical and philosophical tradition.

———. "The Reception of C. M. Wieland in America." In *The German Contribution to the Building of the Americas: Studies in Honor of Karl*

J. R. Arndt, eds. Gehard K. Friesen and Walter Schatzberg, pp. 97–133. Hanover, N.H.: Clark University Press, 1977. A stimulating foray into *terra incognita*.

————. *Die zweite Wirklichkeit. Studien zum Roman des 18. Jahrhunderts*. Chapel Hill: University of North Carolina Press, 1969. Contains chapter on *Don Sylvio*.

LEINERT, MARTIN. "Der Geist von Weimar—Wieland." In *Grosse Seher einer Sozialen Zukunft*, pp. 31–56. Leipzig-Gutritzsch: A. Th. Müller, 1922. Traces the continuous development of Wieland's sociopolitical views from *Cyrus* on. Stresses the importance of justice rather than equality.

LESSING, GOTTHOLD EPHRAIM. *Werke*. Munich: Hanser, 1973.

LEUCA, GEORGE. "Wieland and the Introduction of Shakespeare into Germany." *German Quarterly*, 28 (1955), 247–55.

MARTINI, FRITZ. "Wieland-Forschung." *Deutsche Vierteljahresschrift für Literaturgeschichte*, 24 (1950), 269–80. Historically very important in the renascence of Wieland studies. Still quite valuable.

————. "Wieland—Geschichte der Abderiten." In *Der deutsche Roman*, ed. Benno von Wiese, I, 64–94. Düsseldorf: Bagel, 1963. Good introduction to the form and content of the novel.

————. "C. M. Wielands Oberon." In *Vom Geist der Dichtung. Gedächtnisschrift R. Petsch*. pp. 206–33. Hamburg: Hoffmann and Campe, 1948.

————. "C. M. Wieland und das 18. Jahrhundert". In *Festschrift für Paul Kluckhohn und Hermann Schneider*, pp. 243–65. Tübingen: Mohr, 1948.

McCARTHY, JOHN A. *Fantasy and Reality: An Epistemologic Approach to Wieland*. Berne and Frankfurt: Lang, 1974. An attempt to explain Wieland's style on the basis of perceptual theories. Contains bibliography.

————. "Wieland as Essayist." *Lessing Yearbook*, 8 (1976), 125–39.

————. "Wielands Metamorphose?" In *Deutsche Vierteljahresschrift für Literaturgeschichte*, vol. 49, pp. 149–67. "Sonderheft," 1975. Reevaluation of the transition between the earliest works and those of the Biberach period.

————. "Wieland and Shaftesbury: The Question of Enthusiasm." *Studies in Eighteenth-Century Culture*, 6 (1977), 79–95. Consideration of a central concept.

McNEELY, JAMES. "Historical Relativism in Wieland's Concept of the Ideal State." *Modern Language Quarterly*, 22 (1961), 269–82.

MAURACH, BERND. "Ein Zeitgenosse über Wieland. Unveröffentlichtes aus dem Nachlass K. A. Böttigers, insbes. den *T. M.* betreffend." *Weimarer Beiträge*, 22, no. 7 (1976), 166–75. Some of this interesting material had already been published elsewhere.

MENHENNET, A. "Wieland's "Idris und Zenide": The 'Aufklärer' as Romantic." *German Life and Letters*, 18 (1964–1965), 91–100.

MICHEL, VICTOR. C. M. *Wieland: La formation et l'évolution de son esprit jusqu'à 1772*. Paris: Boivin, 1938. One of the standard works.

MICHELSEN, PETER. *Laurence Sterne und der deutsche Roman des 18. Jahrhunderts*. Göttingen: Vandenhoeck and Ruprecht, 1962. Valuable comparative study.

MILLER, STEVEN R. *Die Figur des Erzählers in Wielands Romanen*. Göppingen: Kümmerle, 1970. Stylistic analyses based on the concept of historical relativity. Good insights.

MINDER, ROBERT. "Réflexions sur Wieland et le classicisme." In *Un dialogue des nations*, pp. 33–42. Munich: Hueber, 1967. Works of the 1760s seen as presaging the style of classical Weimar.

MONECKE, WOLFGANG. *Wieland und Horaz*. Cologne and Graz: Böhlau, 1964. Contains detailed bibliography.

MULLER, JAN-DIRK. *Wielands späte Romane. Untersuchungen zur Erzählweise und zur erzählten Wirklichkeit*. Munich: Fink, 1971. Best full-length study of the late novels with frequent reference to the style and content of the earlier ones.

MULLER, JOACHIM. "Wielands Versepen." *Jahrbuch des Wiener Goethe-Vereins*, 69 (1965), 5–47. Some good insights imbedded in the lengthy plot summaries.

MULLER-SOLGER, HERMANN. *Der Dichtertraum. Studien zur Entwicklung der dichterischen Phantasie im Werk Christoph Martin Wielands*. Göttingen: Kümmerle, 1970. A comprehensive account of Wieland's *Wirkungsästhetik* to about 1780. The role of the dream and imagination in the interplay of art and reality is well delineated.

OETTINGER, KLAUS. *Phantasie und Erfahrung. Studien zur Erzählpoetik Chr. M. Wielands*. Munich: Fink, 1970. Valuable analysis of Wieland's poetics, showing French and English influence and emphasizing an alleged shift from the rationalistic poetics of Bodmer and Breitinger to that of the French and British empiricists.

PELLEGRINI, ALESSANDRO. *Wieland e la Classicità Tedesca*. Firenze: Olschki, 1968. Reinterpretation of Wieland as a classical author.

PREISENDANZ, WOLFGANG. "Die Auseinandersetzung mit dem Nachahmungsprinzip in Deutschland und die besondere Rolle der Romane Wielands *(Don Sylvio, Agathon)*." In *Nachahmung und Illusion*, ed. H. R. Jauss, pp. 72–95. Munich: Eidos, 1964. Important essay for placing Wieland within the aesthetic debates of the eighteenth century.

———. "Die Kunst der Darstellung in Wielands *Oberon*." In *Formenwandel. Festschrift für P. Böckmann*, pp. 236–60. Hamburg, Hoffmann and Campe, 1964. An exemplary stylistic analysis.

———. "Wieland und die Verserzählung des 18. Jahrhunderts." *Germanisch-romanische Monatsschrift*, 43 (1962), 17–31. Wieland's verse tales seen as culmination of the genre.

REICHERT, HERBERT W. "The Philosophy of Archytas." *Germanic Review*, 24 (1949), 8–17. Considers Archytas' views as focus of novel.

SAMUEL, RICHARD. "Wieland als Gesellschaftskritiker: eine Forschungsaufgabe." *Seminar*, 5 (1969), 45–53. Some questions raised here have been answered by Bäppler, Weyergraf, and others. However, the most important question of Wieland's influence on society is still unanswered.

SCHAEFFER, KLAUS. "Das Problem der sozialpolitischen Konzeption in Wielands *Geschichte des Agathon* (1766/67)." *Weimarer Beiträge*, 16 (1970), 171–96. The approach is diametric to Reichert's.

SCHELLE, HANSJÖRG. "Der junge Johann Friedrich von Meyer im Briefwechsel mit Wieland (1792–1797)." *Jahrbuch der Deutschen Schillergesellschaft*, 15 (1971), 36–107.

———. "Wielands Beziehungen zu seinen Leipziger Verlegern. Neue Dokumente." "Teil I," *Lessing Yearbook*, 7 (1975), 149–218; "Teil II," *LY*, 8 (1976), 140–239; "Teil III," *LY*, 9 (1977), 166–258.

———. "C. M. Wielands Briefwechsel mit Friedrich Wilmans." *Jahrbuch des freien deutschen Hochstifts*, (1974), 91–142.

———. "Unbekannte Briefe C. M. Wielands an Carl Leonhard Reinhold aus den Jahren 1787–1792." *Lessing Yearbook*, 3 (1971), 7–24.

———. "Unbekannte Briefe C. M. Wielands und Sophie von LaRoches aus den Jahren 1789–1793." *Modern Language Notes*, 86 (1971), 649–95.

———. "Wieland und die Gebrüder Gädicke." *Modern Language Notes*, 92 (1977), 469–93.

———. "Das Wieland-Museum in Biberach an der Riss und seine Handschriften." *Jahrbuch der Deutschen Schillergesellschaft*, 5 (1961), 548–73.

SCHLAGENFAFT, BARBARA. *Wielands "Agathon" als Spiegelung aufklärerishcer Vernunft- und Gefühlsproblematik*. Erlangen: Palm and Enke: 1935. Judicious appraisal of both enlightened and sentimental influences.

SCHMITT, ALBERT R. "Wielands Urteil über die Brüder Schlegel mit ungedruckten Briefen des Dichters an Carl August Böttiger." *Journal of English and Germanic Philology*, 65 (1966), 637–61. Concise, readable account of Wieland's reaction to W. A. and Fr. Schlegel's criticisms.

———. "Wielands Urteil über Goethes *Wahlverwandtschaften*." *Jahrbuch der Deutschen Schillergesellschaft*, 11 (1967), 47–61.

SCHUMANN, HANNA BRIGITTE. "Zu Literatur über Wielands Sprache und Stil." In *Studien zur neueren deutschen Literatur*. Ed. Hans Werner Seiffert, pp. 7–31. Bellin: Deutsche Akademie der Wissenschaften, 1964. Valuable review of literature concerning Wieland's style. Most of the studies discussed appeared between 1890–1914. Contains detailed bibliography.

Selected Bibliography   187

SEIFFERT, HANS WERNER. "Ergänzungen und Berichtigungen zu den
Prolegomena VIII und IX zu einer Wieland-Ausgabe." *Abhandlungen
der Deutschen Akademie der Wissenschaften*, Klasse für Sprache,
Literatur und Kunst, Nr. 2 (1953). Valuable emandations.
————. "Die Idee der Aufklärung bei C. M. Wieland." *Wissenschaftliche
Annalen*, 2 (1953), 678–89.
————. "Wielandbild und Wielandforschung." In *Wieland: Vier Biberacher
Vorträge*, pp. 80–102. Wiesbaden: Insel, 1954. Summary of research
status as of 1954.
SENGLE, FRIEDRICH. *C. M. Wieland*. Stuttgart: Metzler, 1949. Immensely
influential biography; short on textual anaysis, but extremely good on
intellectual and literary context.
SEUFFERT, BERNHARD. *Prolegomena zu einer Wieland Ausgabe.*
Abhandlungen der Könglich preuss. Akademie der Wissenschaften. Berlin: Akademie der Wissenschaften, 1904–1905. 2 vols. Forms the basis
of the still uncompleted critical edition of Wieland's works.
SOMMER, CORNELIUS. *C. M. Wieland*. Stuttgart: Metzler, 1971. Good introduction to Wieland studies. Bibliography helpful, but by no means
complete.
STAIGER, EMIL. "Wieland: *Musarion*." In *Die Kunst der Interpretation*,
pp. 82–98. Munich: dtv, 1972.
STEINBERGER, JULIUS. *Bibliographie der Wieland-Übersetzungen*. Göttingen: Selbstverlag, 1930. Lists translations of Wieland's works into
other languages.
————. *Wielands Jugendjahre*. Göttingen: Häntzschel, 1935. Good study of
early years; complements Hoppe's investigation.
STERN, GUY. "Fielding, Wieland and Goethe. A Study in the Development
of the Novel." Dissertation, Columbia University, 1954.
SWALES, MARTIN. "An Unreadable Novel?: Some Observations on Wie-
land's *Agathon* and the *Bildungsroman* Tradition." *Publications of the
English Goethe Society*, 45 (1975), 101–30.
TEESING, HUBERT P. H. "Die Motivverschlingung in Wielands *Oberon*."
Neophilologus, 31 (1947), 193–201.
————. "Wielands Verhältnis zur Aufklärung im *Agathodämon*."
Neophilologus, 21 (1936), 23–35, 105–16. Argues that Wieland's own
personal philosophy is not identical to Enlightenment thought.
UNGERN-STERNBERG, WOLFGANG VON. *Chr. M. Wieland und das Ver-
lagswesen seiner Zeit. Studien zur Entstehung des freien Schriftstel-
lertums/in Deutschland.* Frankfurt a.M.: Buchhändler-Vereinigung
GMBH, 1974. Originally published in *Archiv für Geschichte des
Buchwesesn*, 14 (1974), 1211–1534. A most important contribution to
Wieland research. Contains wealth of material and lengthy bibliog-
raphy.
WAHL, HANS. *Geschichte des Teutschen Merkur. Ein Beitrag zur Ge-

schichte des Journalismus im 18. Jahrhundert. 1914; rpt. New York and London: Johnson, 1967. The standard work on the *Teutscher Merkur,* but not exhaustive.

WEYERGRAF, BERND. *Der skeptische Bürger. Wielands Schriften zur Französischen Revolution.* Stuttgart: Metzler, 1972. Read skeptically, although it does draw the general contours of his political thought.

WOLFFHEIM, HANS. *Wielands Begriff der Humanität.* Hamburg: Hoffmann and Campe, 1949. Together with Sengle and Martini, this book started the Wieland renascence.

WÜRZNER, M. H. "Die Figur des Lesers in Wielands *Geschichte des Agathon..*" In *Dichter und Leser. Studien zur Literatur,* pp. 151–55. Groningen: Walters-Noordhoff, 1972. Does on small scale what S. R. Miller does.

YUILL, W. E. "Abderitis und Abderitism. Some Reflections on a Novel by Wieland." In *Essays in German Literature,* ed. Frederick Norman, London: Univ. of London, Institute of Germanic Studies, I, 1965. 72–91.

Index